THE RHETORICAL ACT

THE RHETORICAL ACT

Karlyn Kohrs Campbell
University of Kansas

Wadsworth Publishing Company
Belmont, California
A Division of Wadsworth, Inc.

ISBN 0-534-01008-3

Senior Editor: Rebecca Hayden
Production Editor: Diane Sipes
Designer: Cynthia Bassett
Copy Editor: Carol Dondrea
Technical Illustrator: Joan Carol

Printed in the United States of America

7 8 9 -- 91

Library of Congress Cataloging in Publication Data

Campbell, Karlyn Kohrs
  The rhetorical act.

  Includes index.
  1. Rhetoric. I. Title.
PN187.C3   808   81-7497
ISBN 0-534-01008-3   AACR2

PREFACE

This book takes a traditional humanistic approach to rhetoric drawn from the classical works of Aristotle and the contemporary writings of rhetorical theorist Kenneth Burke. It reaffirms the ancient idea of the relationship between art and practice—that you cannot learn a skill such as speaking or writing unless you understand the theory, the ideas on which it is based.

However, *The Rhetorical Act* departs from traditional textbook approaches in several ways. Most importantly, it treats rhetorical action as the joint creation of rhetor and audience, emphasizing the audience's active, participatory role. In Aristotelian terms, it treats enthymemes, arguments produced cooperatively by speaker and audience, as "the substance of rhetorical persuasion."

Second, it defines rhetoric as "a strategy to encompass a situation" (Kenneth Burke) and as "that art . . . by which discourse is adapted to its end" (George Campbell). It explores the rhetorical obstacles inherent in audience, subject/purpose, and rhetor, and then examines resources available to overcome these obstacles. The purpose of the book is to train students to function as critics or analysts who assess a situation, conceive of rhetorical possibilities, examine actual rhetorical action, and compare the efforts of fellow students with those of journalists, politicians, and other public persuaders.

Third, *The Rhetorical Act* treats all forms of rhetoric as points on a single continuum of influence. Rhetoric ranges from attempts to shape perception, on the one hand, to ritualistic reaffirmations of community membership on the other.

Given these assumptions, there could be no separate treatment of listening or of informative speaking or explanatory writing. Thus, the book minimizes distinctions between oral and written rhetoric, except for recognizing the special role of nonverbal elements in oral persuasion.

The book makes no effort to apply this perspective to communication in small groups or through mass media, although such applications are valid.

The Rhetorical Act is written in the belief that an understanding of rhetorical action enables us to understand the options available, make intelligent choices, evaluate their consequences, appreciate the choices made by others, and protect ourselves from being pawns in the hands of skilled word-users.

This book could not have been written without the challenge provided by the hundreds of students who have been in my classes at the University of Kansas or without the encouragement and support of the SCHR division. My thanks to them all.

My special appreciation to Kathleen Hall Jamieson, University of Maryland, for tapes of Edward Kennedy's speech and of the May 6 Anti-Nuclear Rally, and for being my friend and colleague. My thanks to John Bakke, Memphis State University, for the tape of the last speech of Dr. Martin Luther King, Jr., and for the opportunity to read his analysis of the rhetoric of the Memphis sanitation strike.

Thanks are also due the various readers of all or part of this manuscript, whose comments have been encouraging and valuable. They have made this a better book. I want to express particular gratitude to Mike Halloran of Rensselaer Polytechnic Institute for his many insightful comments and for the thoroughness of his review. I am also indebted to Charles Conrad of the University of North Carolina at Chapel Hill and Joseph L. McCaleb of the University of Maryland for their careful reviews.

Finally, my thanks to Paul, who enriches my life every day.

K. K. C.
Lawrence, Kansas

CONTENTS

To my grandfather, Carl Kohrs (1855–1924),
  whose name I proudly bear.
To my father, Meinhard Kohrs (1888–1967),
  who loved me.
To my uncle, William Kohrs (1904–   ),
  who helped me rediscover my family.

PART ONE

RHETORICAL ACTION

CHAPTER 1

A RHETORICAL
PERSPECTIVE

Through its title, *The Rhetorical Act*, this book boldly announces that it is about rhetoric. Since the mass media often use *rhetoric* to mean "hot air" or "lies," you may well ask why you should study rhetoric in a class or read a book about rhetorical action. One way to answer this question is to define *rhetoric* properly and to show the possible value of a rhetorical perspective on human action.

A "perspective," literally, is a way of looking through (*per* = through; *specere* = to look), an angle of vision, a way of seeing. All perspectives are partial and, in that sense, distorted or biased: each looks at *this* rather than *that;* each has its particular emphasis. Because someone is always doing the looking and seeing, it is impossible to avoid taking some point of view.

Just what is a "rhetorical" (as opposed to a philosophical or scientific) perspective? Whereas the scientist would say the most important thing is the discovery and testing of truth, the rhetorician (one who studies rhetoric and takes a rhetorical perspective) would say, "Truth cannot walk on its own legs. It must be carried by people to other people. It must be made effective through language, through argument and appeal." Philosophers and scientists respond, rightly, that truths must be discovered and tested, through logic and experiment. In fact, they would argue that you and I should pay more attention to how truths are discovered and tested. The rhetorician would answer that unacknowledged and unaccepted truths are of no use at all. Thus, the "bias" of a rhetorical perspective is its emphasis on and its concern with the resources available in language and in people to make ideas clear and cogent, to bring concepts to life. A rhetorical perspective is interested in what influences, in what *persuades* people.

As a result, a rhetorical perspective focuses on *social truths,* that is, on the kinds of truths that are created and tested by people in groups, truths that influence social and political decisions. Among the important social truths a rhetorical perspective might teach you to examine are the processes by which taxpayers, parents, congressional committees, school boards, and citizens treat issues that cannot be resolved solely through logical analysis and experimental testing. For example, should nuclear breeder reactors be built to provide more energy? What should be done about the rising number of pregnancies among teen-agers? What crimes, if any, deserve the death penalty? For social questions such as these, philosophers can point out contradictions in our thinking and spell out the implications of a given position. Scientists can give us the best available data about the storage of nuclear wastes, the ages at which women become pregnant, the rates of commission of capital crimes. When we have looked at the data and examined the logic of the conclusions drawn from them, we still must make decisions that go beyond the facts and make commitments that go beyond logic.

From its beginnings, this emphasis on social truths has been the distinctive quality of a rhetorical perspective. History seems to indicate that rhetoric was first studied and taught by Corax and his pupil Tisias in the Greek city-state of Syracuse in Sicily. A despot had come to power and seized much of the privately owned land. When he was overthrown, former landowners went to court to recover their holdings by pleading their cases. It soon became apparent that those more skilled in arguing were the more successful, and Corax and Tisias began to teach rhetoric—or how to be more skillful in pleading one's case in court.

WHAT IS RHETORIC?

The first major treatise on the art of rhetoric that still exists was written by Aristotle in fourth-century-B.C.E. Athens. Both in the *Rhetoric* and in his other works, Aristotle distinguished among kinds of truth. He recognized that there were certain immutable truths of nature, and these he designated as the province of science (*theoria*). He recognized a different sort of wisdom or knowledge (*phronesis*) as needed to make decisions about social matters. These truths, not discoverable through science or analytic logic, he described as contingent, that is, as dependent on cultural values, the situation, and the nature of the issue. They were the special concerns of the area of study he called "rhetoric." The contingent character of social truths can best be illustrated by looking at what it means to say that something is "a problem."

Put most simply, a problem is the gap that exists between what you think ought to be and what is; it is the discrepancy between the ideal and the real, between goals and achievements. By this definition, a problem for one person may not be a problem for another person. For example, some students are satisfied with C's in most courses. Their goal is to get the "ticket" represented by a college degree with a minimum of inconvenience. They plan to exert their energies after they get into the occupation or position of their choice. Other students are miserable with anything less than an A. Their goal is graduate school or highly specialized study and work. They need very high averages and the best possible preparation and achievement now. For these different students, the same fact—a grade of C—can be a serious problem or no problem at all.

For you as students and for society as a whole, problems depend on the goals desired and the values held. It is in this same sense that social truths—and thus rhetoric—are "subjective" and "evaluative"; rhetoric is grounded in issues that arise because of people's values.

Rhetoric is, of course, also concerned with data that establish what exists and with logical processes for drawing conclusions from facts and implications from principles and assumptions. Indeed, Aristotle considered rhetoric an offshoot of logic, and a rhetorical perspective is characterized not only by an emphasis on social truths but by an emphasis on *reason-giving* or *justification*. Of course, not all of the reasons used by rhetors (those who initiate symbolic acts seeking to influence others) will make sense to logicians and scientists. Some rhetorical reasons will be grounded in facts and logic, but many others will be grounded in religious beliefs, history, or cultural values, in associations and metaphors, in hunger, resentments, or dreams. A rhetorical perspective is eclectic and inclusive in its search for what is influential and why. In fact, rhetoric's concern with justification grows out of its focus on social truths, tested by people in their roles as voters, property owners, and the like. In other words, reasons are presented to those decision makers and evaluators to whom the rhetoric is *addressed*, the audience.

Obviously, in some situations you can say, "Do this and don't ask any questions—just trust me," but these situations are rare. Reasons can be ignored only where your relationship to the audience is so close and strong that the relationship itself is the reason for action or belief.

In most cases, then, even those involving your nearest and dearest, you must give reasons, justify your views, explain your position. And you must do so in terms that will *make sense to others*. Rhetors must "socialize" their reasons. For example, one of my students, a long-distance runner, told me that he ran for the joy of it, for the sheer physical pleasure it gave him. But when others asked him why he ran and endured what they saw as considerable pain, he spoke of developing his body and protecting his health. Those were the "socialized" reasons, reasons accepted by society. United States culture is strongly pragmatic; "good" reasons show that an act is useful. Other societies or subcultures in the United States emphasize the sensual and aesthetic; for them, "good" reasons affirm the pleasure and expressiveness of behavior.

Because rhetoric is *addressed* to others, it is *reason-giving;* and because it is social and public, it uses as reasons the *values accepted and affirmed* by a subculture or culture. In this way, rhetoric is tied to *social values,* and rhetors' statements will reflect the social norms of particular times and places.

Because it is addressed to people, providing justifications that others will understand and feel, rhetoric is a *humanistic* study, and, as such, it examines all kinds of human symbol-using, even the bizarre and perverse. From the beginnings of rhetoric in classical antiquity, rhetoricians have known that persuasion occurs through both argument and association, through the cold light of logic and the white heat of passion, through explicit values and subconscious needs. As a result, rhetoric is a field of study that examines *all* the available means by which we are influenced and by which we can influence others.

In summary, rhetoric is the study of what is *persuasive.* The issues it examines are *social truths, addressed* to others, *justified* by reasons that reflect *cultural values.* It is a *humanistic* study that examines all the symbolic means by which influence occurs.

RHETORICAL ACTS

As I have described it, a rhetorical perspective takes note of the rhetorical or persuasive dimension in all human behavior. Although all human actions can be considered implicitly persuasive, I do not wish to define "the rhetorical act" so broadly. The lines separating rhetorical acts from other acts are difficult to draw, however, and in this book I shall treat the concept of rhetoric in both its broad and its narrow sense. An example will illustrate why this should be.

During the student protests of the 1960s, a group of black students occupied a building on the campus of Cornell University. The incident was widely publicized, and several newspapers and magazines published a photograph showing the blacks leaving the building carrying weapons that included guns. They looked threatening, militant, extreme. But one of the departing blacks also took a photograph. Taken from the opposite direction, it showed what the outgoing blacks faced: a crowd of whites, bunched behind a ring of police wearing helmets and masks and weighed down with weapons. Both police and crowd look angry and dangerous. One picture shows the event as most whites saw it; the other shows the event as the demonstrators and many blacks saw it. Editors who published the first picture probably did not make a consciously racist decision. They published what they saw (and what other whites wished to see, perhaps), and by so doing, they influenced others to see the event as they did, to believe that that was the way it was. The rhetoric of each photograph emerges most clearly when one sees them both.

What the example illustrates is that many acts are rhetorical when you consider the potential of the act to influence others, whatever the actual intentions of its author may have been. Of course, many acts are intentionally rhetorical—advertisements, editorials, book and movie reviews, and essays, sermons and speeches that declare a position and seek to defend it and make it attractive to others. When I address you as speakers or writers, I talk about rhetorical acts as intentional and deliberate attempts to influence others. However, when I function as a critic or analyst and address you as critics and analysts, I comment on all possible persuasive effects, both intentional and unintentional. I do this because, to understand rhetoric, you must understand all the processes of influence and because, as a rhetor, you must come to terms with unintended and accidental effects—especially since some of them may tend to defeat your purpose.

In other words, defined most broadly, *rhetoric* is the study of all the processes by which people influence each other through symbols, regardless of the intent of the source. *A rhetorical act*, however, is an intentional, created, polished attempt to overcome the obstacles in a given situation with a specific audience on a given issue to achieve a particular end. A rhetorical act creates a message whose shape and form, beginning and end, are stamped on it by a human author with a goal for an audience. If you study all forms of influence, you will become aware of all the available resources for persuasion. Similarly, when you analyze your rhetoric and that of others, you must consider persuasive effects that may not have been fully under the control of the speaker or writer.

RHETORICAL PURPOSES

Because intention and effects are so important in a rhetorical perspective, I wish to consider the range of purposes contained in the words *persuasion* and *influence.*

Creating Virtual Experience

First, rhetors intend to communicate. If I write, "The sun shines against a pale blue sky, the snow has melted into dirty slush, blades of grass poke up here and there, and crimson birds chirp in the still-bare trees," you can draw on past sights and sounds and sensations to re-create your own mental picture. Although each reader's picture will be different, and each will reflect the reader's unique past, most will concern spring in the northern hemisphere. To communicate, to act rhetorically, means that you initiate an act that someone else can translate into virtual experience. When something is virtual, it does not exist in fact; it is *as if* it existed. There is no sun, no blue sky, no dirty slush, or crimson bird on this page. But if I write about them vividly enough, you can imagine them; it is as if you saw and heard and felt them here and now. That re-creation in your mind is virtual experience. In response to my words, you imagine a scene, create a mental picture, and what you experience is virtual experience, experience called forth and shaped by your response to the symbols produced by someone else. To communicate effectively means that the image or idea created in your mind approximates the image or idea that the speaker or author wished to convey.

In other words, the fundamental rhetorical purpose, the most basic kind of influence—communicating—requires you to initiate a rhetorical act that can be translated into virtual experience by others. The most basic question in rhetoric is how to do that.

One kind of rhetorical action is intended primarily to produce virtual experience. Most works of literature, for example, are written to expand and shape our experience. In them, one sees, hears, smells, tastes, and touches vividly and concretely, and these sensations are shaped and formed into a satisfying and complete experience. In Tolstoy's *The Death of Iván Ilých*, for example, the reader sees and touches the stuffed furniture and damask draperies; smells Iván's foul breath; hears the crushing of a down cushion; tenses muscles with Iván's struggles. These sensations re-create Iván's fear of death and the horrors of his dying.

Altering Perception

Literary works can also have political effects, however. Charles Dickens's *Oliver Twist* re-created the experiences of orphans in English poorhouses so movingly that readers demanded reform. Harriet Beecher Stowe's *Uncle Tom's Cabin* depicted scenes of slavery so vividly that it became a major force for abolition. The same sensory or aesthetic stimuli that enliven good literature are a major means of persuasion. In other words, by creating virtual experience—the more vivid the better—literature can contribute to the second rhetorical purpose I want to discuss: *altering perception.*

George Washington wrote, "The truth is the people must *feel* before they will *see*." Whether or not you must experience before you can understand or comprehend, it is surely true that vivid experience improves the capacity to understand. Indeed, Washington's statement names the two processes by which persuasion occurs: feeling and understanding.

For a striking example of how an author can change the meaning of a concept for an audience—that is, alter perception—adding to the experiences that are associated with it in the minds of the audience, consider what Tolstoy does to the deductive syllogism that begins: "All men are mortal":

> *Iván Ilých saw that he was dying, and he was in continual despair.*
>
> *In the depth of his heart he knew he was dying, but not only was he not accustomed to the thought, he simply did not and could not grasp it.*
>
> *The syllogism he had learnt from Kiezewetter's Logic: "Caius is a man, men are mortal, therefore Caius is mortal," had always seemed to him correct as applied to Caius, but certainly not as applied to himself. That Caius—man in the abstract—was mortal was perfectly correct, but he was not Caius, not an abstract man, but a creature quite, quite separate from others. He had been little Ványa, with a mamma and a papa, with Mitya and Volódya, with the toys, a coachman and a nurse, afterwards with Kátenka and with all the*

*joys, griefs, and delights of childhood, boyhood, and youth. What did Caius know of the smell of that striped leather ball Ványa had been so fond of? Had Caius kissed his mother's hand like that, and did the silk of her dress rustle so for Caius? Had he rioted like that at school when the pastry was bad? Had Caius been in love like that? Could Caius preside at a session as he did? "Caius really was mortal, and it was right for him to die; but for me, little Ványa, Iván Ilých, with all my thoughts and emotions, it's altogether a different matter. It cannot be that I ought to die. That would be too terrible."** *

Until I read that novel, no one had ever died in a syllogism. Since reading the novel, I cannot hear the syllogism without thinking of my own death.

To recapitulate, the most minimal rhetorical purpose, the smallest effect produced, is to add to the sum of your audience's experience. If you succeed, you start a process that may alter perceptions.

Explaining

If we measured the effects of rhetorical acts by how much they altered belief, nearly all of them would be failures. Normal, healthy human beings whose physical environments are not controlled by someone else do not change their beliefs in response to a single message— whether the message lasts five minutes or five hours. If people do alter their beliefs, they do so over weeks, months, or even years, and in response to many different messages.

Let us suppose that you have read Tolstoy's *The Death of Iván Ilých* and now feel very intensely your own fears about death. But you are puzzled and unsatisfied. You want to understand the processes by which humans avoid thinking about and dealing with death. At this point, you are an ideal audience for the third rhetorical purpose: *explaining* or creating understanding. Such rhetorical acts attempt to order and account for a whole mass of information and experience. For example, Elizabeth Kübler-Ross's *On Death and Dying* explains the psychology of death and helps the reader understand why Ilých's fear of death torments him and why his torment is increased by his family and friends' refusal to acknowledge to him that he is dying.

---

*Leo Tolstoy, "The Death of Iván Ilých," translated by Louise Maude and Aylmer Maude in *The Death of Ivan Ilych and Other Stories* (England: Oxford University Press). Reprinted by permission.

The need to explain often appears when an intense, irrational experience occurs. For example, when a German industrialist, Hanns-Martin Schleyer, was kidnapped and murdered by a group of well-educated young Germans whose middle-class backgrounds provide no obvious reasons for their terrorist behavior, another young German, responding to his need (and ours), wrote an open letter trying to explain such actions. He spoke of the shame that he and other young Germans felt for the Nazi past, especially when postwar affluence seemed to be an obscene reward for the obscene practices of the past. Children of his age learned not to trust parents who pretended never to have known of the death camps and could not trust teachers who reshaped history to emphasize the benefits of the Third Reich in building highways and curbing inflation. He described the efforts of his generation to invent an ersatz (a term borrowed from German referring to an artificial substitute) country and family—by adopting Korean and Vietnamese children, by embracing pentecostal Christianity, by supporting all left-wing causes, by going to work for the United Nations, as he did, or even by joining an international terrorist group. What the author makes us feel and see is the desperate need to belong to something dedicated to good and the intense desire to destroy lies and to act against those who had deceived them about the past. If his letter speaks to us, it helps us share the experiences of bitter young Germans and understand how some, the bitterest perhaps, might see terrorism as a solution.*

Susan Brownmiller wrote a book called *Against Our Will: Men, Women, and Rape.*† Much of the book provides information about the crime of rape—its magnitude and nature—and gives us the virtual experience to recognize it as a crime that real people experience. This evidence is obviously intended to alter perception. However, Brownmiller goes beyond the data to explain—to argue that rape is the logical and necessary outcome of sexism in our society. Her explanation will find a large and ready audience, for women, particularly the millions of rape victims, have usually found rape an unintelligible horror. Most people, in fact, wish they could make sense out of this paradoxical crime—committed by "normal" males who plan their acts before finding an available victim, often committed in groups, the fastest growing violent crime in the United States, and

---

* Frederick Weibgen, "Compensating for a Childhood in Germany," *New York Times*, 17 January 1978, p. A33.

† New York: Simon and Schuster, 1975.

one that is no respecter of persons: neither age, respectability, ugliness, nor staying at home will protect you, your sister, your mother, your friend, your wife, or your daughter. Brownmiller's book provides many data that alter perception and need explaining; then it presents a persuasive, intellectually satisfying explanation.

Formulating Belief

By this time you should begin to see that rhetorical action is not a one-shot event, but a process, and that there is an orderly progression of rhetorical purposes, depending on where a rhetorical act fits into that process. Often when our perceptions are changed by virtual experience, we demand explanations, or the rhetor who has created the virtual experience is moved to explain why these processes occur. Similarly, the next rhetorical purpose emerges out of these: *formulating belief.*

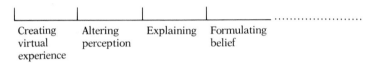

Creating virtual experience	Altering perception	Explaining	Formulating belief

To return to Brownmiller, most people who read this book are probably already concerned about rape or interested in feminism generally. Such readers will, at least, entertain her explanation as possible even if they postpone any further move until they have more data. These readers are now a prime audience for other rhetorical action. They might read a feature story about a rape squad formed on a police force and its effects on the arrest and conviction of rapists and on the protection of persons unjustly accused. Or they might read a San Francisco reporter's story of being raped in her home, or plan to listen to a late-night talk show on which she tells her story.* Such people are testing Brownmiller's explanation. They may now talk to a rape victim. If these experiences and messages confirm Brownmiller's view, they will reach a point at which a new belief will emerge. Many rhetorical acts aim to produce that "precipitating moment" in which everything falls together and the reader or listener says, "That's it.

---

* Marilyn Chase, "Nightmare in California: A Reporter's Story of Her Rape," *New York Times,* 21 January 1978, p. C 25.

That's the way it is." Few rhetorical acts succeed, however, in transforming people's attitudes. Most serve, at best, to confirm a position being considered or to present an explanation the audience is ready to ponder. Indeed, those who achieve such goals have been resounding successes as persuaders!

Initiating Action

Let us suppose, however, that you are present at a rhetorical event that formulates the beliefs of a group of people about rape. The pleased speaker now urges action—but finds that most of the audience is not ready to form a rape squad with some female officers or, in fact, to do anything very concrete. You might doubt that the rhetor has really changed people's belief, and your doubts would have merit, because belief and action are related. But a survey of rhetorical purposes may show that a normal process is occurring. The speaker may merely have tried to move too fast, skipping one or two steps in the sequence of rhetorical goals and purposes. Even when belief is formulated, it will not result in action unless the general belief is reinforced and then channeled so that action seems appropriate and necessary:

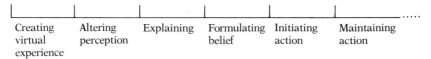

| Creating virtual experience | Altering perception | Explaining | Formulating belief | Initiating action | Maintaining action |

Once again, messages must be supported by other events. If a series of rapes occurs on your campus and they are publicized, generalized belief will be reinforced, and concerned groups and individuals will seek to protect potential victims and create procedures that will increase the chances that the rapist(s) will be caught. Under such circumstances, reinforcement may happen almost instantly for friends and families of the victims, but can happen fairly soon even for those not directly involved. In the face of such events, people discuss alternatives, argue their merits, consider what is feasible, decide the extent of their commitment, and choose what actions, if any, they will take.

Rhetorical acts aimed at initiating action will appear. An editorial will urge a special rape squad; a women's group will press the school administration to provide facilities for a crisis line for rape victims and hold a rally at which speakers urge this; the police chief will promise anonymity to witnesses; a local student organization may urge formation of a special student police group to protect women students; and so on.

Maintaining Action

And then, when the furor dies, rhetorical acts will be needed to keep the crisis line and the special police rape squad in operation. Rhetorical acts will appear to sustain the commitment to continued action (maintaining action, the sixth and last of our rhetorical purposes). Such rhetorical action perpetuates institutions: the Sunday sermon to the regular churchgoer, which urges continued support and attendance; the regular report on the activities of the Rotary Club, which reaffirms the club's successes and values; the weekly ritual at Eastern Star, which reinforces Masonic principles; the daily repetition of the national anthem at baseball games in summer, which proclaims the patriotism of sport.

This progression reflects the rhetorical dimension in all human behavior and indicates the processes involved in the most ordinary sorts of rhetorical acts. It should suggest to you as a prospective rhetor that your choice of a rhetorical purpose should reflect the prior experiences of your audience and should be attuned to the events taking place in your environment. Your potential purposes will depend on the issue, the audience, and the context, as well as on you. (Your role in a rhetorical act is considered in Chapters 3 and 6.)

THE DISCIPLINE OF RHETORIC

A discipline is a field of study, an area of expertise, a branch of knowledge. A discipline provides *theory, application,* and *experimentation,* and *criticism* to test them all. Theories are explanations that seek to account for processes and data. Rhetorical theories seek to account for the processes in language and people that influence belief and action. Applications are rules for action that are developed from theory. Rhetorical applications suggest how you can use rhetorical principles to be an effective moral agent and to protect yourself as you participate in rhetorical action initiated by others. Experimentation seeks to isolate variables or elements in the persuasive process and to test theoretical explanations as carefully as possible. Critical analysis examines rhetorical acts in order to describe processes of influence and explain how they occur. Both experimentation and criticism (of theories, applications, experimental research, and rhetorical action) contribute to the modification and application of theory.*

In the chapters that follow, I develop theory about the nature and application of rhetorical processes, which is supported by experimental research and by critical analysis that qualifies, refines, and illustrates these theoretical concepts.

In its theory, the discipline of rhetoric examines the symbolic dimensions of human behavior in order to provide the most complete explanations of human influence. This broad view is tested by critical analysis. Rhetorical application focuses more narrowly on rhetorical acts—written and spoken messages designed to achieve predetermined effects in an audience. Experimental studies of persuasion focus more narrowly on rhetorical acts and test the adequacy of explanations of them and the appropriateness of rules for application.

As a discipline, *rhetoric is the study of the art of using symbols.*† It provides theory, application, experimentation, and critical analysis. It studies the *social use* of words by people in groups, the *political use* of words to decide who shall make what kinds of decisions, and the *ethical use* of words to justify belief and action through cultural values. It is related to logic and empirical validation because it uses these materials. It is different from philosophy and science because it studies all the available processes for influencing people, and it defines influence broadly. As a result, it considers how people use language to alter perception, to explain, to change, reinforce, and channel belief, to initiate and maintain actions. Put more traditionally, it studies all the ways in which symbols can be used to teach, to delight, and to move.

This book is based on the ancient idea of the relationship between art and practice—the belief that you cannot develop a skill such as speaking or writing unless you understand the theory, the concepts, and the ideas on which it is based. Conversely, you cannot understand the theory unless you use it and test it in practice. In my view, this ancient relationship demands that those who would learn about rhetoric must take the posture of a rhetor–critic. The rhetor is an

---

* Karlyn Kohrs Campbell, "The Nature of Criticism in Rhetorical and Communicative Studies," *Central States Speech Journal* 30 (1979): 4–13.

† This conception is reflected in many well-known definitions of rhetoric: "The art or talent by which discourse is adapted to its end" (George Campbell); "The use of language as a symbolic means of inducing cooperation in beings that by nature respond to symbols" (Kenneth Burke); "The faculty of observing, in any given case, the available means of persuasion" (Aristotle).

initiator of rhetorical action who tries to make the choices that will make her or him the most effective moral agent. As a rhetor, you come to understand all the forces at work in persuasion, some of which are outside your control. The critic analyzes, describes, interprets, and evaluates rhetorical acts to understand what they are, and how and for whom they work. As a critic, you learn to criticize your own rhetoric to improve it, and you learn to analyze the rhetoric of others in order to make decisions as intelligently as possible.

CRITICISM IS FEEDBACK

Every book addressed to students of communication begins with a model of the process that looks something like this:

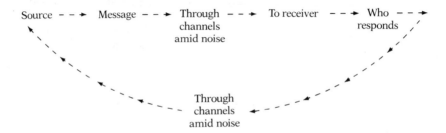

Most of you already know that the name for the receiver's response is "feedback," the kind of information used in missile guidance systems to keep projectiles on the correct path. When you speak, the immediate audience gives you useful but limited feedback. They look at you intently, smile in amusement, frown in puzzlement, look away in annoyance or boredom, take a note to check out a statistic, and the like. If you are in a class and your instructor has the other students write comments and discuss your speech, you will discover that most of their reactions were not evident from their faces and bodies. You will also discover that the messages you could not read are very important—perhaps the most important. Similarly, when your instructor comments orally and in writing, you will discover that the written comments are different—less superficial, more helpful, tied to ideas you have studied. Such feedback is criticism—the careful analysis and evaluation by an experienced student of rhetoric who has heard and read many rhetorical acts, read many critical analyses, studied available theories, and read many experimental studies. Ideally, you should aspire to be such a critic. If you understand rhetorical processes, you have the best chance of consistent success in rhetorical action. You will be able to help yourself improve, and you will be able to consider the rhetoric of others most carefully.

The perspective of this book is a critical one. In each case, theory and application are related to critical analysis of rhetorical acts, with the goal of making you an effective critic of rhetoric, your own and others'. Then, the process of learning that begins in class can continue outside the classroom and throughout your life.

SOURCES

Aristotle, *Ethica Nicomachea*. Translated by W. D. Ross. (*The Student's Oxford Aristotle*, Vol. V.) London: Oxford University Press, 1942. See Book Six for a discussion of the different kinds of knowledge.

Aristotle. *Rhetoric*. Translated by W. Rhys Roberts. New York: The Modern Library, 1954. The definitions of rhetoric used in this chapter are drawn from this source.

Brownmiller, Susan. *Against Our Will: Men, Women and Rape*. New York: Simon and Schuster, 1975.

Burke, Kenneth. *Language as Symbolic Action*. Berkeley: University of California Press, 1966. See particularly the essays entitled "Definition of Man," "Terministic Screens," and "What are the Signs of What?"

Kennedy, George A. *Classical Rhetoric and Its Christian and Secular Tradition from Ancient to Modern Times*. Chapel Hill: The University of North Carolina Press, 1980. As its title indicates, this is a history of rhetoric. It is concise and readable.

Kübler-Ross, Elizabeth. *On Death and Dying*. New York: Macmillan, 1969.

Langer, Susanne K. *Feeling and Form: A Theory of Art*. New York: Charles Scribner's Sons, 1953. This work is the source of the phrase "virtual experience," one phrase the author uses to describe the artistic form created by *poesis* or imaginative literature.

Langer, Susanne K. *Philosophy in a New Key: A Study in the Symbolism of Reason, Rite, and Art*. 3d ed. Cambridge, Mass.: Harvard University Press, 1957. This is one of the most important contemporary studies of human symbolization.

EXERCISE

The history of rhetoric and of communication is embedded in and revealed by the meanings, usage, and origins of these terms. Both the history and the varied meanings of these words can be discovered this way: ask each student or assign groups of students to look up *rhetoric* and *communication* or *communications* in one of the following:

The Oxford English Dictionary

Roget's Thesaurus or any dictionary of synonyms and antonyms

Encyclopaedia Britannica (Compare the essay in the eleventh edition with that in the fourteenth; then look at the Macropedia and the Micropedia of the latest edition.)

Bartlett's Familiar Quotations or *The Oxford Dictionary of Quotations*

The Encyclopedia of Philosophy

A Dictionary of Contemporary American Usage

A Dictionary of Word Origins

The Oxford Classical Dictionary

The Dictionary of the Social Sciences

Black's Law Dictionary

M. H. Abrams, *A Glossary of Literary Terms*

And any other dictionary, encyclopedia, or other reference work.

In class, share all the definitions, meanings, and information about word origins that were found. How old is the study of rhetoric? How old is the study of communication? How do their word origins reflect their meaning? What differences are there in these two terms?

CHAPTER 2

THE RHETORICAL ACT

In the first chapter, I discussed rhetoric, the rhetorical dimension in all human action, and rhetorical acts in general. In this chapter, I examine a particular rhetorical act in some detail, and in Chapter 3, I discuss *your* rhetorical act, the special relationship between you as a specific individual and the choices to be made when *you* speak and write to achieve the range of rhetorical purposes I have described.

In this chapter I play the role of critic, analyzing and interpreting a rhetorical act. As the analysis proceeds, I develop a lexicon or set of terms that can be used to talk about the elements or parts of a rhetorical act.

The act I examine was printed on the Op-Ed (opposite the editorial) page (p. 21C) of the *New York Times* on September 24, 1977. It was written, not by a journalist or member of the *Times*'s editorial staff, but by Melvin J. Konner, an associate professor of biological anthropology at Harvard University.* I have chosen the act because, as you will see, it works well to illustrate the various elements in rhetorical action and because it treats a typical rhetorical issue, a question of public policy that rests on cultural values and requires the creation of social truths. The broad issue is what public policy should be about providing contraceptive information and abortions to teen-agers.

---

* This information about the author appeared in a note at the end of the essay.

ELEMENTS OF RHETORICAL ACTION

The terminology I shall use allows critics and rhetors to describe the parts and elements of rhetorical action. The terms name seven general categories as follows:

1. Purpose: the conclusion argued (thesis) and the response desired by the author.

2. Audience: the author's target; those listeners or readers selected by the act; the audience's role.

3. Persona: the role adopted by the persuader in making the argument (such as teacher, preacher, reporter, prophet, etc.).

4. Tone: the author's attitude toward the subject and the audience (such as personal, sarcastic, instructive, etc.).

5. Structure: the way the materials are organized to gain attention, develop a case, and emphasize certain elements.

6. Supporting materials: different kinds of evidence for the argument.

7. Strategies: adaptation of language, appeals, and argument to shape the materials to overcome the rhetorical problem.

Here is the rhetorical act I shall describe as it appeared in the *New York Times:*

Adolescent Pregnancy

1 *Cambridge, Mass.* —The United States faces a problem that has reached the dimensions of a national disaster, comparable to a flood, epidemic or famine—and one that results, similarly, from a colossal flaw of nature. That flaw is the precipitous, unprecedented drop in the age of puberty; the problem is the spread of teen-age pregnancy.

2 In 1840, the average young woman in Europe and the United States menstruated for the first time at the age of 17; her modern counterpart reaches the age of menstruation at about 12. Well known to biological anthropologists as the "secular trend," this crash in the age of sexual maturity has proceeded at the rate of four months per decade, and, in most populations, continues.

3 The age of first possible parenthood has declined comparably, and early literary references to teen-age marriage and

parenthood have been shown to be completely unrepresentative, exaggerated or false.

4   In much of the third world, we can watch the trend beginning. Among the Kung San, an African gathering–hunting people believed to model the original human way of life, the age at first menstruation is 16 1/2 and the age at first birth 19 1/2 (within a very narrow range). Sex play in childhood and adolescence is ubiquitous, 99 percent of girls are married by age 20 (half of them before their first menstruation) and no contraception is in use.

5   There is thus no explanation for the late age at first birth except late menstruation and adolescent sterility.

6   Human beings are not designed by evolution either in body or in spirit for the experience of adolescent pregnancy. In the United States, from 1940 to 1960, births in the 15–19 maternal age group about doubled. After 1960, out-of-wedlock births in the 14–17-year age range rose steadily until 1973, when legal abortions halted the rise. But teen-age pregnancy has continued to rise to the present rate of one million a year. The fastest rise is in the youngest group, 11–13 years.

7   As maternal age drops from age 20, mortality risks for mother and child rise sharply as does the probability of birth defects. Offspring of adolescent mothers, if they survive, are more likely to have impaired intellectual functioning. Poverty, divorce, inept parenting, child neglect and child abuse are all more frequent in teen-age parents.

8   The baby, of course, is not the only sufferer. For women of all ages, the incidence of onset of mental illness increases fivefold to fifteenfold during the first month after delivery. What sort of effect may we expect it to have on a junior high school girl? Little stretch of the imagination is required to conclude that denying her an abortion is in itself a form of child abuse, even leaving aside the kitchen-abortion horror tales.

9   In every other arena of life, including the criminal court, we absolve her of responsibility for her actions; in the maternity clinic we avert our eyes and condemn her.

10   Consider the plight of these children. Assaulted by culturally sanctioned sexual innuendo and borne along by physical and physiological events that have never before befallen such young children, they are at the mercy of their own and one another's impulses, having five years' less experience and mental growth than their pubescent counterparts of a century ago.

11   To guide them through these biological storms, we offer religion's thick counsel that is vague, timid, false, irrelevant or

negligible, and teachers who, on the subject of contraception, are silenced by rule of law.

12   The people who keep children in the dark about contraception have now deprived them of a major source of rescue from the accident caused by this legislated ignorance. An estimated one-third of the 250,000– 300,000 abortions funded by Medicaid each year go to teen-agers, and it is easy to see how ignorance kept a ceiling on this figure even before the law withdrew the funds, bowing to a superstitious campaign against women's rights to govern their bodies.

13   The effect of this capitulation is the moral and practical equivalent of sabotaging a lone remaining dam above an already inundated flood plain. Its result will be a lock-step cycle of children born to children, inadequately parented and inadequately parenting, condemned to poverty, with a generation turnover time approaching one decade.

14   Let us hope that the proposed substitute—bounty payments to foster parents—is merely ill-advised, because if it is not ill-advised, it is simply cynical.

15   Foster care is such a well-studied failure that it is difficult to be charitable to its promoters, except where the only alternative is the orphanage.

16   We may sympathize with the impulse of those whose private views make them oppose abortion on ethical grounds. But their personal reading of the human moral law need not constrain the rest of us from exercising a more complex judgment.

17   We must now evidently fight for the right to do so. In the meantime, the law may yet provide some protection for pregnant children. The arguments that I give, though they must not be taken as a substitute for a woman's right to choose, produce the conclusion that an abortion must always be available to a teen-ager. Modern teen-agers are the victims of a physiological blight, the capacity for immature pregnancy—a tragic, anomalous, biological novelty. It is our clear duty to help save them from this blight, not condemn them to it.

18   A little moment ago in European history, the intense convictions of some people led them to enjoin others—on pain of torture and death—from believing that rulers derived their power from the governed, that many religions were possible, that animal species were mutable, and that the planet Earth revolved around the sun.

19   In another moment, the high-minded stricture against women's rights over their bodies will seem, in retrospect, comparably arbitrary and bullying.

20   But for the transient, rather desperate, here and now, some of us have a moral sense that enables us to feel obligated to several hundred thousand pregnant children.*

The opening paragraph is an *introduction,* a part of the **structure** of the rhetorical act. In broad terms, rhetorical acts are divided into three major parts: (1) an introduction that gets attention and introduces the subject; (2) the body, composed of the thesis (the central point the rhetor argues and wants the audience to accept) and the arguments, appeals, explanations, and evidence that support it; and (3) the conclusion, usually a summary and a forceful appeal for the position being advanced.

In this case, the introduction begins by announcing that a problem exists and by describing the problem in a dramatic, vivid **tone**—it is a "national disaster"; in size and seriousness, it is like a "flood, epidemic or famine" and, like them, it is the result of "a colossal flaw of nature." These opening lines catch our attention because the comparisons call up vivid images of death, suffering, and destruction and feelings of fear or insecurity. These comparisons are a kind of **supporting material**—they are a special type of comparison, *the figurative analogy.* The rhetor here assumes his readers will have strong emotional and aesthetic (sensory) responses to such natural disasters as floods, epidemics, and famine. The rhetor hopes that the comparison will create an association so that readers will feel and imagine about teen-age pregnancy what they feel and imagine about floods and famines. But the introduction also says something important about the similarity among all these: that they all are the result of a common cause—a flaw in nature. The author is saying that teen-age pregnancies are caused by biological, physiological, *natural* processes, not by a moral flaw. It is this idea that the essay seeks to establish and it is this **strategy** that makes this rhetorical act distinctive.

What is the "colossal flaw of nature"? The "precipitous [abrupt], unprecedented [nothing quite like it has occurred in the past] drop in the age of puberty [the state of physical development or maturity when it is first possible to beget or bear children]." This claim has force only if it is a conclusion drawn from evidence. The next paragraph provides two kinds of **supporting materials** or evidence: *statistics* and *literal analogy.* The author compares two cases that are obvi-

---

* M. J. Konner, "Adolescent Pregnancy." © 1977 by The New York Times Company. Reprinted by permission.

ously and literally alike—the ages at which young women reach menarche (first menstruation) in two different eras. The comparison is expressed in numerical or quantitative terms—dates and age. The accuracy of this statistical comparison is claimed by reference to *authority:* "Well known to biological anthropologists as the 'secular trend' . . ." and this is followed by additional statistical evidence stating relatively precisely the rate at which this process occurs: four months per decade. The use of authority is indirect and general. The author cites no specific authorities; he simply asserts that this is commonly accepted knowledge in a given area of expertise, an area of expertise that he shares. He supports the appeal to authority by the use of a technical term, the "secular trend." The term is technical because it is particular to a special area of expertise, and it is in quotation marks because it is a special usage that differs from ordinary usage. Ordinarily, the word *secular* refers to something non-religious or nontheological. But here the term is used to mean "of an age or generation," and this meaning is derived from the Latin word *saeculum,* meaning age or generation. That a technical term exists suggests that the phenomenon is so familiar experts have coined a term for it.

The next paragraph states the implication of this decline in the age of puberty, which is parenthood, and attacks evidence that would refute the decline as untrue, atypical, or misinterpreted. This is a **strategy,** the strategy of *refutation,* in which a rhetor shows that the opposition's evidence is inadequate or that the conclusions drawn from the evidence are inappropriate. In this case, the refutation is merely an *assertion,* or statement, and it is convincing only to the degree that you accept the author's authority or expertise.

Paragraph 4 presents more evidence for the author's claim that the decline in puberty is the cause of increased pregnancy among teenagers. The author presents an *example* **(supporting material)** of a people, the Kung San, whose gathering–hunting way of life is similar, presumably, to the way of life of the original humans. Among this people, the age of menarche is quite close to that of women in Europe and the United States in 1840, and the age of first birth is comparably later. Some details are provided to strengthen the example. We are told that sexual activity among adolescents is very common (*ubiquitous* means existing everywhere), that half are married before menarche, and that no form of contraception is in use. By providing these details the author is attempting to prove that only the higher age of puberty prevents this people from having a high rate of teenage pregnancy, the conclusion that he asserts in paragraph 5.

The *thesis* or major conclusion **(purpose)** is stated at the beginning of paragraph 6: "Human beings are not designed by evolution either in body or in spirit for the experience of adolescent pregnancy." If the act is well constructed, everything presented to us should support this claim, and everything argued should follow from it.

Paragraph 6 contains more *statistical* evidence **(supporting material).** This evidence details the specific size and location of the problem and describes the rate of increase. These statistics are specific for an American audience, and the details are presented, I think, to reinforce the seriousness of the problem. We are told that in a 20-year period, the birth rate doubled among teen-agers aged 15–19. More recently, from 1960 to 1973, births to unmarried teen-agers aged 14–17 rose steadily. The author asserts that the rise in births was halted by legal abortions. Teen-age pregnancies have continued to rise, however, now numbering one million per year, and the fastest rise is among the youngest group, those aged 11–13. These statistics say this is the problem, this is its size, this is how it is developing, this is where it is located. Numbers make the problem more specific and real, and the trends and ages support the author's earlier explanation of the phenomenon. Once again, the author has combined *statistics* with *literal analogy* (comparing teen-age pregnancies in one period with such pregnancies in another).

Paragraph 7 supports the idea that human beings are not physically ready for maternity before age 20. According to the author (and he cites no sources; one must rely on his authority), women under 20 have a greater chance of dying in childbirth, bearing a dead child, or bearing a child with birth defects. He adds that social and economic problems—poverty, divorce, inept parenting, child neglect, and child abuse—are more likely to afflict teen-age parents because of their age. Once again, readers are asked to accept these statements because of the rhetor's authority and/or because they are plausible (given what is known about employment, causes of divorce, and causes of poor parenting).

Paragraph 8 supports the idea that teen-agers are not psychologically ready to bear children. The argument is *a fortiori* (a Latin phrase meaning "for the stronger reason" or "all the more"): If this one thing is true, then this other thing is all the more likely to be true. Here, the author tells us that all women, even those over 20, run a substantially increased risk of mental illness (fivefold to fifteenfold) during the first month after childbirth. When the author asks, "What sort of effect may we expect it [childbirth] to have on a junior high school girl?" he expects us to say that if the danger of mental illness is so great at this time for all women, will it not be that much greater for teen-agers who, because of their age, are less able to cope with stress, for example? (Note that this conclusion may be false. Teen-agers may be more resilient and flexible because of their youth.)

The next sentence is a long argument abbreviated to a sentence or presented in a kind of shorthand that the reader must decode. One must, as the author says, "stretch the imagination." If we do so, according to the author, we will conclude that to deny a teen-ager an abortion is a form of child abuse. To reach that conclusion, one must see teen-agers as children who are the innocent victims of a flawed natural process. To punish a child for such a natural flaw (as for a cleft palate, or some other handicap) is a form of child abuse. Since children born to children (teen-agers) have a greater chance of dying, being physically or mentally defective, and/or being badly parented, refusing an abortion to a teen-ager is to abuse her and, indirectly, to cause the abuse of her child. The final clause in the sentence adds another element to the argument: "the kitchen-abortion horror tales." It says, in effect, that if denied legal abortions, teen-agers will seek out illegal ones, and they will die or be rendered sterile by procedures done poorly in filthy surroundings. To allow this to happen is also child abuse, according to the author.

Since ancient times, arguments the audience must complete have been called *enthymemes*. Such arguments require that the audience share certain values with the speaker or have certain kinds of knowledge and experience such that, when given fragmentary cues, they can and will complete the argument or thought. When they work, such arguments are strong because the audience cooperates in creating the proofs by which it is persuaded and thus becomes more deeply persuaded.

The idea that we "abuse" these "children" is expanded in paragraphs 9 and 10. Paragraph 9 argues that we behave inconsistently. It says that in all other areas of life, we treat the teen-ager as a minor with "diminished responsibility"; in the maternity clinic, however, we treat the teen-ager as a fully responsible adult and condemn her, presumably for immorality.

Paragraph 10 describes the various forces working on teen-agers: "Assaulted by culturally sanctioned sexual innuendo [sexually suggestive material bombards them in television programs, magazines, advertising] and borne along by physical and physiological events [carried and moved by natural forces]," "at the mercy of their own and one another's impulses [adolescents always have strong urges to experiment with sex, but today's adolescents are at the mercy of these urges because they are no longer protected by sterility]," having five

years less experience and mental growth than their pubescent counterparts of a century ago [compared to young persons in the past, they
have fewer resources on which to draw to handle these pressures]."
Note that the description shows natural and social forces acting on
teen-agers, forces that are outside their control.

In paragraph 11, the author considers how *we* **(audience)** help these
children in the midst of these "biological storms" (the same kind of
figurative analogy as in paragraph 1). According to him, we offer, on
the one hand, the counsel of religion, which he calls thick (dense or
unclear), "vague, timid, false, irrelevant or negligible." Once again,
this is just an assertion supported by a series of adjectives. The effect
depends on the reader. If you think of religion's counsels as unclear
and vague because of prudery, or as downright false, as in the scare
story that masturbation will stunt your growth or make your sex
drive uncontrollable; if you think that the admonition to pray is timid
or irrelevant or that religionists' advice is rarely helpful, the argument will be forceful. Conversely, if you hold strong religious beliefs,
if your rabbi, priest, or minister has been understanding and helpful,
the argument is weak.

On the other hand, we offer teen-agers sex education that the author correctly says is silenced by law on matters of contraception. And
contraceptive information is crucial for sexually active teen-agers,
in his view.

Paragraph 12 is a dramatic attack on those who deprive teen-agers
of contraceptive information and of legal abortions. Such information
is " a major source of rescue from the accident"; children are kept "in
the dark." The campaign against women's rights to control their
bodies is "superstitious." These are dramatic phrases, *labels*. The
strategy of *labeling* is intended to pin certain positive or negative
associations on a process or person or object by calling it a certain
name. Similarly, as noted in paragraph 13, giving in to this campaign
is "capitulation" [surrender]; it is the same thing as "sabotaging a
lone remaining dam [abortion becomes the last barrier against total
disaster] above an already inundated flood plain [when the dam goes,
it will add disaster to disaster]" (*figurative analogy*). The effect will be
an unbreakable cycle of children born to children, with all the terrible effects he has described, says the author.

Paragraphs 14 and 15 attempt to dismiss an alternative, that is,
placing children born to teen-age mothers with foster parents. The
author calls payments to foster parents *"bounty* payments," a label
that literally refers to rewards for catching outlaws or killing preda-
tory animals, but has come to carry connotations of actions done
purely for money. Paragraph 15 asserts that foster care is a proven

failure, and thus not an acceptable choice except where the only alternative is the orphanage. In effect, the author argues that there is no satisfactory alternative to legal abortion and contraceptive information.

Paragraph 16 defines the **audience** to whom the appeal is made. The author recognizes that he cannot persuade those "whose private views make them oppose abortion on ethical grounds." He is not addressing members of right-to-life groups or those whose religious beliefs condemn abortion. It is to the "rest of us" that he is speaking.

Paragraph 17 describes the alternative view as pro-choice (we must fight for the right to exercise a more complex judgment). But this paragraph narrows the issue **(structure).** The author favors choice for all women, but there is a special and dramatic need to provide "protection for pregnant children"; "an abortion must always be available to a teen-ager." For him, these very young women are a special case; they are physiologically blighted, "a tragic, anomalous, biological novelty," he says, repeating his earlier views. Because of their special situation, they must be our first concern.

Paragraphs 18, 19, and 20 are the *conclusion*. Following the *summary* **(structure)** in paragraph 17, the author makes a series of appeals through historical *analogy* **(supporting material).** In paragraph 18 he *alludes* to **(strategy)** past fanatical and religious resistance to concepts of democratic government, religious freedom, and evolution, and to new theories about the movements of the planets. The current resistance to acknowledging women's rights over their bodies, he says, is like earlier resistance to these other new ideas—with the passage of time, the current challenge to these rights will seem as inappropriate as the earlier resistance seems to us now. But, he reminds us, right now there are still several hundred thousand pregnant children to whom he, at least, remains morally obligated.

ELEMENTS OF DESCRIPTIVE ANALYSIS

The seven elements of descriptive analysis can now be explained in greater detail and illustrated from this rhetorical act:

1. Purpose

     a. Thesis: the specific purpose, central idea, or major conclusion: "Human beings are not designed by evolution either in body or in spirit for the experience of adolescent pregnancy."

b.   Narrowing the subject: limiting the aspect of the issue to be treated. In this case, the author treats the problems of contraception and unwanted pregnancy only for persons under the age of 20.

c.   Response desired: the beliefs and actions the author seeks from the audience. Konner wants us to believe the thesis, and, as a result, to support the act of providing contraceptive information and legal abortions to teen-agers.

2.   Audience

a.   Those selected by the act: the target group the rhetor seeks to influence. Notice that although many different people read the *New York Times*, Konner is addressing adults (see paragraphs 11, 17, and 20) and only those *adults whose moral positions let them consider abortion ethically possible*. In addition, Konner seems to select intelligent and well-educated people by the vocabulary he uses.

b.   The role prospective audience members are asked to play: in this case, *agents of change* to alter our laws.

3.   Persona

a.   The role(s) adopted by the rhetor in making the case: Konner adopts two *roles* —that of a *scientific expert* with the authority and competence to provide and interpret accurate information, and that of *moralist*, one who feels in a position to tell us what is ethically proper and morally right. He condemns the actions of those who withhold contraceptive information and abortions from teen-agers on moral grounds (see paragraphs 12, 13, 20).

4.   Tone

a.   Attitude toward the subject: In this case, I described this facet of tone as "dramatic" and "vivid" (see page 23). There is a great deal of *personal* involvement with the subject, a strong *emotional* commitment to it (in this sense, the tone is angry and horror-rousing), illustrated by the use of emotive and loaded language or labels.

b.   Attitude toward the audience: This varies, depending on the rhetor–audience relationship. Rhetors may approach the audience as peers, as inferiors (e.g., as students to be taught), or as superiors (e.g., as when addressing God in prayer, as a student addressing teachers, a lay person addressing experts, and so on). In this case, the speaker acts as an authority and seeks to teach and advise. The tone is *authoritative* ("I know," "I am the expert")—in this case, that of an expert and moral adviser.

5. Structure

a.   Introduction: gaining attention, introducing the subject/ issue or the perspective to be taken, narrowing the subject, creating a relationship between rhetor and audience. Not all of these are done in every introduction. In this case, the introduction is paragraph 1; it gains attention by introducing the author's perspective and by the use of vivid figurative analogies.

b.   Body: the development of and justification for the purpose. It is here that you should expect to find most supporting materials (some may appear in the introduction and conclusion) and here that the strategies become apparent. Ordinarily, development and justification occur along one of these lines:

(1)   Chronological development: This is development over time (starting with the earliest and working toward the latest event) or in sequence. In this case, paragraph 6 develops a trend historically, or chronologically.

(2)   Topical development: This organizes material in terms of its parts or aspects. In this case, paragraph 7 illustrates a topical exploration of the problems of teen-age pregnancy: (a) mortality, (b) birth defects, (c) mental retardation, (d) socioeconomic problems, and (e) psychological problems. These "topics" are answers to the question: What kinds of problems result from teen-age motherhood?

(3)   Logical development: This type of organization examines processes that are necessarily related, such as the relationship between problems and solutions. Here, the whole act is organized logically. The author asserts that the cause of increased teen-age pregnancy is earlier menarche, and he describes the problem of teen-age motherhood and proposes solutions he believes are most desirable.

c.   Conclusion: summarizing the major ideas and reinforcing the purpose. In this case, the conclusion is paragraphs 17 through 20; 17 summarizes, 18 and 19 make comparisons to emphasize and reinforce, and 20 places special emphasis on the particular aspect of the issue that has been Konner's concern—the moral obligation of adults to pregnant children.

d.   Transitions, often internal summaries: These are explanations and comments made to show relationships. They are re-

minders of what has gone before and preparations for what is
to come. These should enable the audience to follow the author's structural plan. Paragraph 5 is an internal summary or
conclusion drawn from what has just been presented. The beginning of paragraph 8 is a transition. In paragraph 7 we have
read of the problems for the child; the first sentence in paragraph 8 prepares us for the remainder of the paragraph, which
discusses the problems of the teen-age mother. This sentence
also connects the problems of the two paragraphs so that we
consider them together and their impact is increased by the
combination.

6. Supporting materials: evidence that describes, explains,
enumerates, and proves.

> **a.** Examples: instances or specific cases that illustrate con-
> cretely and often in detail. In this act, the story of the Kung
> San is an example.
>
> **b.** Statistics: numerical measures of size, scope, or frequency
> of occurrence. There are many in this essay, for example, "at
> the rate of four months per decade" (paragraph 2), "99 percent
> of [Kung San] girls are married by age 20" (paragraph 4),
> "births in the 15–19 maternal age group about doubled" and
> "the present rate of one million a year" (paragraph 6).
>
> **c.** Authority: quotation of an opinion or conclusion drawn by
> someone with expertise and experience in an area relevant to
> the issue. Presumably, such a person has special abilities to
> interpret information. No specific authority is cited in this es-
> say. The author relies on his own credentials, cited at the end of
> the published essay, and on a general reference to authorities:
> "Well known to biological anthropologists as the 'secular
> trend' " (paragraph 2).
>
> **d.** Analogy
>
>> **(1)** Literal analogies, usually called comparisons, com-
>> pare events, objects, persons, and so on that are obviously
>> or literally (on the face of it) alike, or in the same
>> category—for example, comparing two quarterbacks, four
>> pies, ten funerals, two sewage systems, three modern
>> poets. In this essay, the literal analogies are also statisti-
>> cal; that is, the comparisons are numerically measured.
>> For example, the author compares the average ages at
>> menarche of American and European women in 1840 and

today, and the incidence of mental illness among women both in general and during the month after childbirth.

(2) Figurative analogies are imaginative comparisons between things, events, and persons that are not obviously alike at all but that nevertheless resemble each other in some way. According to this author, the spread of teen-age pregnancy is like a flood, epidemic, and famine because both have natural causes and widespread and disastrous effects. The author also compares the failure to provide teen-agers with contraceptive information to keeping "children in the dark," and the removal of funding for abortion to removing "a lone remaining dam above an already inundated flood plain." Such comparisons make ideas vivid, and associate what is familiar with what is unfamiliar and alien.

7. Strategies: the selection of language, appeals, arguments, and evidence and their adaptation to a particular audience, issue, and occasion.

a. Language: the selection of terms and labels for their appropriateness and impact. "Pregnant children" is a shocking phrase that immediately suggests that teen-age mothers are thrust into an inappropriate situation and are in need of help; "secular trend" is a bit of technical terminology that lends authority to the assertion.

b. Appeals: to needs, drives, and desires; to cultural values. Konner appeals to adults to protect the survival of their teen-age children—and the future of society—by preventing teen-age motherhood. Since adults in our society are supposed to protect children, we can see this as an appeal to a cultural value about adult responsibility. The most important strategy is the appeal on scientific or naturalistic grounds: pregnant teen-agers are not moral deviants, but victims of a natural disaster, and so deserve our help (not our condemnation) just as would the victims of flood, epidemic, or famine. The issue has been cast in a different perspective from the moral one in which it is usually considered.

c. Selection of specific discursive and aesthetic techniques: Out of the many persuasive strategies available, this editorial uses these, among others:

(1) Refutation: stating an opposing argument and showing its weakness.

(2)   Enthymemes: presenting an argument in such a way that the audience participates in its completion.

(3)   *A fortiori* argument: a special form of argumentative comparison that says, in effect, if it happens in that case, how much more likely it is to occur in this one.

(4)   Allusion: a reference to historical events, literature, mythology, or some other repository of cultural wisdom. In this case, the allusions occur in the conclusion and are all very indirect references to past history, to the French Revolution, the Inquisition, the Scopes trial, and the trial of Galileo.

These categories (and their subcategories) provide a set of labels or terms that lets a critic or rhetor talk about a rhetorical act in order to analyze it (divide it into its parts) and describe it as fully and accurately as possible. Some of these categories are basic and are essential starting points. For instance, as a rhetor, you must immediately decide your purpose and determine just whom you are addressing. You must select a method of organization and the supporting materials you will use. Your simplest role would be to speak or write as a peer to your classmates (but there are always the problems of the teacher, who is not a peer, and of a subject on which you are more expert than your classmates). You may also try to treat tone very simply, by saying, "Oh, I'll be objective." But in most cases, you will find that you have beliefs and commitments and personal involvements, and you must decide how to handle these. The category of strategy is the most difficult, and it requires the greatest experience. You will need to read and hear many rhetorical acts to see the possibilities, and you will also need to use your instructor as a resource to get suggestions about approaches you might use to overcome special elements of the rhetorical problem.

As you will discover, these elements are always present and almost always important in understanding how and why a rhetorical act succeeded or failed in its purpose. If you are to talk to yourself and to others about anything, you must share a common language. This chapter suggests some crucial terms in the language needed to talk about rhetorical acts.

Descriptive analysis provides you with a vocabulary for discussing rhetorical action and with a method of identifying what is distinctive about a particular persuasive effort. Both a vocabulary and a method are needed if you are to become sophisticated consumers of contemporary persuasion. Skillful rhetors understand both their own acts and those of others. Your ability to initiate rhetorical action and to control how others influence you depends on your accuracy in describing discourse.

EXERCISES

1. Select an editorial from your local or school newspaper, and make a descriptive analysis of it. Write the results in an outline similar to the one in this chapter. What did you discover from your analysis that was not apparent from a casual first reading?

2. Read Benjamin Hooks's speech at the end of Chapter 4. Then apply the relevant and appropriate categories of descriptive analysis (purpose, rhetor, tone, structure, support materials, strategy, audience) to each of the following in order to explain its function in the discourse:

Sample   **a.** "In the words of one of the first black Republicans, Frederick Douglass, 'Unless there is struggle, there will be no progress'" (paragraph 4). This is authority evidence from a famous black speaker and abolitionist. It works well because Douglass is an authority (one of the first black Republicans) for the immediate audience and for blacks in the larger audience. Douglass's position creates a common bond between the immediate Republican audience and blacks in the television audience; it reminds both groups of the historical connection between blacks and the Republican party. Douglass's statement is also related to Hooks's purpose. Hooks is asking Republicans to do hard things, and Douglass is recalling tough decisions of the past (abolition of slavery) that Republicans can be proud of.

b. "I come today not in a partisan position, for I intend to present this same position paper to the black delegates and alternates at the Democratic Convention . . ." (paragraph 3).

c. "For this large number of unemployed black youth, in the words of Mr. Jones, Chairman of General Electric, 'constitute a ticking time bomb that would threaten to destroy the whole of our nation'" (paragraph 10).

d. "The common thread which runs throughout our concerns for each of these issues is, in part, because of uneven treatment on the basis of race, sex, or poverty. We urge you to reexamine your positions to make sure that the American values of equality of opportunity are guaranteed on these issues of such vital concern. For instance, on the issue of abortion, whatever your personal position might be, we at the NAACP believe that any rights and options which are wanted and available to the rich must be available to the poor" (paragraph 13).

e.   "As a black, growing up in a rigidly segregated society, I have felt the sting of overt, blatant prejudice and segregation. But like the overwhelming majority of black Americans, I remain loyal to the American dream" (paragraph 22).

CHAPTER 3

YOUR RHETORICAL ACT

Early in most practical courses, students and teachers face a dilemma. On the one hand, students need to begin applying their developing skills in order to understand problems concretely and to discover ways to handle specific situations. On the other hand, students do not yet know many of the concepts they need to cope with difficulties, and teachers have not had time to present them. Clearly acknowledging this dilemma, this chapter is intended to give you practical advice on preparing your first classroom exercise.

At the end of the chapter, there is a strategy report and a list of assignments your instructor may wish to use for your first exercise. The strategy report is designed to make you aware of your choices and their implications, and to develop your skills as a critic. Each of the exercises presumes that your first classroom effort will be directed toward the most limited and manageable rhetorical purposes: to alter perception and/or to explain, the two purposes that have traditionally been referred to as informative. The suggestions in the rest of the chapter, however, are appropriate for preparing any kind of rhetorical effort.

The prospect of initiating rhetorical action is frightening, even for the most skilled practitioners. Those of us who lecture daily never overcome the fear of seeming trivial or boring, of saying something foolish, of forgetting important material. These are normal and appropriate fears. Anyone can misread an audience, presenting material the audience already knows and, hence, produce a humdrum act. Anyone can forget important material, be ill prepared, or make a silly or foolish statement. The material in this chapter is intended to provide you with the best possible insurance against all these prospects when you speak or write for an audience. I divide my suggestions into four areas: picking a topic, researching a subject, organizing your material, and preparing for the final presentation.

PICKING A TOPIC

Much of the fear you feel in a rhetorical situation arises from a sense that the situation is not under your control. Admittedly, unforeseen things can happen. But they are much less likely if you choose your topic well. The most basic advice to the rhetor is: *Speak and write from your own knowledge and experience!* If you do, you will prepare with greater ease and confidence because you are working out of familiarity. You will have general knowledge against which you can test information from articles and books. Your own experiences will provide a stock of examples that will make the subject more personal and vivid for the audience. If you share values and experiences with members of your audience, your relationship to the topic will make it easier to show their relationship to the topic. In addition, your research will be easier as you will probably have access to firsthand information, from people who work with or experience the topic directly every day. Here are some general questions that will help you find suitable topics for speeches or essays:

1.   Where did you grow up? Each of you has special knowledge and experiences from growing up on a farm, in the inner city, on army bases, in a mining town, in the mountains, or in the desert. These experiences can be the starting point for a speech or essay. In the past, students who have grown up on farms have given exciting speeches on support prices, insecticides, fertilizers, beef imports; students from cities have written about red-lining, street repair, and variations in police protection in areas of the city. In no case was the personal experience and knowledge of the student sufficient, but in each case, the research was easier, and familiarity with the subject increased the rhetor's confidence.

2.   What are your parents' occupations? As the child of a plumber, a lawyer, a store manager, or whatever, you have a special store of firsthand experience and access to a source of firsthand information. For example, in the past, students have used this experience to speak or write on how plumbers are licensed and why they command such high pay, on the feasibility of converting factories from oil to coal (the father sold such machinery), medical malpractice

awards from juries (the child of a lawyer), and the nature of capital gains taxes (the child of an accountant). Once again, your experience can be the starting point for your rhetorical act, and you will speak from special knowledge and familiarity.

3.   What jobs have you done? Even temporary or part-time work teaches you a lot. For instance, a grocery clerk discussed the arguments for and against automated check-out equipment; a student who had worked as a building inspector wrote about city laws governing apartments and how to make complaints to compel landlords to meet the requirements of the building code; a student who had worked as the manager of a fast-food restaurant discussed franchises.

4.   What are your hobbies and interests? In past classes, a member of the track team talked about why some shoes increase your speed and last longer; a collector of stamps argued for their value as an investment; a student who had raced cars claimed that 55 mph is the safest maximum speed limit; an auto buff spoke about why changing the oil regularly is the single most important maintenance task a car owner can perform.

5.   Have you family or friends with special problems, distinctions, or unusual characteristics? Many rhetorical acts spring from tragedy. An alcoholic father prompted a speech on organizations that help the families of alcoholics; a schizophrenic sister prompted a speech on megavitamin therapy—what it is and how it works; the suicide of a friend's brother prompted an essay on suicide among college students; an epileptic brother occasioned a speech on misconceptions about epilepsy; a father's death from a shot of penicillin inspired an essay on the dangers of allergies. Success and honor can also be the source of topics: the daughter of a mother who patented a new chemical process talked about the two-income family; the brother of a professional baseball player discussed the antitrust suits against baseball; a scholarship student in ballet demonstrated and explained the basic movements of ballet as part of a speech to increase appreciation of ballet performances.

6.   Have you had unusual experiences? The survivor of a severe automobile accident talked about seat belt safety; a girl who was threatened by a drunken boy with a loaded gun argued for gun control; a foreign exchange student spoke about currency problems.

These are only a few examples of the many instances in which students have drawn on their special experiences.

Speaking or writing from your own experience has additional benefits. In most cases, you will be deeply involved in your topic and your sincerity will be catching—the audience will care too. When you draw on personal experience, your audience will find you knowledgeable and credible, worthy of being believed. Your rhetorical act will not seem a mere exercise for a class; rather, the audience will hear you telling them something you know about firsthand, that you care about, and they will consider what you write or say seriously and with respect. You will be on the way to a successful presentation.

If you have considered these questions carefully, you will recognize some weak approaches. Don't write from research you did on last year's debate topic unless you can personalize the topic for yourself and your audience. A similar warning goes for a rhetorical act drawn from last semester's term paper. Don't pick a topic from an article in a magazine just because you happened to find it in the dentist's waiting room. Again, do pick a subject that is close to you as a person, one with which you have had firsthand experience.

Firsthand experience and personal knowledge alone, however, are not sufficient. You must test your experience and broaden your knowledge with information drawn from other sources.

RESEARCHING A SUBJECT

If you wish to be an effective speaker or writer, you must become familiar with the library. It is the primary resource for testing personal experience, refining understanding of the subject, and collecting concrete material that will explain and prove your claims and make your subject vivid.

Begin with a general survey of the library (try both your school and your public library). Find out where things are and what procedures you must follow. For example, locate the card catalog, the reference room, the periodicals room, the reserve room, the government documents area, if any, and the microfilm area. Learn how to take materials out of the library and what procedures must be followed to use books, magazines, and microfilm. Are there open stacks where you can browse, or must you ask for all materials? Does a computer printout show which periodicals the library holds and where they are? Is there a computer printout that will tell whether someone has the book you want? Are there special libraries for certain kinds of materials? Many libraries provide tours, and you would be wise to take one or to get the library's brochure on its materials and procedures. In other words, "case the joint" carefully before mounting an assault to find specific materials.

What will you need to know and how can you find it? Obviously, your needs and problems will differ (for each effort), but there are some general procedures you can follow. First, since personal experiences are ordinarily narrow and limited, you will need general background on a particular subject and an understanding of terms and concepts. Begin in the reference room. In this room you will find all the general sources of information and the indexes that will help you find more detailed information.

General Sources

There are three basic general sources to help you: encyclopedias, dictionaries, and almanacs and statistical yearbooks. The least specialized and most general sources are large encyclopedias such as the *Encyclopaedia Britannica* or the *Encyclopedia Americana*. These will give you general and historical information on people, places, concepts, and events. The articles are written by authorities, and each ends with a list of books and articles that will provide more detailed information. You may also find it helpful to look up your topic or related subjects in a slightly more specialized but still encyclopedic reference, such as the *Encyclopedia of Philosophy*, the *Encyclopedia of Social Work*, or the *American Negro Reference Book*. Once again, these will give you background plus a list of more detailed sources.

You are all familiar with general dictionaries such as *Webster's International Dictionary* and the *Oxford English Dictionary* and their more compact and abridged versions. You can check the meanings of terms in them, the history of changes in meanings, and the etymology or the linguistic origin of meanings. As with encyclopedias, specialized dictionaries may be helpful. For example, the *Dictionary of the Social Sciences* explains terms peculiar to or with special meanings in the social sciences, the *Oxford Classical Dictionary* focuses on figures from ancient Greece and Rome and on concepts needed to study classical literature and philosophy. There are similar dictionaries for medicine, law, sociology, psychiatry, and the like.

If you seek more recent information, particularly quantitative information, as background for your research, turn to almanacs and statistical yearbooks. These books contain information, usually for a single year, and are compiled by a variety of agencies usually named in the titles—the *CBS News Almanac*, the *New York Times Almanac*, the *Reader's Digest Almanac, World Almanac, Information Please Almanac,* among others. These sources are usually current within a few months of the events you may be researching. Similarly, the *Statistical Abstract of the United States* provides quantitative information of all sorts for a single year (often with comparisons to other, recent years).

Specific Sources

When you have gathered this general background and statistical information, you will need more detailed information and specialized analyses. Begin with the card catalog; since it is organized by subject, author, and title, you can look up your subject. You can also look up the books, by author or title, that you found in general references.

Before you approach the subject index, make a list of related topics or subjects suggested by your general background research, under which you might find information. Remember that every filing system, including the card catalogs of libraries, reflects a way of looking at reality. Since your perceptions and those of the catalogers may differ, a list of subjects will be more helpful in finding what you need. For example, if you want to show that 55 mph is a good national speed limit, you will find information listed under:

Speed limits
Traffic regulations
Traffic accidents
Automobile driving
Gasoline consumption

and possibly under:

Weather and driving
Aging and accidents
Stimulus and response (reflexes)
Highway conditions
Highway repair
Fuel shortage
Highway safety or fatalities

A list of such topics will help you find all relevant information on your topic in the card catalog organized by subject.

How do you decide which books to use or take out? Initially, you will have to make some guesses based on limited information. You might begin with works cited in the encyclopedia article(s), or by the authors of such articles. You may decide to include the most recent works available. In addition, you can get some clues from a book's title. But the best information comes from the subject classification found at the bottom of the library card. For example:

Pomeroy, Sarah B.	Name of author
Goddesses, whores, wives, and slaves.	Title of book
Bibliography	The book has a list of the sources used and is indexed.
Includes Index.	
1. Women—History—To 500. 2. Rome—Social conditions.	These subject listings are helpful. They indicate the book is a history, they indicate the time period covered, and they show that there is an emphasis on social conditions in Rome.

Here, by contrast, is one that is not particularly helpful:

Kingston, Maxine Hong. The woman warrior. 1. Kingston, Maxine Hong. I. Title	From the card, you would not know that this is the autobiography of an American woman of Chinese ancestry.

If you are in a library with closed stacks, such cards will have to serve, however limited they are. If you are in a library with open stacks, go to the places where the books you have chosen are shelved. Browse in these areas for books that you have overlooked in the card catalog. Before you decide to take any book out, look at the preface and table of contents. The preface will indicate the author's point of view and purpose; the table of contents will tell you precisely what areas of the subject are covered.

Because of the delays involved in publishing books, you must go elsewhere for information more recent than two or three years old. The *Readers' Guide to Periodical Literature* is an index to general subscription magazines from 1900 to the present. (The first page lists the periodicals and reports it indexes.) Since articles are indexed by subject, come armed with a list of possible headings. An item looks like this:

TRAFFIC accidents

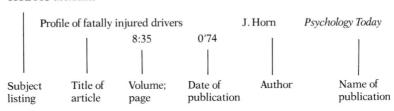

| Subject listing | Title of article | Volume; page | Date of publication | Author | Name of publication |

Another large and helpful index is that of the *Congressional Record*. The *Congressional Record* is a record of debate in Congress and contains all articles and items that are inserted into it by members of Congress. As a result, it covers many topics and contains much useful information. Some newspapers, including the *New York Times*, the *Wall Street Journal*, and the *Washington Post*, also have indexes. Check to see which indexes your library holds, keeping in mind that if you seek information from an unindexed newspaper, you will have a hard time.

In addition to general subscription periodicals and newspapers, there are specialized academic and professional journals in many subject areas, and these create difficulties because they are sometimes indexed individually. *The Humanities Index* and the *Social Sciences Index* list articles published in scholarly journals. For even more specialized information, you may need to talk to a librarian or to someone in the field in which you are interested.

There are also indexes to special kinds of information. For example, the *Book Review Digest* and the *Index to Book Reviews in the Humanities* will guide you to what reviewers have said about books you may be using as sources. And the *Dramatic Criticism Index* cites reviews of plays.

As a rhetor, you need outside opinions of books that you cite. You will also need to know the qualifications and experience of persons you quote as authorities. Among the special references that can help you are the *Directory of American Scholars, American Men and Women of Science,* and *Who's Who in America.* Sources such as these will help you judge the authority and credibility of a source and indicate to the audience how much weight should be given to a person's statement.

As you expand your knowledge of library resources, you will find that you are expanding your abilities as a rhetor.

TAKING NOTES

Like all researchers, rhetors need to learn to take notes so citations are accurate and complete and so they can return to a source easily if they need to. The ideal way to take notes is on note cards because they are easily filed and rearranged, and can be used easily in speaking or writing. If you plan to take small amounts of information from many sources, 3"-×-5" cards are suitable; however, in most cases 4"-×-6" or 5"-×-7" cards will be more convenient because there is more space on which to write or type. A note card with only one note from a source should look like this:

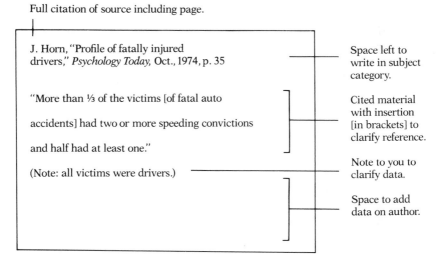

Full citation of source including page.

J. Horn, "Profile of fatally injured drivers," *Psychology Today*, Oct., 1974, p. 35 — Space left to write in subject category.

"More than ⅓ of the victims [of fatal auto accidents] had two or more speeding convictions and half had at least one." — Cited material with insertion [in brackets] to clarify reference.

(Note: all victims were drivers.) — Note to you to clarify data.

Space to add data on author.

Note that there is a full bibliographical citation for the source and that an insertion and a note are added to make the information clear to you. In addition, a space is left in the upper right-hand corner for a subject category. It is a good idea to write the subject category in pencil so it will be easy to change if you need to reorganize your material. If several note cards are used to record material from the same source, shorten the bibliographical entry but be sure to record the page number from which material is entered. For example, you might write:

Horn, PT, O '74, p. 36.

The only reasonable alternative to note cards is a notebook in which you record all your notes on a subject together. This is less convenient because you cannot discard material or reorganize as easily. If you do use a notebook, be sure to leave spaces in margins for classifications by subject so you can find the notes you need. In this case, you must recopy your data onto cards if the information is to be used in a speech.

Whether you are speaking or writing, your notes need to contain all necessary information about the source. Some of this material may be omitted in speaking, but in writing, it must all be produced in footnotes or the bibliography. This is a good time to buy a style sheet, such as the *Modern Language Association Style Sheet*, third edition, to learn the proper form for footnotes and bibliography. A style sheet will also help you with rules for writing. If you learn the proper form to use on note cards, you will find it easy to write correct footnotes for papers and articles.

ORGANIZING YOUR MATERIAL

Chapter 10 discusses organization in detail. You may wish to consult that chapter when you have finished reading this material. What follows are some preliminary and general considerations to use in limiting your topic and in planning the structure of your rhetorical act.

Narrowing or Limiting Your Topic

Most rhetorical acts, whether spoken or written, are relatively brief. Our culture is fast-paced; even most presidential addresses can be fitted into a half-hour for transmission by television or radio. Because of school schedules, speeches and essays for classes have to be fairly short. Your first concern, then, is to narrow your topic. Three questions will help you do this: (1) What parts of this topic are most significant and interesting for this audience? (2) What parts of this topic are most important, most serious, or have the broadest implications? (3) What aspect of the topic is most easily explained or what aspect can be discussed most fully in the time or space allotted?

The first question focuses your attention on the audience that is here at this time. What aspects of the topic will be new to them? What parts of the topic touch their lives or are directly related to their immediate circumstances? As an example, imagine that you want to talk about the problems of energy. Most college students do not pay utility bills directly, and many do not own cars, so the price of gas may be remote. Few live in houses heated by solar energy; in most cases, few will have the necessary expertise to compare coal and gas as sources of energy. If there is no nuclear plant in the area and none proposed, even the dangers of nuclear power may not be particularly relevant.

However, assume that student activity fees have been raised because of the increased costs of heating and cooling the student union, and that fees for board and room in dormitories have been raised for the same reason. Some research leads to the discovery that these buildings waste energy because of the way they were built. Perhaps your topic should be narrowed to the relationship between architecture and construction and energy consumption. Recognize that you are trying to alter the perceptions of *this particular audience,* and that your first concern should be to approach the topic so that its significance *for them* is apparent.

The second question is designed to fit your subject to the particular circumstances of the audience. Consider here what any audience should know about this subject. On the basis of your research, you may decide that the problems of nuclear energy are the most pressing despite their remoteness from the immediate concerns of the audience. If so, you need to think carefully about how you can make this facet of the energy question interesting and significant for the audience. You might decide to begin with the nuclear plants built 15 years ago that are now obsolete and that no one knows how to protect, make safe, or dismantle. Such dangers can be made concrete and personal for a community and for individuals. Members of the audience can identify with dangers to people like themselves and to communities similar to their own.

Whatever facet of the subject you choose, this second question will help you explain to the audience why you have chosen it. If you decide to discuss the relationship between building construction and fossil fuel consumption, you may need to explain briefly why you are not discussing nuclear power but instead have selected what may appear to be a less important part of the subject of energy. (Obviously, the need for energy in general and for nuclear energy in particular would be lessened if consumption dropped. You might argue that that makes the question of construction a very important one.)

The third question, what aspect of the topic can be most easily explained or fully discussed in the time or space allotted, is designed to call the rhetor's attention to clarity and intelligibility. In Part Two, which examines the rhetorical problem, I discuss the problems created by the complexity of some topics and purposes. The decision you make on this question is intended to simplify as much as possible so the audience will understand what you are discussing.

For example, the problems of energy are many, and each is complex. The problems of nuclear power alone cannot be discussed in 5 minutes or in 1,000 words. In order to make sense of the subject, you might decide to limit your discussion entirely to the problem of what to do with existing nuclear plants that are out of date. This choice ignores a great deal—whether there is sufficient uranium, whether nuclear wastes can be disposed of, whether the products of breeder reactors can be kept from terrorists, whether alternative energy sources exist, and on and on. But it focuses on a concrete problem that already exists: 20 nuclear power plants have been closed in the Western industrialized world—15 in the United States and 5 in Western Europe. By the year 2000, there will be more than 100 inactive atomic plants, and hundreds of smaller nuclear installations, such as nuclear medicine facilities and navy ship reactors, will have ceased to operate. All of them will stay radioactive for hundreds or even thousands of years, and they remain a serious threat.*

A rhetorical act on this subject may serve as a case study of the problems of nuclear power, as a concrete way for you to explore the kinds of problems that exist in the use of atomic energy. It's important, it's concrete, and it is sufficiently limited to be fully explained and explored in a relatively short rhetorical act. In other words, the third question should bend your energies toward finding a facet of the subject that you can cover thoroughly and clearly in the time or space allotted.

In sum, narrowing the topic should take into consideration the ways in which the subject is significant for the audience, the most important facets of the topic, and which aspects of the subject can be treated fully and carefully in a limited time or space.

Choosing a Thesis

Narrowing your topic leads naturally into the most important decision you make about organization: the selection of a thesis. Ordinarily, the general purpose of a rhetorical act is determined by the occa-

---

* Some information on this problem is given in "A-Plant Builder Turns to Dismantling Old Ones," by Jonathan Kandell, *New York Times*, 17 June 1978, late edition, pp. 23, 27.

sion or the assignment. For example, editorials, feature stories, and general news stories have rather clearly defined general purposes, but the writer must choose how she or he will translate the general purpose into a specific purpose. Occasions for speeches also usually define a general purpose—commencement speakers are expected to praise the new graduating class and talk about their future; sermons are intended to reinforce belief; reports are expected to provide information and create understanding. And again, in each case, the rhetor must decide just how he or she will translate the general purpose into a specific thesis.

Deciding on a thesis or central idea is difficult, and you should expect to find it troublesome. First, it represents a commitment that is hard to make—"I want the audience to know and understand precisely this: 'Storage facilities for nuclear wastes cannot be guaranteed safe for longer than 20 years.' " When you choose such a thesis, you make a claim to knowledge; in effect you say, "I have researched this topic, and I stake my credibility and authority on the accuracy of my research." In addition, you eliminate material, and limit yourself drastically. In this case, all research that does not bear directly on storage of nuclear wastes must be discarded. So the choice of a thesis is an extreme decision that specifies the precise claim you want to make and represents a drastic limitation of the topic. The thesis should be a simple declarative sentence that answers the question, "Just what do I want the audience to know or understand (or believe or do) when I finish?"

Here are some examples of good theses:

Building a solar home or converting a home to solar energy is a practical solution to the energy crunch for individuals.

Note that the topic is narrowed in two ways: to solving the energy problem for individuals (not industry, for example) and to solar energy. It is a good thesis because it focuses on practicality. As the audience for this rhetorical act, we would expect to hear about costs of building and conversion, availability of materials, ease of construction, availability of materials and knowledge for maintenance, climatic conditions needed, and so forth. It is also good because the claim of the rhetor is explicit and clear, and we know how to judge whether or not the claim is adequately supported.

Nuclear breeder reactors are unsafe.

This is a larger and more difficult claim that is aimed at a speech to formulate belief. It is good, however, because it narrows the topic to *breeder* reactors and because it narrows the perspective to questions of *safety*. As an audience, we would expect such a rhetorical act to focus on the problems of disposing of plutonium wastes and of preventing nuclear material suitable for explosive devices from falling into unauthorized hands.

> *55 mph is the maximum safe speed limit.*

This is a good thesis because the claim is specific—the fastest safe speed limit is 55 mph. Note that it ignores questions of energy altogether and focuses only on questions of safety. We would, as an audience, expect to hear about reaction times, stopping distances at various speeds, statistics on auto deaths, and the relation of auto deaths to speed. Note again that the thesis is clear, explicit, and limiting.

Here are some poor thesis statements:

> *The deregulation of natural gas.*

This is poor because it isn't a sentence and doesn't make a claim. It isn't clear what we are to know or understand about deregulation. That makes it a poor thesis, although it does a good job of narrowing the subject to natural gas and to questions about the relationship between price, availability, and government controls. Contrast this statement with a more explicit version:

> *The deregulation of natural gas will increase both the supply and the price.*

The following is a very poor statement that reflects a common error:

> *How a nuclear plant runs.*

It is not a sentence and does not state a purpose or a goal. One may rightly ask, *Why* should I know how a nuclear plant runs, and the thesis ought to give an answer. Contrast this statement with a more explicit one:

A nuclear power plant has a major impact on the environment.

This claim cannot be substantiated without explaining how a plant runs, but it also says, Here's why you should know how it runs. Recall that you, as rhetor, must always concern yourself with relevance and significance. Just as you may ask about classes and lecture materials—Why should I learn that—your audience will *always* ask, Why should I know? Why should I care? What difference does it make to me? Your thesis should be a statement that gives an answer.

People should drive more carefully.

This statement is a sentence, and it has a purpose. But it's hard to imagine how anyone could disagree. It's also hard to see how it could be developed or argued. No matter how careful drivers are, they could still drive more carefully. This seems to put the statement beyond argument. Just what is meant by "more carefully"? That very general phrase, open to many interpretations, ought to be translated into more concrete terms: not driving while on medication, while ill, while drunk, or in a car with poor brakes. A speech or essay on a particular kind of carelessness would come to grips with an issue that should challenge you and the audience.

People drive too fast.

This statement is a sentence, and it has a purpose. Its problems arise from its very general nature. The rhetor who uses this thesis will be all right if she or he narrows and specifies in the speech or essay just what benefits are to be derived from slower driving. Contrast it with a more specific statement:

You can save lives and money by driving no faster than 55 mph.

The following sentence is a problem because it contains two theses and implies two different rhetorical acts.

We must build nuclear power plants and convert industries to coal.

Each claim is adequate separately, but the rhetorical act that combines them will be somewhat schizophrenic. Each could be stated more clearly. For example, "There is no economically feasible alternative to nuclear power" is a clearer statement of the first claim. It is still very general, and it implies that the speaker will prove that natural gas, oil, solar energy, geothermal energy, and coal will all be proved inadequate. Actually, the only economically feasible alternative to nuclear energy that has been proposed, at least in the short-run, is coal, so the best statement would be:

Our supplies of coal are inadequate to meet our energy needs.

That statement explains why the two theses were combined. If coal is not adequate to our needs, then nuclear plants will have to be built (unless we reduce consumption greatly). However, the rhetor in this case should consider whether all of this can be treated in a single rhetorical act, given the constraints of space or time.

A good thesis statement should:

State a specific claim
Express a single unified purpose
Indicate significance and relevance

You will have conquered many of the problems of organizing your material when you have decided on a thesis and stated it clearly. As will be evident from the examples I have given, clearly stated theses imply the internal organization of the speech or essay. The structure of your rhetorical act is the development of your thesis. The main points of the rhetorical act should be statements (sentences making claims) that prove and explain the thesis. These main points should answer the questions Why? or How do I know? For example, the thesis "The deregulation of natural gas will increase both the supply and the price" implies a two-part development:

A. It will increase the supplies available across state lines.

B. It will raise the interstate price to the level of the intrastate price.

The statement "Nuclear breeder reactors are unsafe" implies that the main points will give reasons why such power plants are unsafe.

A. There are no safe methods for storing plutonium wastes.

B. There is no way to prevent the theft of plutonium.

Note that these reasons will need to be developed, in turn, by statements that show how the rhetor knows these things to be true or highly probable.

The specific purpose, making people believe that "55 mph is the maximum safe speed limit," suggests a development with main points like these:

A. Under ideal conditions, a car traveling at 55 mph requires a distance of more than seven car lengths to stop.

B. Road and weather conditions limit visibility and maneuverability.

C. Reaction times of drivers are increased by age, medications, and the consumption of alcohol.

D. The substantial decline in deaths in auto accidents since the speed limit has been lowered demonstrates the greater safety of lower speeds.

For your initial exercise, you should do only two additional things to organize your material: indicate how you will develop these main points, and plan an introduction and conclusion. For example, if you were to take as a thesis the statement "The 55 mph speed limit on our highways saves lives and money," your outline might look like this:

A. The 55 mph speed limit is better suited to actual driving conditions.
  1. Under ideal conditions, an alert, healthy driver needs about seven car lengths to stop a car going 55 mph.
    a. This distance includes reaction time (thinking distance) and braking distance.
    b. Small increases in speed make a difference because the distance needed to stop and the force of impact increase geometrically.
  2. Many drivers aren't in ideal condition.
    a. We have an aging population that will see and hear less well and react less quickly.

    b. Medicines and alcohol are even bigger problems.
       1. Over-the-counter remedies affect driving ability.
       2. Many commonly used prescription drugs are a serious threat to safe driving.
       3. Even relatively small amounts of alcohol impair driving ability.
  3. Road and weather conditions are often less than ideal.
    a. Many sections of our best highways are in poor condition.
    b. More limited visibility at night has always required lower speed limits.
    c. Rain, as well as ice and sleet, is a serious driving hazard, especially on limited access roads.
  4. Many cars are poorly maintained.

B. The 55 mph speed limit also saves lives.
  1. Since its enactment, for the first time in our history, there has been a dramatic drop in the number of highway fatalities.
  2. This drop is caused by lower speeds as well as less travel.

C. The 55 mph speed limit also saves money and energy.
  1. Most cars burn fuel with maximum efficiency at about 50 mph.
  2. Efficient gas use by all Americans saves energy.

Now two things need to be added, an introduction and a conclusion. The introduction should get the attention of the audience and indicate the significance of the topic for us. If you chose this topic because of a tragic or near-tragic personal experience, that story might be the ideal way to begin. A student who made a speech on this topic came to class scratched and bruised. He told of the miraculous survival of himself and his companions in an accident in which the driver had avoided a head-on collision only by taking to the ditch and hitting a tree. He told the story of the accident, reported that they had been traveling between 60 and 65, and said that he, personally, was now convinced that speed kills. He talked about his attitude and the attitudes of other people he knew about the 55 mph limit. He said his purpose was to defend that limit, not just because it saved energy, but because it saved lives. That was a superb introduction. It was vivid, personal, attention-getting. It located accurately the attitudes of the audience. It showed his personal commitment to the topic and purpose. It prepared us for what followed; we knew what to expect. In other words, a good introduction:

Gets the audience's attention

Creates accurate expectations about what will follow

Suggests the relationship of the topic to the audience

In this case, the introduction also showed the relationship between the rhetor and the subject, a highly desirable characteristic of introductions.

The conclusion of a rhetorical act is good if it is such that the act ends rather than stops. Ideally, a conclusion should do two things: (1) summarize the major ideas that lead to the claim embodied in the thesis and (2) fix the specific purpose in the audience's mind. What is most important is that you plan carefully just how you will end. In the case of the student who had the near-tragic accident, the speaker said something like this: "I've shown you that if you are healthy and alert, if your car is in good mechanical condition, and if you're driving 55 mph, it will take you 218 feet from the time you see a problem until you can stop. If you're tired, if you've had a drink or have taken an antihistamine, if your tires are worn or your brake fluid is down, if it is dusk or raining, it will take you longer. When you drive over 55, you are not only breaking the law and wasting gas, you may be driving too fast to avoid an accident. And I've got the cuts and bruises to prove it."

That conclusion is simple and effective. It recalls most of the major ideas of the speech so that it summarizes, but it does so in concrete terms that will be relevant and intelligible to each member of the audience. That helps to make each idea memorable. In addition, the speaker uses himself as a vivid visual reminder of the dangers of fast driving. The conclusion illustrates another useful technique for concluding—the explicit reference to an anecdote or example that was used in the *introduction*. This creates the effect of "completing a circle" and hence a very strong impression of completeness.

PREPARING YOUR PRESENTATION

The quality of your final oral or written presentation depends on your skills as a critic and on your willingness to practice or rewrite. You can develop and refine your critical skills through preparing the strategy report described at the end of the chapter. A strategy report is a written analysis of the choices you made in preparing your rhetorical act, in light of the obstacles you faced and your purpose. In addition, if the act is oral, you must practice it aloud, standing, and, at the same time, try to imagine yourself as a member of the audience. If your act is written, you must learn to polish and refine your efforts through rewriting.

At this point, you have an outline that states the specific purpose, lists the main points, and cites the evidence you will use to explain and prove your assertions. You have made some rough notes for what you will say in the introduction and conclusion. You now need to move from the outline toward the composition of a complete and finished rhetorical act. Your first concern should be clarity. Focus your attention on two areas: the clarity of the relationships among ideas and the clarity of each piece of evidence you will present.

The clarity of the relationships among the main ideas depends on the soundness of the argument's structure and on the kinds of transitions or bridges made between ideas. If you have done your outline carefully and have made certain that your main points answer the questions Why? and How do I know? the relationships among the main points should be clear. There is a relatively simple test you can apply to determine the adequacy of your argument. If your main points are A, B, C, and D, then, if the argument is sound, it should be the case that:

If A is true, if B is true, if C is true, and if D is true, then it should necessarily and inevitably follow that the claim you make in your specific purpose is true.

If you apply this test to the outline about 55 mph speed limits, you will notice the "fit" between the main points and the specific purpose. However, the material under A.1. will need some explanation to show how these figures were arrived at. In main point A.3., the rhetor is saying that ideal driving conditions rarely exist. After you eliminate stretches of limited access superhighways, the places with the best visibility, fewest traffic problems, and best surface, driving hazards are likely to increase. That needs to be clear as the argument is presented. Point A.2. is really saying that even young and healthy persons can have slowed reactions from cold medicine or a couple of beers, and this fact needs to be emphasized. Also, the audience may wonder about enforcement—are people really driving more slowly? If you think about the whole argument, you will realize that the rhetor is admitting that there may be places and persons and times that it's safe to drive faster than 55 mph; but he or she is saying that 55 mph is the maximum realistic speed limit, and a speed limit should not be made for ideal but for real and normal driving conditions. The rhetorical act should emphasize that point if it is to be really effective. Note that such a survey of the outline helps to clarify for the rhetor just what the purpose is, what should be emphasized, and what qualifications may need to be made, as for example, the recognition that it might be safe to drive faster under some conditions. In spite of such qualifications, you can make a strong and forceful argument, and by qualifying your claim you may avoid resistance from members of the audience who recognize exceptions.

Transitions are statements you make to ensure that the audience understands and recognizes the relationships among ideas. Although some members of your audience will listen or read actively, testing your arguments and trying to understand, others will listen or read relatively passively and will not see relationships unless you make them explicit. Here are some examples of transitions that might be used in the rhetorical act on 55 mph speed limits:

A good speed limit is geared to averages —normal reaction time, normal mechanical conditions, normal conditions of visibility and road surfaces. As a result, I'll begin by talking about optimums — ideal reaction time, ideal mechanical conditions, ideal visibility and road conditions. But I shall also talk about the prevalent use of medication and alcohol and about the conditions of roads and the problems of weather.

That statement creates connections and also previews what will happen in the speech. It is the sort of transition that usually connects the attention-getting introduction to the body of the rhetorical act (the section that develops the specific purpose). It clarifies by creating expectations: here is what I shall do and here is the general relationship among all these ideas.

The next transition explains two parts of one subpoint: the distance it takes to stop a car at a particular speed.

Two elements are involved in stopping a car: thinking distance and braking distance. The first refers to the distance you will travel during your reaction time. The second refers to the distance you travel after you've stepped on the brakes. It is a measure of the distance it takes for your car to stop mechanically. Let's consider reaction times first.

This transition clarifies by reminding the audience that there are two parts and allows the speaker to talk about each separately while creating in the audience an awareness of their relationship.

The next transition is really an explanation of how you and the highway department arrived at certain conclusions.

> *To understand how far you travel at different speeds, the Kansas Highway Department talks in feet per second. The math works like this: there are 5,280 feet in a mile (as you remember from elementary school). At speed 60, you travel one mile per minute or 5,280 divided by 60 or 88 feet per second.*

The transition clarifies by explaining, but it also shows the relationships among speed, reaction time, and the distance it takes to stop.

Here's another kind of transition and explanation, one on the deregulation of natural gas:

> *I've shown you how and why federal deregulation will increase the supplies of natural gas across state lines. What I've told you should make it pretty obvious that increased supplies depend on and are a result of higher prices for interstate gas shipments. In fact, deregulation will raise interstate prices to the intrastate level and will probably raise the prices for both in a few years.*

This is a transition between two main points to indicate their relationship to each other. In addition, the transition is a preview of what the rhetor intends to do under the second main point. It clarifies by showing the relationship between these two parts of the argument.

Practicing aloud and rewriting are the processes by which rhetors prepare oral and written rhetorical acts, respectively. Both are essential to produce a good final product. Practicing aloud serves two purposes: first, it creates a physical memory of what you intend to say that will help you speak smoothly. It prevents your oral presentation before the audience from being frightening because it is the first time you make your speech. Part of the fear associated with speaking is the fear each of us has about doing things that are new and different and in which we feel unskilled. You can diminish that by oral practice. Stand up as you intend to before the audience, hold your notes as you intend to, and speak your speech as you plan to do it on the actual occasion. If there are tongue twisters, you'll find them and be able to overcome them or make changes. If there's complicated material that's hard to explain, you'll discover it and have time for extra practice. Moreover, by the time you give your speech, it won't be the first time—it will be the ninth or tenth—and the material will feel familiar when you begin once again to present your speech. Second, it is the means for refining and reorganizing. For example, you practice your 5-minute speech aloud, and it runs 15 minutes. Clearly, you haven't narrowed the topic enough, and you need to do some cutting. Or, as you listen to yourself, you realize that to be clear you have to add something—and you can add it and plan carefully how to make the idea clearer. Please note, however, that none of these benefits occurs unless you practice aloud *exactly as if you were presenting the speech to your audience* and listen to yourself critically. You must pretend to be your own audience, listening to the speech as someone unfamiliar with the subject. It is such listening that enables you to catch problems and make needed changes. (Of course, you can also snag a cooperative roommate or friend and ask that person to respond candidly about questions and problems that she or he has in listening to what you say. But such a person is only a poor substitute for developing your abilities as your own best listener.)

Your speech should be presented from notes, not from a manuscript on which you have written out, word by word, what you intend to say. Presenting a speech from a manuscript is a difficult skill, as illustrated by former President Carter's difficulties delivering speeches. Do not add to your problems by attempting this in the initial exercise. Tailor your notes to your personal needs. In my case, I memorize the introduction and write only one or two words from it on a card. You may need a chain of terms to create associations to help you remember all the elements of the story you want to tell and the order you want to follow.

After these terms, write a phrase or word that will suggest the transition into the thesis or specific purpose, and then write out the purpose in full. Next write a word or phrase suggesting the transition into the first main point and write this main point out in full. You should depart from outline or key term form only for evidence that should be written out in full so you can cite it accurately and completely, along with its source. Here is an example of the notes for the speech on 55 mph speed limit.

(intro.)   alive today bec lucky
Friday nite, returning KC, hwy 10
60–65 mph, car passing, head-on collision
couldn't stop, into ditch, hit tree
injuries—minor bec of seat belts
I now believe speed kills

(trans.)   attitudes of others; possible change in national policy

(thesis)   The 55 mph speed limit saves lives and money.

(trans.)   ideal vs. real: reaction time, mechanical condition of car, road and weather conditions

A. 55 mph better for actual driving conditions

    1. Under ideal conditions, ideal driver needs 7 car lengths to stop going 55 mph.

        a. Combines reaction time (thinking distance) and braking distance.

(evidence) At 55 mph, travel 80.66 ft. per second, so takes 218 ft. to stop from time see problem.
Ks. Driving Handbook, p. 42.

(trans.)   what difference if lower only 5–15 mph?

        b. Small increases in speed make big difference.

(evidence) Distance needed to stop and force of impact increase geometrically; if double speed, 4 times distance to stop.
Ks. Driving Handbook, p. 42.

(trans.)   but drivers, roads, and cars aren't in ideal condition

    2. Many drivers aren't in ideal shape.

        a. aging population

        b. over-the-counter remedies, e.g. Dristan or
(evidence) Sinutabs. Ks. Driving Handbook, p. 46

        c. warnings about drowsiness on prescription drugs, e.g. tranquilizers, pain remedies, antihistamines.

        d. alcohol

(evidence) Driving is impaired by as little as 1 drink of whiskey or 2 beers. Ks. Driving Handbook, p. 46.

(trans.)   boast of our fine roads, but many problems, and these compounded by weather

(evidence) 3. Many sections of best highways in poor condition, e.g., Interstate 80. Grace Lichtenstein, N.Y. Times, 6/18/78

    4. Weather conditions: ice and sleet obvious; also rain esp. on limited access highways.

(evidence) hydroplaning: when so much water on highway tires can't "wipe" the road so car starts to run on film of water. Starts at 35 mph, by 55 car traveling entirely on water and out of control. Ks. Driving Handbook, p. 45

(trans.)   can be more realistic and save money and energy and
              lives
              B. 55 mph saves lives
                  1. For first time in history, sudden and dramatic drop
(evidence)   in number of highway fatalities. Fred Gregory,
                      Motor Trend, August 1974, p. 97.
                  2. Drop came from a combination of less travel and
                      less speed.
(evidence) Study of 31 turnpikes showed that traffic was down 18%
              but fatalities were down 60%. Gregory, MT, p. 98.
              C. 55 mph also saves $ and energy.
                  1. Most cars burn fuel with maximum efficiency at
                      about 50 mph, so get most for gas $.
                  2. Efficient gas use by all Americans would save
                      energy—travel farther on energy $
(concl.)   if healthy and alert
              if car well maintained
              if drive 55, need 7 car lengths to stop
                      BUT
              if tired, had a drink, or taken a Dristan
              if tires worn or brake fluid down
              if dusk, night, raining
              —takes longer
              when drive over 55, breaking law, wasting gas
              may also be driving too fast to prevent accident
              I have cuts and bruises to prove it.

As you practice, add whatever notes you need for changes or additions. Be sure that what you have written on the cards is easily legible. Hold your notes slightly above waist level and use them every time you practice. Do not try to avoid looking at them (you will lose your place, fail to shift the cards as you progress, and have to search desperately if you need to consult them). Practice looking at them regularly, and plan to consult each card, moving the top card to the bottom as you finish the ideas it covers. Stand up firmly, speak aloud, try to imagine the audience in front of you. Practice until you can present the whole speech smoothly and easily. When your moment arrives, you will be well prepared to make a competent presentation.

If your rhetorical act is written, you need to move from the detailed notes to a complete first draft, typed or written with adequate margins and double-spaced so that corrections are easy to make. Struggle to complete a first draft even if you discover some problems along the way. The whole act will help you clarify your purpose and indicate what kinds of changes are needed. As with a speaker, concern yourself with the clarity of supporting materials. At this point, read to simplify. Shorten sentences and simplify sentence structure. Change terms that seem confusing or ambiguous. Check syntax and punctuation so they are correct and help the reader to understand. Read for repetition and redundancy. Unlike a listener, a reader can reread, check an earlier paragraph, and stop to think. For this reason, you should edit to eliminate repetition although you should not eliminate transitions. Check to be sure that no part of the argument is unstated and, thus, unclear.

A second draft is now in order. When it is completed, check it for syntax, punctuation, and spelling. Now polish for forcefulness and accuracy. Consider terms that are more vivid, precise, explicit. Read it in its entirety again and mark sections that seem less clear and forceful than you wish. Now try for a final draft that is as polished as you can make it. At this point, your instructor's comments should help you revise once again to produce a finished essay, news or feature story, or editorial.

Space does not permit a detailed exploration here of suggestions for editing and polishing. However, what I have written about selecting a topic, narrowing it to a specific purpose, researching the subject, organizing the material, taking notes, and preparing notes for yourself for a final presentation apply equally to speaking or writing a rhetorical act. Also, a strategy report is equally useful for oral and written rhetoric.

At this point you, the rhetor, have the preliminaries to produce your first rhetorical act and to do it with some competence. In the next chapter I explore the difficulties and obstacles that require more complicated and detailed analyses of the parts of a rhetorical act.

SOURCES

Fowler, H. W. *A Dictionary of Modern English Usage.* 2d ed. New York: Oxford University Press, 1965. Useful pointers on grammar and style, punctuation, spelling, and pronunciation are provided.

MLA Handbook for Writers of Research Papers, Theses, and Dissertations. New York: Modern Language Association of America, 1977.

Strunk, William, Jr. Revised by E. B. White. *The Elements of Style.* 3d ed. New York: Macmillan, 1979. A most readable, basic work on usage, composition, and style.

Turabian, Kate L. *A Manual for Writers of Term Papers, Theses, and Dissertations,* 4th ed. Chicago: Univ. of Chicago Press, 1973.

EXERCISES

1. Prepare a 5–7-minute speech to alter perception that includes an excerpt from a novel, a short story, or a poem as a major piece of evidence.

2. Prepare a 1,500-word essay that applies a fable, tale, myth, or story to a current problem; use such stories as Aesop's fables, Greek or Roman mythology, or the fairy tales of Hans Christian Andersen or the brothers Grimm.

3. Prepare a speech or essay that combines detailed personal experience with research from secondary sources in order to explain something—for example, to lessen the controversy around an issue or to demystify a process.

4. Prepare a speech or essay to intensify beliefs already held by the audience by providing detailed information. Look at "Memorial Day in Stony Creek, Conn.," printed at the end of Chapter 10, as an example of this kind of effort.

STRATEGY REPORT

For each rhetorical act, prepare a written strategy report to be turned in at the time of your presentation. The report makes explicit at least part of the process you go through in preparing for rhetorical action. As such, it is not an end in itself, but a tool for learning. It should help make you aware of the choices that you make in initiating rhetorical action.

The strategy report has seven parts, some of which can be quite short:

1. Purpose

2. Persona (role) and tone

3. Audience

4. Outline

5. Source sheet

6. Strategies

7. Special remarks

1. *Purpose*

First, try to define the rhetorical purpose of your speech in terms of the general response you seek from the audience: to alter perception, to explain, to formulate belief, to initiate action, to maintain belief or action. Recall that each of these purposes is related to assumptions you are making about what your audience knows, feels, and believes.

Second, try to state as briefly and precisely as you can what you would like the audience to know, feel, believe, or do when you are finished. In other words, indicate what you would consider an ideal response from your audience.

2. *Persona (role) and tone*

A speaker or writer assumes a persona or role in relation to the audience, and the "tone" of the language reflects her or his attitude toward the subject and relationship to the audience. Indicate whether you will speak as a peer or as an expert, and if you will shift roles during the act. Similarly, indicate whether your tone will be relatively impersonal and objective (appropriate for an expert, for instance) or personal and conversational (appropriate for a peer) or ironic (appropriate for a skeptic).

3. *Audience*

Discuss whether the exposed audience is your target audience and whether it includes agents of change. If there are discrepancies between those exposed and those you seek to reach or who can act (and if there are not, why rhetoric?), discuss some specific obstacles you face from this audience in transforming them into an ideal audience.

4. *Outline*

With some practice, most students have little difficulty in making outlines. Look at the examples in Chapter 10, and be sure that your outline is in complete sentences, particularly as it expresses your thesis and your main points. Leave a wide margin on the left in order to label what you are doing at each point, such as kinds of evidence, transitions, organizational patterns, and strategies. Use the margin for an abbreviated descriptive analysis of your own rhetoric.

5. *Source sheet*

In preparing for a speech or essay, your personal experience and your imagination are important sources from which to draw material and shape it for your audience. But almost no one's personal experience is so broad or insight so penetrating that she or he cannot benefit from the knowledge in secondary sources or the challenge of responding to the ideas of others.

For each rhetorical act, provide a list of annotated sources, that is, sources for which you write a short paragraph describing the nature of each and telling what you used it for.

Sources may be of four types. Use all these types in rhetorical acts throughout this course so you become familiar with different kinds of resources.

a. *Popular sources.* Mass circulation newspapers and magazines are popular sources. Articles in *TV Guide* or *Newsweek* or the *Kansas City Star* are intended for general audiences. They provide useful evidence and often stimulate thinking.

b. *Specialized sources.* Periodicals intended for limited audiences of specialists are specialized sources. They present articles by experts for specialists, and they analyze more thoroughly topics that are discussed generally or superficially in popular sources. In the *Quarterly Journal of Speech, Signs, Foreign Affairs,* or the *Monthly Labor Review,* for example, you can gain greater understanding, gather data, and verify claims made in popular sources. You should learn to do research that takes you beyond the *Readers' Guide to Periodical Literature. Note:* A distinction between popular and specialized sources can be made, in many cases, between books written for the mass market and those written by specialists for a specialized audience.

c. *Interviews.* The world is full of all kinds of experts, and you should take the opportunity to talk to those available in your area on your subject. Such interviews should be listed as part of your source materials.

d. *Personal experience.* You may have direct knowledge of your subject that goes beyond the ordinary. If you have such experience, and it is relevant to your subject, cite your own expertise and describe its nature. Be reminded, however, of the importance of testing your experience against data gathered by others and the opinions of experts.

Cite your sources in proper bibliographic form. Here are examples for a periodical and a book:

Modleski, Tania. "The Disappearing Act: A Study of Harlequin Romances." *Signs* 5 (Spring 1980):435–448.
Weibel, Kathrun. *Mirror Mirror: Images of Women Reflected in Popular Culture.* Garden City, N.Y.: Anchor Books, 1977.

If your source is an interview with an expert or personal experience, simply make a note of the nature of the interview or the
experience. For example:

On October 20, 1980, I interviewed Elaine Showalter, a
professor of English at Rutgers. She provided me with data about
images of women in popular literature in the Victorian era in Great
Britain and contrasted them with images of women in literary
masterpieces of the period authored by women. Her work is strong
support for the claim that images of women in popular literature
and images of women in the masterpieces of women writers differ
significantly.

From September 1978 to September 1979, I was the manager of
a McDonald's restaurant in Lawrence, Ks. As a result of that
experience, I have detailed knowledge of food preparation,
overhead, construction, and other parts of the franchise operation
that are standardized to appeal to customers, use national
advertising, and ensure a profit.

6. *Strategies*

It may take you only a sentence or two to describe your purpose,
your persona and tone, and your audience, but it will take you
several paragraphs to describe your strategies adequately. In this
section, you must discuss the means you will use to achieve your
purpose and the choices you will make to overcome the obstacles
you face. Your statement should have two parts.

First, given your subject and purpose, how is your audience
likely to respond? Here you should explore the rhetorical obstacles
of complexity, cultural history, cost, control, and reasons why the
audience might be hostile or indifferent to your subject or to what
you propose. (See Chapters 4 through 7.)

Second, discuss specific choices you made to create your audience, to transform the exposed audience into the target audience
and agents of change. Specifically, discuss your choice of perspective, evidence, organizational patterns, introductory and concluding remarks, appeals to needs or values, and statements made to
indicate your relationship to the subject. Strategies should reflect
the ways in which you have adapted materials for your audience in
order to achieve your purpose.

7. *Special remarks*

Use this section to discuss anything you believe significant that
does not fit into the other sections. It may be that you have no
special remarks, but many rhetorical acts are unusual, and you
may need this section to talk about elements you believe are
unique or out of the ordinary.

PART TWO

THE RHETORICAL PROBLEM

CHAPTER 4
OBSTACLES ARISING FROM THE AUDIENCE

A problem is the gap between what you have and what you want. In rhetorical action, a rhetor confronts an audience that perceives, understands, believes, or acts in one way and wants that audience to perceive, understand, believe, or act in another way. The *rhetorical problem* is an umbrella concept that covers all of the obstacles rhetors face. In Part Two, I examine obstacles arising from the audience (Chapter 4), from the subject and purpose (Chapter 5), and from the rhetor's need to be credible (Chapter 6). In Chapter 7 I show how descriptive analysis and the rhetorical problem fit into evaluation and criticism.

In practice, of course, obstacles arising from audience, subject, and rhetor cannot be isolated so neatly. For example, suppose that your subject were the bloodlines of the Chihuahua breed of dogs. Even if your purpose were merely informative (and not getting the Chihuahua named the national mascot), you would have a fairly hard time holding the interest of an audience of teen-agers or lawyers. But your rhetorical problem would be much smaller if your audience were a group of dedicated dog breeders, preferably sprinkled with Chihuahua enthusiasts. In other words, whether or not your subject and purpose create obstacles depends partly on the nature of your audience.

Think of these three aspects of the rhetorical problem as forming a triangle:

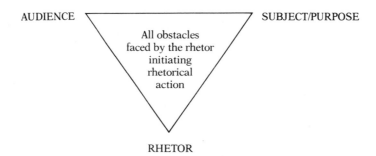

The interrelationships among the aspects symbolized by the triangle can be expressed in three questions: (1) What does the audience require to participate in rhetorical action? (2) What does the subject/ purpose demand of the audience? (3) What are the demands of the subject/purpose and of the audience on the credibility (ethos) of the rhetor?

Beginning rhetors tend to make two common errors in thinking about audiences. First, they assume that most audiences (particularly classmates, friends, colleagues) are just like themselves, with the same experiences, values, religious beliefs, political preferences, and life goals. They are shocked to discover within the same culture or community—or even in the same rhetoric class—wide divergences in belief. But people do differ. All audiences, even close friends, need explanation, adaptation, and effort to see the importance and significance of the issue and the purpose.

Your assumption that members of the audience are just like you, the rhetor, takes several specific forms. Sometimes, for example, you might take it for granted that those you address are, like you, rational, impartial, interested, informed, and concerned. Though people can be all these things, we are also creatures of deep feeling who are, at the same time, likely to be apathetic toward issues of great importance to others. And your audiences are people. As a rhetor, you must treat them as many-faceted and not assume they are well informed and curious unless you make an effort to provide information and arouse curiosity. In this sense, you create your audience—you provide the materials that will enable them to become the ideal respondents to your message.

The second common error rhetors make is to transform the audience into vicious monsters eagerly waiting to jeer at them and to discredit their messages. The sense that those for whom you write or speak are different from yourself can help you when you try to imagine yourself as a member of the audience. But this feeling can be carried too far. Audiences *are* like you. Although not identical, they have needs and fears similar to yours. You and they share many values. Generally, an audience can share your experiences and come to understand a differing point of view.

To be successful as a rhetor requires that you induce the audience to cooperate and participate in the rhetorical act. You and the audience must identify with each other and come to some kind of common understanding if the message you produce is to be a communication. With some experience, you will discover that one of your assets as a rhetor is your individuality—your special experiences, biases, fallibilities, especially as you are able to recognize them and share them with the audience.

Your goal as a rhetor, then, is to avoid both these errors: to recognize differences between yourself and members of the audience and yet create common bonds between you from what you do share. In other words, prepare your rhetorical act to overcome the obstacles represented by these differences.

Beliefs about persuasion are also relevant to the rhetorical obstacles arising from the audience. At various times in American history we have demonstrated our fears of the power of persuasion. We have banned certain books and movies as heretical or obscene and forbidden Nazis and Communists to speak in certain forums, as if exposure to a book, a movie, or a speech could cause good Christians to lose their faith and become ravening sex fiends, or patriotic Americans to become traitors or Communists. As I hope this chapter will indicate, normal people are not transformed by a single rhetorical act. Audiences, in fact, show considerable resistance to persuasion in all forms. Indeed, considering all of the obstacles to persuasion that arise from audiences, you may well marvel that any persuasion ever occurs.

THE AUDIENCE

There are at least four ways to define an "audience." An audience is : (1) those *exposed* to the rhetorical act, the *empirical* audience; (2) the *target* audience, the *ideal* audience at whom the act is aimed; (3) the *agents of change,* those who have the capacity to do as the rhetor wishes, who can make changes; and (4) the *role* the audience is asked to play, the audience as it is *created* by rhetorical action.

The Empirical Audience

Most simply, the audience is all those exposed to the rhetorical act, whether it be in a face-to-face encounter or through the mass media.

Obviously, if people do not encounter the rhetorical act, nothing can occur. The channels through which rhetorical acts are transmitted select and limit the potential empirical audience. An essay printed in *Mother Jones* reaches a relatively small audience of subscribers and others—at a friend's or at the dentist's office—who pick up the magazine and read it. Those who read *Mother Jones* are likely to be different from those who read the *National Review* or *TV Guide*. A rhetor who wishes to reach the appropriate audience must try to find the channel that will expose her or his ideas to the ideal or target audience.

The Target Audience

All rhetorical acts are shaped and planned to reach a certain group of people with certain characteristics. These people are the target audience. They are the ones most likely to be responsive to the issue and capable of acting on it. The target audience is likely to share basic assumptions with the rhetor; ideally, they have common experiences and shared longings. Patterns of television advertising illustrate this concept. For example, the demographic analyses of television viewers made by the Nielsen Company indicate that a large proportion of viewers of network news are older people. As a result, if you watch the news on any network, you will see advertisements for such products as Geritol, Fixodent, and Ex-Lax because older viewers are thought more likely to have "tired blood" (whatever that is), loose false teeth, and constipation. Similarly, razor blades and after-shave lotions are advertised on the World Series because Nielsen studies indicate that many viewers are male. In each case, the ads are targeted at audiences most likely to have needs these products can fill.

In the case of the Konner editorial on adolescent pregnancy in Chapter 2, the target audience is adults whose religious and moral views allow them to consider abortion and contraception as possible solutions to the problem of teen-age pregnancy. These adults are likely to be parents, to fear this problem with their own children, and to be particularly concerned about preventing and solving this problem. They are especially interested in rhetorical action on this issue.

The Agents of Change

Konner's choice of a target audience also illustrates another facet of the audience. You should select those who have the power to act, those with the political ability, the economic power, and the social influence to alter the situation. Only a tiny minority of teen-agers (those 18 or over) can vote; very few have the wherewithal to exert economic power, and almost none have social influence as members of school boards, deacons in churches, or leaders of the PTA or the Chamber of Commerce. Konner chooses to talk to adults although teen-agers have an equally direct, personal interest in the issue, because it is adults who can act as agents to bring about change. Effective rhetors aim their messages at those who can do what they desire.

Such a description of the audience seems to make it a power elite, but other factors are also at work. Advertisers, for example, have learned that they can be effective if they reach those who influence the agents of change. Toys, candy, and sugar-coated cereals are advertised on children's television programs despite the fact that few children make such purchasing decisions. But children influence the decisions made by their parents.* The agents of change are not only those with the power to act but also those who can influence them. In addition, participation in rhetorical action can create agents of change.

The Created Audience

Rhetorical action is participatory; it involves a reciprocal relationship between those involved in it. Just as the rhetor plays a role and takes on a persona, audiences are asked to play roles and take on a persona.† For example, cosmetic ads invite the viewer to be a glamorous, seductive sex object with long, bouncy hair (buy our shampoo), glistening lips (buy our lipstick), and sultry eyes with long dark lashes (buy our eye shadow and mascara). Richard Nixon invited Americans to be "the great silent majority" that supported Administrative policy toward Vietnam, to behave like Good Samaritans toward their "neighbors" in South Vietnam.‡

---

* A Harvard Business School study determined that mothers fulfill their children's requests 88 percent of the time when buying cereal and 40 percent of the time when buying candy. Cited in "Children and TV Commercials," *Intellect* (May–June 1976), pp. 552–553.

† Edwin Black, in "The Second Persona," *Quarterly Journal of Speech* 56 (April 1970): 109–119, discusses the persona of the audience.

‡ See Richard Nixon's address of November 3, 1969, on Vietnamization, in the *Congressional Record*, Vol. 115, Part 24, pp. 32784–32786.

The importance of creating the audience, of inviting them to play a role, is illustrated by the problems of female audiences. An audience must not only *have* the power to act, it must also *believe* that it has it. Several studies show that women have negative self-images, that they see themselves as passive, helpless, patient, silly, grateful, and so forth.* In fact, women *can* act as agents of change. They can vote and work as volunteers, they can write letters to influential people, they can influence businesses through purchasing decisions, and they can form groups that will influence school policy, television programming, and police action. They can run for office and get elected. But they can do these things if and only if they come to believe that they can. The so-called consciousness-raising groups in the women's liberation movement can be seen as transforming women into audiences—that is, into people who believe that they are agents of change.

The common kinds of audience-related rhetorical obstacles are

1. Inattention
2. Misperception and misinterpretation
3. Lack of motivation
4. Inertia

In other words, if a rhetorical act is to have any chance of succeeding, audience members must participate in it from beginning to end. They must perceive its ideas accurately and internalize the "virtual experience" presented. They must see the information and arguments as coming from an informed and trustworthy source† and the rhetorical act as relevant to their needs. In addition, the audience must see the purpose of the act and the means to achieve it as consistent with their values, and they must come to believe that they can take action, here and now, that can reasonably be expected to achieve the goal desired. These requirements suggest the dimensions and the facets of the obstacles that arise from the audience.

---

* See Jo Freeman, "The Building of the Gilded Cage," in K. K. Campbell, *Critiques of Contemporary Rhetoric* (Belmont, Calif.: Wadsworth, 1972), pp. 152–173. These studies do not reflect changes in women's self-images produced by contemporary feminism.

† This part of the rhetorical problem is the subject of Chapter 6.

ATTENTION

Although you may not appreciate it, as a student you are in a rare and highly privileged rhetorical situation: you have a captive audience. Your teacher is paid to read your essay or listen to your speech, and your classmates are required to attend class. Unlike most rhetors, you do not need to struggle to gather an audience, to get your name recognized, or to gain media coverage.

As a college teacher, I also have a more or less captive audience. Yet I compete directly during any given lecture with the university, town, and Kansas City newspapers, letters from parents and friends, and assignments for other classes.

And like all other rhetors I compete indirectly with the hundreds of eager persuaders my audience encounters daily: newspaper editorials and letters to the editor; television, radio, and magazine advertising; telephone and door-to-door solicitors; billboards; political candidates; family and friends. If this bombardment does not create resistance to persuasion by its sheer volume, it may outclass me in slickness or entertainment quality. Although I come in three dimensions and the mass media persuaders do not, and though we are both in "living color," I cannot make eight retakes, do a dissolve, edit the tape, or cut to an animated cartoon when attention flags.

If my students could choose whether or not to come to class, I would encounter another audience-related obstacle. Let us call it *selective exposure*. This term means just what it seems to mean: audiences choose what rhetorical acts they will expose themselves to. Not surprisingly, as research has shown, people expose themselves to messages that support their beliefs, attitudes, and behaviors. Republicans, for example, are far more likely to watch a Republican candidate on television than a Democrat or a Peace and Freedom candidate, and voters generally select persuasive messages favoring candidates of their own party or positions reflecting their own beliefs. You know this from your own experience. If you are a political conservative, you are likely to read magazines, books, and newspapers that support your beliefs and to enjoy TV programs such as William Buckley's "Firing Line." If you are a liberal, you are more likely to read journals or books that support your views, to heed the charitable appeals of the Southern Poverty Law Center, and to prefer magazines such as *The New Republic*.

As a rhetor, however, you need to know that under certain circumstances people are willing to expose themselves to information that conflicts with what they know and with views that challenge their own. At least three factors modify the common sense picture just presented: the audience's level of education, the usefulness of the information to be presented, and the audience's past history of exposure. One study concludes: "Clearly the most powerful known predictor of voluntary exposure to mass communications of an information or public-affairs sort is the general factor of education and social class."* More simply, people with more education and higher incomes choose to expose themselves to more news and information on public affairs in the mass media. They buy more magazines and newspapers; they watch more public affairs programs on radio and television; they are more likely to be active in groups that spread such information. In fact, education and social class may be a more significant factor in exposure than ideological agreement.

Another factor influencing selective exposure is the immediate usefulness of the information to the recipient. In two studies subjects preferred the more useful information to the less useful, regardless of which supported their previous beliefs.† A lack of shared beliefs and attitudes is a serious barrier, but one that can be overcome if the recipients see a direct use for the information now.

Finally, past exposure to the issue will influence selection in ways that are not necessarily related to the compatibility of beliefs. Three studies indicate that where subjects were initially exposed to one-sided or biased information, they later preferred opposing information whether or not it supported the position they had taken.‡ Such studies, along with others indicating tolerance for and interest in new and challenging data, suggest that it would be a mistake to assume that audiences will not attend to information that conflicts with their beliefs and attitudes.

---

* D. O. Sears and J. L. Freedman, "Selective Exposure to Information: A Critical Review," *Public Opinion Quarterly* 31 (1967): 175. Other studies mentioned in this section are cited and analyzed here.

† L. K. Canon, "Self-confidence and Selective Exposure to Information," in *Conflict, Decision and Dissonance*, ed. L. Festinger (Stanford, Calif.: Stanford University Press, 1964); J. L. Freedman, "Confidence, Utility and Selective Exposure: A Partial Replication," *Journal of Personality and Social Psychology* 2 (1965):778–780.

‡ J. L. Freedman and D. O. Sears, "Selective Exposure," in *Advances in Experimental Social Psychology*, Vol. 2, ed. L. Berkowitz (New York: Academic Press, 1965); D. O. Sears and J. L. Freedman, "Effects of Expected Familiarity with Arguments upon Opinion Change and Selective Exposure," *Journal of Personality and Social Psychology* 2 (1965):420–426; D. O. Sears, J. L. Freedman, and E. F. O'Connor, "The Effects of Anticipated Debate and Commitment on the Polarization of Audience Opinion," *Public Opinion Quarterly* 28 (1964):617–627.

The first challenge you face as a rhetor in relation to an audience, then, is gaining and maintaining attention. As indicated here, the individual rhetor competes for attention with many other persuaders and meets obstacles having to do with the selection of messages by members of the audience. A tendency to seek information compatible with beliefs we already hold is balanced by the generally high level of exposure to information among the more educated and affluent, by a desire for useful information, and by a desire for opposing information if the initial exposure has been one-sided or biased.

PERCEPTION AND INTERPRETATION

"Selective perception" names a second kind of audience-related obstacle you will face. It refers to the human ability to function rather like a radio—to tune one channel in and another out, turn the volume down or up, fade the sound in and out, or turn the set off entirely. We do not "perceive" all the stimuli to which we are exposed—we would go crazy if we did. We sort out what is relevant, for example, and ignore the rest. The basis for this ability remains largely a mystery. However, there is evidence that our attitudes influence what we perceive and how we interpret it.

Attitudes

No one has ever seen an attitude. *Attitude* is a concept developed by researchers to describe some of the mental (emotional *and* rational; logical *and* psychological) processes and behaviors of human beings. The concept is particularly difficult because it is complex, and not all researchers agree on how to define attitudes or on whether and how they can be distinguished from "beliefs" and "values."

Attitudes are likes or dislikes, affinities for or aversions to situations (discussing a grade with a student one has failed), events (weddings), objects (motorcycles), people (children), groups (Methodists), or any identifiable aspect of one's environment (the humidity). Attitudes are a mental readiness or a predisposition to react that influences a fairly large class of one's evaluative responses consistently or over a significant period of time.

Attitudes are expressed in statements like these: I don't like big parties; I love ice cream; I like assertive people; the *New York Times* is the best newspaper in the United States. Presumably, as a result of direct experience (at parties, eating ice cream, reading many newspapers) and of other kinds of learning (from school, parents, and peers, among others), people develop evaluative categories so they are prepared to respond, favorably or unfavorably, with varying degrees of intensity (strongly or mildly favorably or unfavorably) to the items they encounter.

Attitudes are relatively generalized (they tend to refer to categories or classes rather than to individual items) and they are enduring (they persist over time). They are also learned. People probably learn likes and dislikes as they learn nearly everything else, and they categorize their evaluative experiences in order to simplify the world. For example, if you have an aversion to dogs, it is likely that you were frightened or bitten as a child or have a parent, friend, or sibling with a strong dislike. In most cases, the attitude will apply to most or all dogs (variations in size may create exceptions), and it is likely that if you dislike them today, you will continue to dislike them next week and next month, although change is possible based on new experiences and learning.

In addition, your aversion to dogs would probably influence reactions to related areas: to dog shows, to dog owners, to leash laws, and so on. Obviously, the rhetor who tries to alter audience attitudes like this one or whose purposes run counter to intensely held attitudes of audience members will run into trouble. Attitudes are learned over a period of time from your experiences or from credible sources; they are reinforced by later experiences; they are also patterns of response that make it easier to cope with the world. This rhetorical problem is compounded by the fact that attitudes influence what we perceive and how we interpret it.

A famous study of the influence of attitudes on perception used a particularly controversial football game between Dartmouth and Princeton as its raw material. The researchers showed students from both schools the same film of the game and tested their perceptions of who broke the rules how many times and in what ways. From the test results, you might have thought the two groups of students had seen two different events. For example, Princeton students "saw" the Dartmouth team break the rules more than twice as many times as the Dartmouth students "saw" their team do so. The researchers concluded that the same data transmitted in the same way create different experiences in different people, and that the significance of an event depends on the purposes different people bring to it and the assumptions they have about the purposes of other people involved. They wrote: "It is inaccurate and misleading to say that different people have different 'attitudes' concerning the same 'thing.' For the 'thing' simply is *not* the same for different people whether the 'thing' is a football game, a presidential candidate, Communism, or spinach."*

You can probably think of many similar examples from the sports world in which partisanship strongly influences what the fans see. And such responses are not surprising, given the nature of attitudes. Avid Kansas City Royals fans want the Royals to beat the Yankees. Because the Yankees stand between the Royals and the World Series, the Kansas City fans dislike them—that nasty Eastern team with its overpaid players. In such a situation Kansas City fans assume that an injury to a Royals base runner sliding into third base is deliberate spiking, because that is the sort of behavior they expect of nasty, overpaid Eastern baseball players.

And what happens in sports can easily happen in other areas. An attitude is a readiness to respond favorably or unfavorably. It represents an expectation of favorable or unfavorable qualities and behaviors. In other words, we tend to "see" the qualities and behaviors in objects, events, persons, and so forth that we expect to be there. As a result, our attitudes influence our perceptions and our interpretations of events.

Beliefs

The influence of attitudes on perception and interpretation suggests that there is a close relationship between information and evaluation. A belief is a judgment about what is true or probable, real or likely. Beliefs may refer to the past (Americans consumed 15.4 lbs. of candy, per capita, in 1977), the present, or the future (there will be too little oil and gas by 1990 to maintain current levels of industrial production). They may assert a causal relationship (per capita consumption of candy declined in 1977 because candy bars were smaller and more expensive) or evaluate the credibility of sources of information (seeing is believing; Juanita Kreps is an expert on U.S. economic matters; Walter Kerr is a reliable authority on the American theatre; the speaker knows what she's talking about).

Insofar as attitudes are learned from our own experiences or those of others, they are based on beliefs, on what we consider true, or likely. For example, if you hate dogs, you probably believe that they bite many people each year, that they often bite without provocation,

---

* A. Hasdorf and H. Cantril,"They Saw a Game: A Case Study," *Journal of Abnormal and Social Psychology* 49 (1954):133.

and that they are the source of some serious diseases of children. These beliefs not only describe dogs, as you may see them, but predict future situations.

Note that insofar as attitudes rest on beliefs, they can be influenced by future learning. Hence the rhetor who wants to change attitudes tries to alter perception (and beliefs) through "virtual experience." Conversely, as the Dartmouth–Princeton example shows, attitudes influence perception in ways that undermine this process, and even conflicting information is perceived as compatible with the perceiver's attitudes.

A recent study illustrates the influence of attitudes on perception. The subjects were viewers of the comedy program "All in the Family," whose central character, Archie Bunker, is a bigot. Defenders of the program have argued that its satirical presentation of prejudice can have a beneficial effect on the audience by making them aware of their own undesirable prejudices and making fun of bigotry. The study tested whether or not prejudice is correlated to exposure and whether viewers differ in their interpretations. The researchers studied a sample of adolescents who were classified as high or low in prejudice based on a questionnaire. The researchers concluded that highly prejudiced adolescents were more likely than less prejudiced ones not only to watch the show (selective exposure), but to admire Archie, to perceive him as making sense, and to see him as winning at the end of the program.*

Decoding

Attitudes influence perception and interpretation so strongly that rhetors cannot be sure their audiences will perceive information as they do. In fact, the interpretation of information and argument is a problem with all audiences, however well intentioned they may be. *Decoding* is a term used to refer to this interpretative process by which listeners or readers translate and interpret messages from outside, assign meanings, determine relationships, and draw implica-

---

* N. Vidmar and M. Rokeach, "Archie Bunker's Bigotry: A Study in Selective Perception and Exposure," *Journal of Communication* 24, no. 2 (1974):36–47. See also, in *Journal of Communication* 26, no. 4 (1976):61–84, Stuart H. Surlin and Eugene D. Tate, " 'All in the Family': Is Archie Funny?"; John C. Brigham and Linda W. Giesbrecht, " 'All in the Family': Racial Attitudes"; and G. Cleveland Wilhoit and Harold de Bock, " 'All in the Family' in Holland."

tions. Audiences obviously find decoding hard to do. Thus, much of the impact of a rhetorical act is lost unless rhetors make special efforts to organize material, to state conclusions, and to show the relationships among ideas. For example, in one study, an audience of unusually bright college students became confused when conclusions were not stated explicitly. Other studies confirm this finding.* The rhetorical problem is that the audience resists or botches decoding unless conclusions are stated explicitly. At a minimum, the rhetor must state conclusions, organize materials clearly, and provide transitions that show relationships if the audience is to decode the material accurately.

NEEDS AND VALUES OF THE AUDIENCE

Needs

People act for reasons. They pursue goals, they are motivated, they try to satisfy their needs. The significant role of needs and goals has already been indicated by the fact that people expose themselves to messages containing information they believe will be useful—to satisfy needs. What are these "needs"? Among the many lists of human needs, one of the most useful is Abraham Maslow's. Maslow, a psychologist, sets up a hierarchy (or ranking) of human needs, suggesting that some needs may be more intense and basic than others. The most fundamental and intense needs are physiological—the needs for food, water, sleep, and protection from exposure. Only when these are relatively well satisfied do needs for safety (stability, order, freedom from violence and disease) become predominant. When these, in turn, are relatively well met, needs for love and acceptance (affection, giving and receiving love, touching and being touched) emerge. And when these are satisfied, needs for esteem (recognition, respect from others and for ourselves) emerge. Finally, when all of these are relatively

---

* The original study was done by C. I. Hovland and W. Mandell, "An Experimental Comparison of Conclusion Drawing by the Communicator and the Audience," *Journal of Abnormal and Social Psychology* 47 (July 1952):581–588. These findings were confirmed in studies by Fine; Irwin and Brockhaus; and Thistlethwaite, DeHaan, and Kamenetsky listed at the end of the chapter. These findings are one reason for my emphasis on the statement of the thesis, organization, and transitions in Chapter 3 and for a separate chapter, Chapter 10, on the structuring of a rhetorical act.

well met, the need for self-actualization—to be all that one is capable of being, to develop one's unique potential—becomes dominant. All humans experience all of these needs and seek to have them met.*

This pyramid of needs can help us to understand the successes and failures of some kinds of rhetorical processes. We may wonder why parliamentary democracy has not attracted more Third World nations. But most citizens of these countries do not have their physiological and safety needs met. They are still at the more basic levels of the pyramid, whereas democracy is an ideology that emphasizes satisfying individual needs for esteem and self-actualization, needs at the top of the pyramid.

Likewise, the successes of charismatic and mystical religious movements should not be too surprising in our culture. We are a nation of transients (one of four families moves every 5 years) with a diminishing sense of community; our families are a less stable source of love and acceptance—two of every five marriages ends in divorce. In such a climate, the community of believers becomes most attractive; if no one else loves you or cares for you, God does. Similarly, the current vogue in books on self-development (*Looking Out for #1, Your Erroneous Zones, The Joy of Sex, How to Flatten Your Stomach, Pulling Your Own Strings*) reflects a society in which the basic needs of many persons are relatively well met so that the focus of interest is on self-actualization.

Because the concept of "needs" focuses on deprivation and because it does not take into account the extent to which our needs are modified by socialization and acculturation, values also need to be considered.

Values

Attitudes, our predispositions to respond favorably or unfavorably to elements of the environment (including invitations to rhetorical action), are influenced not only by beliefs about what is true or probable but by goals or *values*. Like "attitude" and "belief," "value" is a construct describing a pattern of human behavior. It cannot be touched or seen. Values are usually defined as judgments about what is moral (good or right), important (worthy, significant), or beautiful (moving, expressive, pleasing), or as fundamental preferences for cer-

---

* Abraham Maslow, *Motivation and Personality* (New York: Harper, 1954).

tain ends (such as equality, freedom, self-actualization) or for certain modes of conduct (such as honesty, courage, or integrity). In other words, values express strong, basic, and very general views of how one should act or what goals one should seek (what goals are worthy of seeking).

Values seem to arise from three sources: our biology, our cultures, and our unique qualities as individuals. These sources suggest the relationship between values and needs. Some values arise from *biological needs or genetic characteristics* (birds need to fly; salmon need to swim upriver to spawn). Despite the many lists in psychological works and Maslow's hierarchy of needs (leading to a hierarchy of motives), there is no list of needs that satisfactorily describes human motivation. Consider Maslow's hierarchy. It cannot explain artists who are driven to paint or sculpt even though they cannot buy enough food to eat and are scorned by others. Nor can it explain religious people who act altruistically. Maslow himself recognizes these exceptions and discusses the problems involved in establishing any needs as basic or in describing motivation as arising from deprivation. As he notes, rats seem to run mazes as fast out of curiosity as out of hunger, thirst, or sex drive. Obviously, human beings need nutrition, safety, shelter from exposure, and affection, but we have modified these needs culturally and socially. The Masai of Africa, for example, seem to thrive on a diet composed largely of the blood of their cattle, a diet that would nauseate most people. Dwellers in tropical and even Mediterranean climates meet part of their sleep needs by the siesta, a practice unintelligible to those from more temperate climates. In other words, what begin as organic or biological needs are shaped by culture and society.

In every community, there are norms about what is good and proper to eat, and what is a delicacy to one group may be nauseating to another. Values arise, then, not only from biological requirements, but also from *the norms of the groups we belong to*, groups ranging in size from the nation to the gang on the block. Group values are expressed in such statements as, "That is un-American," "It is the Hopi way," "No Cleary ever cries in public." These values, affecting every facet of life, are so fused with biological needs that no one can find where biology stops and socialization begins.

A third source of values is idiosyncrasies, the *unique qualities of the individual.* Each of us is physiologically different. Because I have an unusually acute sense of smell, I have a strong aversion to many perfumes; because tobacco smoke gives me sinus headaches, I support strong regulations on smoking. Epileptics place a special value on sleep. Some people have intense aesthetic needs, some have few sexual needs, some enjoy food and others merely eat to survive. As you will note from these examples, such individual values are refinements or modifications of cultural values and biological needs. Values arising from the special qualities of individuals may account for some unusual responses to rhetorical efforts. Individual values are also a source of variation in the importance or priority given to one value over another.

Attitudes, our predispositions to respond, are a product of values and beliefs. The emotive and affective component of attitudes (reflecting our desires) and goals comes from our values; the cognitive component of values (based on information and inference) comes from our beliefs. Clearly, however, these concepts and the processes they represent are inseparable because evaluations are based on what we believe to be true, and our evaluations, in turn, influence what we perceive and how we interpret it.

SPECIFIC AND FEASIBLE ACTION

The concept of *inertia* is by now a familiar one. Inertia is the tendency of an object to continue doing whatever it has been doing—to rest if it has been resting, to move in a straight line unless disturbed by an outside force, and so on. When applied to people, it refers to an audience's resistance to the rhetor's purpose. Inertia is a complex psychological matter, but from a rhetorical viewpoint, it usually has to do with a feeling of powerlessness. Audiences will resist changing their ideas, and will ignore all calls to action unless that action is within their capabilities, can be done here and now, and has a reasonable chance of being effective.

A speech given by one of my students illustrates the problem. As she reported, the University of Kansas proposed a major renovation of the football stadium, to be paid for by raising the price of season tickets for students. Almost none of the renovations was necessary for the health and safety of fans or players, and a major item was building glass-enclosed boxes so that the press, celebrities, or alumni (such as Morris Moneybags, Arthur Affluent, and Walter Wealthy) could enjoy the games in bad weather. She listed names, addresses, and phone numbers of the Athletic Board members who would be making the decision in three days. She showed which members were wavering and thus particularly vulnerable to phone calls from parents and alumni.

The following week she asked whether anyone had called or written or induced their parents to do so. None had. The students sheepishly said that although they agreed with her strongly and resented the action, they did not believe that their actions would make any difference. She had made the action both specific and easy (one only had to dial a phone), but even then, feeling powerless, the audience did not respond.

Those who write about attitudes argue that they have three parts: cognitive (beliefs), affective (values), and behavioral. Attitudes do not exist apart from behaviors, but the relationship between them is complex. First, there is no simple correlation between an attitude and a particular behavior. For example, one can agree with my student about the stadium project and behave in various ways. One can stop buying season tickets. One can stop attending the games. One can tear down the new fence that shuts off the view of the playing field formerly available to students without tickets who sat on the hill. One can decide that, given inflation, the increase in price is too small to be significant and pay it without irritation. Or, one can do nothing at all. Either attitudes and behavior correlate very poorly, or people's reported attitudes differ from their actual attitudes.*

Just as attitudes can influence behavior, so behavior can also influence attitudes. Studies comparing listening to a speech or reading an essay by someone else with composing one's own speech or essay or with recording the arguments made by others are illustrative. In the studies, even for those hostile to the specific purpose of the speech or essay, there was considerable change in attitudes with greater participation.† Advertisers who promote contests in which participants write "Why I like X . . ." in 25 words or less are using behavior to influence attitudes. This process is sometimes called "self-influence," and it may occur because the people involved try to make their attitudes consistent with their behaviors.

At a minimum, an action is a commitment, often a public commitment, to an attitude. It expresses the recipients' participation in the persuasive process and involves them in the process of influence. Participation in the rhetorical act may be a most effective way of influencing attitudes, and inducing a specific action may be just the reinforcement needed to ensure that a belief will persist. In all cases,

---

* Two classic studies of the differences between reported attitudes and behavior are: R. Lapiere, "Attitudes vs. Actions," *Social Forces* 13 (December 1934):230–237; B. Kutner, C. Wilkins, and R. R. Yarrow, "Verbal Attitudes and Overt Behavior Involving Prejudice," *Journal of Abnormal and Social Psychology* 47 (1952):649–652.

† O. J. Harvey and G. D. Beverly, "Some Personality Correlates of Concept Change Through Role Playing," *Journal of Abnormal and Social Psychology* 63 (1961):125–130.

as mentioned above, rhetorical acts that propose specific, feasible, and immediate actions for the audience will be the most successful.

These, then, are the rhetorical obstacles arising from the audience: inattention, misperception and misinterpretation, lack of motivation (different needs, values), and inertia. In the next section I offer three examples—capital punishment, teen-age pregnancy, and nuclear power—to illustrate these facets of the rhetorical problem.

EXAMPLES OF RHETORICAL PROBLEMS

Consider, for a moment, why it is hard to mount a campaign to alter the status quo (what exists now) on these issues: the death penalty, contraceptive information and legal abortions for teen-agers, and the development of nuclear power.*

If you have followed the persuasive histories of these issues, you will know that without dramatic incidents, it is hard to persuade an audience that there is any need for change. Even with such incidents, social change of this size requires highly committed and sustained efforts that are costly for supporters. Consider the difficulties that have faced the Equal Rights Amendment although a majority of Americans support it. The same is true of regulation of handguns. In each case, the successful persuader must find dramatic materials that will gain the attention of the audience, present convincing evidence, show that the needs and values of the audience are directly related to this proposal, and finally, show that action can be taken to produce the desired results.

Capital Punishment

Dramatic murder cases have often attracted attention to this issue. On the one hand, the fact that execution is so serious an act and that a mistake cannot be corrected helps sustain attention on this much-debated topic. Because it touches on our needs for safety and security, many people see this topic as relevant to them. On the other hand, the small number of people executed or even eligible for execution makes

---

* The status quo on these issues varies among the states; some have the death penalty and some make contraceptive information and abortion available. Our current national policy generally favors the development of nuclear power.

this topic seem remote and relatively unimportant. It is hard to convince an audience that they might be threatened with execution. And because executions have been rare lately, the concern for mistakes may be small. In addition, this issue suffers the disadvantage of requiring such familiar but unpopular actions as writing your legislator or signing a petition, actions that few people still believe are effective. Note that remoteness from the immediate needs of the audience is the greatest barrier to arousing concern for this topic and to inducing people to take it seriously and make a strong commitment.

As a way of clarifying the problem, consider who would make up an ideal audience for a speech on capital punishment. The friends, relatives, and families of victims and criminals; prison guards; and judges and lawyers with extensive experience with criminal cases are those likely to be most involved with the issue. For them, the topic is highly salient; it is related to their immediate needs and to their values. Some of them are natural agents of change in this area. Note, however, that whichever position you took on the issue, some members of this audience would be hostile and difficult to reach. All of them would have direct personal experience against which to test whatever evidence you presented. They are, then, an ideal audience to make a decision on the issue; they are also an extremely challenging audience that would test your knowledge and skills to the utmost.

Teen-age Pregnancy

This is a newly prominent issue. The state of New York has only recently begun to expand services to prevent such pregnancies and to provide care for pregnant teen-agers and teen-age mothers. These efforts, initiated by Governor Carey, are a response to a report showing the substantial increase in such pregnancies and noting the medical and social problems listed by Konner.* (See Konner's article printed in Chapter 2.)

Several elements help make messages on teen-age pregnancy effective. As a society, we listen to messages about young people because they are our future and because we see them as innocent and helpless victims for whom we are responsible. In addition, available statistics show dramatic and attention-getting changes in the rate of teen-age

---

* Sheila Rule, "New York Acts on Teen-Age Pregnancy Problems," *New York Times,* 16 July 1978, p. 38.

pregnancy, and the effects on all those involved are not only very serious—death, severe disability, and the like—but long-lasting. Teen-age parents and their children will feel them for years, perhaps for their entire lives.

Teen-age pregnancies also represent a substantial cost in welfare, in social workers' time, and in time and space in medical facilities. Hence there is practical as well as humanitarian motivation to prevent such occurrences. In this case, persuaders have reached a particularly important agent of change—the governor of New York. It is now easier for others to act because, with his support, their actions will more likely produce effects.

Consider the most resistant kinds of audiences. Some people believe sexual matters should not be discussed publicly; others think contraception is wrong or that it encourages sexual promiscuity. Still others believe that pregnancy is just punishment for sinful sexual behavior. Others might resist because of the costs of providing contraceptive information, abortions, and other social services. Others may believe that nothing can be done because even informed teen-agers with access to contraceptive devices do not always use them. Still others have no children or teen-age relatives and may see the issue as irrelevant, the fault of bad parents.

Note that the same problems arise over and over: How can the issue be made salient for the audience? How can it be related to their needs and values? How can they be convinced to act?

Nuclear Power

Similar problems arise with the many facets of the nuclear issue. The success of the Clamshell Alliance in slowing down the construction of nuclear plants shows that opposition can have an impact.* There is enough drama in the issue to attract attention—reports of accidents in nuclear plants, an oil embargo, sharp increases in oil prices, severe shortages of heating fuels in midwestern states, and a clear relationship between our personal needs for warmth and light and jobs and the needs of our society as an industrial nation. There are conflicting viewpoints, but they should generate lively discussions.

Many specific actions have been proposed: a return to coal, recycling garbage, heating and cooling and lighting less, raised fuel prices,

---

* Charles Mohr, "Antinuclear Drives: Diffuse but Effective," *New York Times*, 24 June 1978, p. 6.

rationing gas, and so on. But the complexity of the issue is such that, as individuals, we cannot be sure what is true; we have to rely on others. We face the terrible problem of determining who is knowledgeable and trustworthy. These questions, leading to the rhetorical obstacles originating with the rhetor, are the subject of Chapter 6. They also are part of the rhetorical obstacle of complexity arising from the nature of this subject, which is discussed in Chapter 5.

SUMMARY

This chapter has argued that certain rhetorical obstacles routinely arise from the audience, although their specific form depends on the particular topic/purpose, occasion, and audience. These obstacles, arising from the requirements every rhetorical act must meet, can be grouped under headings of inattention, misperception and misinterpretation, lack of motivation (different needs and values), and inertia. Every rhetorical effort must overcome these obstacles in order to reach the audience and have an opportunity to influence.

Obviously, rhetors need to understand their audiences: those exposed to a rhetorical effort, those chosen as the particular target for influence, and those able to produce change. The audience-related aspects of the rhetorical problem are also related to important psychological concepts: the predispositions of humans to react favorably or unfavorably to what they encounter (attitudes), beliefs held about what is true or probable, and values that indicate goals and preferences. In every case, you must consider how to use the beliefs, attitudes, and values of the audience in order to reach them and induce them to participate.

SOURCES

A review and analysis of studies of selective exposure and perception is found in C. David Mortenson, *Communication: The Study of Human Interaction* (New York: McGraw-Hill, 1972), pp. 100–106.

Problems in the study of attitudes are explored in C. A. Kiesler, B. E. Collins, and N. Miller, *Attitude Change: A Critical Analysis of Theoretical Approaches* (New York: John Wiley and Sons, 1969).

An excellent basic source on beliefs and attitudes is Daryl J. Bem, *Beliefs, Attitudes, and Human Affairs* (Belmont, Calif.: Brooks/Cole,

1970). More detailed analyses are found in Milton Rokeach, *Beliefs, Attitudes and Values* (San Francisco: Jossey-Bass, 1968) and Rokeach, *The Nature of Human Values* (New York: Free Press, 1973).

The importance of structural clarity and transitions is supported in these studies: B. J. Fine, "Conclusion-drawing, Communicator Credibility and Anxiety as Factors in Opinion Change," *Journal of Abnormal and Social Psychology* 54 (1957):369–374; J. V. Irwin and H. H. Brockhaus, "The 'Teletalk' Project: A Study of the Effectiveness of Two Public Relations Speeches," *Speech Monographs* 30 (1963):359–368; D. Thistlethwaite, H. DeHaan, and J. Kamenetsky, "The Effects of 'Directive' and 'Non-directive' Communication Procedures on Attitudes," *Journal of Abnormal and Social Psychology* 51 (1955):107–113.

MATERIAL FOR ANALYSIS

The kinds of obstacles that can arise from the audience are illustrated by two speeches delivered at the Republican National Convention in 1980. Benjamin Hooks, Executive Director of the National Association for the Advancement of Colored People (NAACP), spoke during prime time on the Tuesday evening of the convention, and Ronald Reagan made his nomination acceptance address during prime time on Friday evening. Consider, for a moment, the very different situations they confronted. Prior to the convention, everyone knew that Reagan would be the nominee and that his acceptance speech would be the climax of the convention. By contrast, Hooks's speech was unscheduled, a last-minute addition after black delegates threatened a symbolic walkout.* The convention itself was a triumph of conservatism and a celebration of Republican unity. Although Hooks is Republican, the organization he heads, the National Association for the Advancement of Colored People, espouses positions different from many in the Republican platform; Hooks was a potential source of disunity.† The delegates were familiar with Reagan's rhetorical

---

* Hedrick Smith ("Republican Leaders Open Wide Attacks on Carter Policies," *New York Times*, 16 July 1980, p. A 1.) reported that the invitation was extended to head off a threatened symbolic walkout by some black delegates. Howell Raines ("Reagan Seeks to Placate Minorities and Moderates," *New York Times*, 16 July 1980, p. A 1.) reported that Hooks was invited to make the address after Reagan had given his approval. The situation arose because Reagan declined an invitation to speak at the NAACP National Convention (the invitation was said not to have reached him).

† Efforts had been made by the Republican party to appeal to black voters. See Martin Tolchin, "Republicans Make New Efforts to Win Black Voters," *New York Times*, 13 July 1980, p. A 12. The 1980 Republican Platform had a special section on

style; Hooks was probably unknown as a speaker. Reagan's role was clearly defined: political columnist and speech writer William Safire listed the requirements for an acceptance speech.* Hooks's role was not. Reagan's speech echoed the themes of the convention; Hooks's speech was a departure from them. In other words, all elements in the situation worked to enhance Reagan's rhetoric and to diminish Hooks's impact.

Given these obstacles, here is what Benjamin Hooks said on the night of July 15, 1980, to the delegates to the Republican National Convention assembled in Joe Louis Stadium in Detroit:†

1 Thank you. Mr. Chairman and delegates, alternates, and guests, I am honored and delighted to have been extended this opportunity to address the thirty-second Republican National Convention.

2 It is significant to note that this year's convention is being held in the state of Michigan. As most of you know, the first Republican convention was held in Jackson, Michigan, in 1854. (*Applause*) Six years later, this infant Republican Party nominated Abraham Lincoln who became the 16th President of the United States of America. Today, 126 years later, many of the problems in transferring blacks from chattel status to first-class citizenship still exist. It is also significant that you have chosen to come to Detroit, which in many ways is symptomatic of both the possibilities and the problems that plague the American urban community today.

3 I come today not in a partisan position, for I intend to present this same position paper to the black delegates and alternates at the Democratic Convention as well as to the entire Democratic National Convention to be convened in August in New York City. I represent an organization that does not engage in partisan politics, but we have traditionally acted as a catalyst to move this nation forward.

4 America today stands at a crossroads in its history. We must decide as a nation if we are to become prisoners of our past or

---

Black Americans that promised to solve their economic problems with "the same answer we make to all Americans—full employment without inflation through economic growth." See "Excerpts from Platform to Be Submitted to Republican Delegates," *New York Times*, 13 July 1980, p. A 4. The platform was approved without amendment by the convention. On July 15, 1980, Reagan made a speech in Detroit to the National Black Republican Council. Fifty-six of the 1,994 delegates were black, and a black physician called the roll of the states for all votes.

* "How to Accept," *New York Times*, 17 July 1980, p. A 19.

† The text is a transcription by the author of the speech as delivered. Reprinted by permission.

possessors of an enlightened and progressive future. The task before us is a difficult one indeed. In the words of one of the first black Republicans, Frederick Douglass, "Unless there is struggle, there will be no progress."

5   No one who has even a passing understanding of American history can argue the fact that America today is a vastly improved society than it was in 1854. No one in his right mind can refute the statement that blacks have come a long way as a people in the last 126 years. We must not, however, allow ourselves to be lulled into a sense of false security or be placated by the progress we have achieved. For today, in this America, the richest nation on the face of the earth, fully one-fourth of its black citizens live below the poverty level. We are relegated to substandard housing, unequal representation in the professions, over-represented among our prison population, and under-represented in the halls of government. We in the NAACP do not accept the fact that these circumstances are just coincidental. Rather, we believe, and history attests to the fact, that as a result of systematic discrimination and the legacy of the institution of slavery, blacks have been relegated to second-class citizenship. We believe that the greatest dilemma facing America today is how to eradicate, in the best manner possible, racism, sexism, and poverty in our society, and to afford to those who have been historically denied it equal access to opportunity. (*Applause*)

6   If we are to meet these challenges, it is incumbent upon the major political parties, those formed or those about to be formed, and all institutions of America to address forthrightly these vexing problems. As you meet here this week in national convention, we would remind you that among the many adverse conditions facing black Americans are these:

7   In 1980, one-third of all black Americans live in substandard housing. Black unemployment is twice as high as white unemployment. The black median family income is 57% of that of white families. Black youth unemployment is officially 30%, but in many urban centers it is as high as 40 to 60%. Blacks are 11% of the population, yet we represent less than 2% of the lawyers, doctors, and dentists, and less than 1% of the engineers. We are disproportionately the victims of police brutality and increasingly the victims of violence from hate groups like the Ku Klux Klan and the American Nazi Party. Our urban centers are decaying, yet it is hard to visualize life in America without decent cities. The high rate of infant mortality continues to deny black children an equal start in life. And black businesses are deprived of equal access to loans, equity capital, and procurement opportunities in all levels of government and private industry.

8 But we have come, not simply to recite problems, but we have come to offer what we believe are positive solutions. We invite your careful consideration. For even though we may disagree on some issues, we ought to be able to disagree without being disagreeable. (*Applause*) We, therefore, suggest the following as an agenda for the '80s:

9 Full employment. Priority should and must be given to economic policies that create jobs and commit this nation to a policy and practice of full employment. (*Applause*) There must be a vigorous commitment to achieve the goals and objectives of the Equal Employment Opportunity Law of 1964. This will require vigorous enforcement of that act by the appropriate federal, state, and local agencies to assure adequate black representation in all levels of employment.

10 In addition, the disastrously high level of youth unemployment must be reduced. Therefore, we urge your support for legislation that provides tax incentives to the private sector for recruiting and training disadvantaged black youth so that they may eventually be able to compete in the American work force. For this large number of unemployed black youth, in the words of Mr. Jones, Chairman of General Electric, "constitute a ticking time bomb that would threaten to destroy the whole of our nation."

11 We need each and every one of you to relentlessly pursue a policy of quality, integrated education for all Americans in public schools and to promote the concept of accountability on the part of school personnel. This includes adequate funds.

12 There is no question but that the energy crisis is real. There is no question also that the response on the part of the political leadership in Congress regarding a comprehensive energy program has been inadequate and unimpressive. We, therefore, urge a decisive plan for the conservation of energy that produces equity for the poor, and we support the immediate implementation of a fuel stamp program. We also urge support for programs to increase aid for clean, safe, efficient, low-cost public transportation in the inner city and policies of urban revitalization which include the development of racially and economically integrated housing.

13 As a civil rights organization, we may differ with many of you on the issues of abortion, capital punishment, and the Equal Rights Amendment. The common thread which runs throughout our concerns for each of these issues is, in part, because of uneven treatment on the basis of race, sex, or poverty. We urge you to reexamine your positions to make sure that the American values of equality of opportunity are guaranteed on these issues of such vital concern. For instance, on the issue of abortion, whatever your personal position might be, we at the NAACP believe that any rights and options which are wanted and available to the rich must be available to the poor. (*Applause*)

14   We urge full support of a health insurance plan which covers all Americans with a comprehensive range of benefits.

15   As political leaders of this nation, if you are serious about eliminating all forms of racial discrimination in housing, you must support policies and programs that will provide an adequate, affordable supply of housing, particularly for the low and moderate income family. It is time for the U.S. Senate to pass the 1980 Fair Housing Act as adopted by the U.S. House of Representatives. We note that several Republican members of the House Judiciary Committee provided real leadership in securing the passage in the House of the 1980 Fair Housing Act.

16   The heavy involvement of American capital in South Africa supports the continued exploitation of the black majority. We, therefore, submit that American investment should not be used to support the evils of apartheid. We urge this party to forthrightly demand of South Africa that they and their policies be denied American aid that supports, directly or indirectly, apartheid.

17   The appointments to the U.S. Supreme Court and the Federal Judiciary must continue to include more blacks, Hispanic Americans, and women. We call for a Supreme Court that will be faithful to the majesty of the Constitution and sensitive to the sweep of racial history in America.

18   While we have increased the number of black elected officials over the past ten years, of the more than 4,000 black elected officials, less than 10% are Republicans. We call upon this party to vigorously seek out and support black Republicans for public office. (*Applause*)

19   At virtually every stage of the criminal justice system, there are racial disparities, gross inequities, and patterns of injustice. In the final analysis, however, crime will be controlled by the expansion of equal opportunity, the proper hiring and training and deployment of law enforcement officers that respect the rights of all persons who are arrested.

20   We are concerned and disagree with the recent decision of U.S. Supreme Court in the Mobile, Alabama, case, and we pray for legislative changes permissible under the Supreme Court decision that will eliminate districting that has a discriminatory effect. And we urge endorsement or ratification of the District of Columbia voter representation amendment.

21   Finally, key provisions of the Voting Rights Act of 1965 would expire in 1982 unless extended. It is essential to pass legislation providing for such an extension in order to complete the job of full enfranchisement commenced by the passage of the 1965 Act. We urgently ask your support of such legislation.

22 As a black, growing up in a rigidly segregated society, I have felt the sting of overt, blatant prejudice and segregation. But like the overwhelming majority of black Americans, I remain loyal to the American dream. (*Applause*) Throughout our long and tortured history, we as black folk have been sustained by the faith that one day America would truly be the land of the free and equal opportunity for all. We remain committed to that goal. Black folk, through slavery, through second-class citizenship, through separate but unequal, through the long and difficult days, have remained true to the goals of America. We remain faithfully committed to those ideals today.

23 I learned a song many years ago. It speaks of the glory and grandeur that is America. I close with that song tonight.

O Beautiful for spacious skies,
For amber waves of grain,
For purple mountain majesties
Above the fruited plain!
America! America!
God shed his grace on thee

24 And now, let us, from this time and this place, united in heart and head and hands, black and white, Jew and Gentile, rich and poor, learned and unlearned, male, female, Catholic, Protestant, believers, nonbelievers, and other believers, let us boom out

And crown that good with brotherhood and sisterhood
From sea to shining sea!

Peace and freedom! (*Applause*)

Hooks's speech is an excellent example of a speaker's attempts to overcome the rhetorical problem. After you have done a descriptive analysis of the speech, consider these questions:

1. How does Hooks create identification between himself and his views and the audience and their views? How does he tie his speech to the setting, the occasion, to the Republican party? How are the introduction and conclusion adapted to achieve these goals?

2. How does he handle audience hostility, indifference? What specific things does he do to minimize sources of conflict?

3. Political conventions not only nominate candidates, they write and endorse a platform that expresses the philosophy and policy of the party. How are Hooks's tone, the role he assumes, and the structure of his speech adapted to these convention functions?

4. What kinds of difficulties are created by issues that are highly salient for the NAACP but matters of indifference for the Republican Party? Is this an inevitable problem given his nonpartisan stance?

5. Hooks addresses two audiences, the delegates and television viewers. He is also speaking to whites (given the race of the vast majority of delegates) while being overheard by blacks on television. What special problems of ethos does this create?*

For purposes of comparison, consider the conclusion of Ronald Reagan's Acceptance Speech.† Like Hooks, he is addressing two audiences, Republicans and others—Democrats and Independents. The tension between the two audiences is evident in the conclusion of the speech as delivered (only the first two paragraphs were included in the prepared text). The first two paragraphs are ideally suited to appeal to non-Republicans, but the last paragraphs demand a kind of participation that can only occur for true believers.

Conclusion of Ronald Reagan's Acceptance Speech at the Republican National Convention, July 17, 1980

1   And the time is now to redeem promises once made to the American people by another candidate in another time and another place. He said, "For three long years, I have been going up and down this country preaching that government, federal, state, and local, costs too much. I shall not stop that preaching. As an

---

* On Monday, July 14, when former president Ford spoke, CBS had 18 percent, ABC 16 percent, and NBC 14 percent of the national television audience. The overall audience was down "several million people" from 1976, an ABC official estimated. See Steven Rattner, "Convention News Coverage Questioned," *New York Times*, 17 July 1980, p. B 8. For a discussion of the dilemma faced by black rhetors, see Robert L. Scott and Wayne Brockriede, *The Rhetoric of Black Power* (New York: Harper and Row, 1969), pp. 112–131.

† The text of the entire speech, as prepared for delivery, can be found in the *New York Times*, 18 July 1980, p. A 8. As printed here, the conclusion is a transcript by the author of the speech as delivered. Dots are used to indicate pauses, not omitted material.

immediate program of action, we must abolish useless offices. We must eliminate unnecessary functions of government. We must consolidate subdivisions of government and, like the private citizen, give up luxuries which we can no longer afford." And then he said, "I propose to you, my friends, and through you, that government of all kinds, big and little, be made solvent and that the example be set by the President of the United States and his cabinet." That was Franklin Delano Roosevelt's words as he accepted the Democratic nomination for President in 1932. (*Applause*)

2   The time is now, my fellow Americans, to recapture our destiny, to take it into our own hands. And to do this will take many of us working together. I ask you tonight, all over this land, to volunteer your help in this cause so that we the people carry out those unkept promises, that we pledge to each other and to all America on this July day, forty-eight years later, that now we intend to do just that? . . . . .

3   I have thought of something that's not a part of my speech and worried over whether I should do it . . . . .

4   Can we doubt that only a Divine Providence placed this land, this island of freedom, here as a refuge for all those people in the world who yearn to breathe free? Jews and Christians enduring persecution behind the Iron Curtain, the boat people of Southeast Asia, of Cuba, and of Haiti, the victims of drought and famine in Africa, the freedom fighters in Afghanistan, and our own countrymen held in savage captivity? . . . . .

5   I'll confess that I've been a little afraid to suggest what I'm going to suggest. I'm more afraid not to.

6   Can we begin our crusade, join together in a moment of silent prayer? . . . . .

God bless America.

Thank you. (*Applause*)

Like Hooks's conclusion, this is the climax of Reagan's speech. Compare the two conclusions, then consider these questions:

1.   Why is the quotation from Franklin Roosevelt's 1932 acceptance speech particularly appropriate for the speaker, for the audience, and for the start of the campaign?

2.   Contrast the conclusion of the prepared text, paragraphs 1 and 2, with the conclusion Reagan added when he delivered the speech. In terms of strategies, style, tone, and persona, how do they differ?

3. Why might the second conclusion be considered controversial?

4. The second conclusion is enthymematic; it implies a subtext. Try to make explicit what is implicit in it. How does this help to define the audience that can participate in its creation?

5. "God Bless America" is the title of a song. Why might that be an evocative symbol for Reagan and for his immediate audience?

The acceptance speech by a party nominee is the start of the presidential campaign, and it is expected to fire up delegates and other party members to work hard in the coming months. Reagan faced few obstacles in that effort. There was little dissent about him as a nominee, and the convention was unified. The morale of the delegates was high, and other Republicans were probably optimistic given polls showing the declining popularity of the incumbent Democratic president and the likelihood that Reagan would beat Carter if the election were being held at the time of the convention. As a result, Reagan's speech illustrates a high level of audience participation while Hooks's address illustrates the struggles of a rhetor attempting to overcome a multitude of obstacles.*

EXERCISE

Discovering Audience Beliefs and Attitudes

For this exercise, you must design an interviewing instrument (a series of planned and interrelated questions on a subject) and use it to interview seven to ten persons on the subject of your rhetorical act. The exercise has three purposes: (1) to give you experience with the problems involved in developing questions that elicit accurately what others know, believe, and feel; (2) to give you experience in creating an atmosphere in which others are willing to tell you what they know, believe, and feel; and (3) to provide you with information about the knowledge, beliefs, and attitudes of others to help you adapt a rhetorical act to a general or heterogeneous audience.

The intent of the interviews is to gather information that would help you, as a rhetor, prepare a rhetorical act more likely to be attended to and influential for a general audience. You are attempt-

---

* Reagan found himself in a position analogous to that of Hooks when he addressed the NAACP National Convention in Denver on June 29, 1981. His efforts to overcome similar rhetorical obstacles may be compared to those of Hooks. Excerpts from his address appear in the *New York Times*, 30 June 1981, p. D 21.

ing to discover the causes of resistance to your purpose and the sorts of obstacles you might face. You are also trying to find out what bases there are for appeals that might cause this audience to give your point of view a fair and open hearing. In order to be an effective interviewer, you need to be well informed on the subject yourself.

A general audience is really a cross section or random sample of the population. For this reason, you should try to interview people representing diverse interests and situations. Ideally, those interviewed should differ in age, sex, ethnic group, socioeconomic level, occupation, and religious and political affiliation. *Do not* interview friends or roommates; do interview people who are complete strangers.

You need to plan an opening that introduces you, indicates what you are doing and why, introduces the subject, and tells the person to be interviewed how much time will be involved and why it is important that he or she participate. Plan a series of questions that progress through the areas of the subject you think most important. Begin with basic questions to determine just what the person knows. Plan a closing that expresses appreciation and that will end the interview comfortably.

Problems to be avoided: not knowing the questions well enough and/or reading them mechanically, lack of warmth and eye contact suggesting disinterest, speaking too softly or too quickly, rushing the interview so that answers are superficial, apologizing, asking biased questions, suggesting answers if the person hesitates, mentioning how others answered, taking too many notes, and taking too much for granted (such as how much is known about the subject or familiarity with vocabulary).

1.   Turn in a copy of the questions you used, together with an evaluation of them as a means of getting useful and accurate information about knowledge, beliefs, and attitudes.

2.   Briefly evaluate your strengths and weaknesses as an interviewer and indicate what kinds of things were successful and unsuccessful in creating an atmosphere in which people were willing to be interviewed and to take the questions seriously. What places were the best for doing the interviews?

3.   Briefly evaluate the information you obtained in terms of using it for a rhetorical act on this subject for a general audience. Indicate what assumptions were confirmed or disconfirmed; consider how your class differs from this wider audience; indicate some ways you might proceed that you think would be effective in gaining a hearing for your point of view.

CHAPTER 5

OBSTACLES ARISING FROM SUBJECT AND PURPOSE

Although the audience is central in an analysis of rhetorical obstacles, subject and purpose are almost equally important. Actually, of course, the problems discussed here arise out of the interrelationship between the audience and the issue: the subject the audience must consider and the purpose, the response that the rhetor wishes to evoke from the audience. Again, no subject is without interest for some audience, and no subject is of interest to everyone.

To give you a feeling for the kind of rhetorical problem discussed in this chapter, consider this paragraph from a recent review of a book on toxic wastes:

> It is sometimes difficult to find the right words for describing this situation —the right notes for sounding a general alarm —because the vocabularies and images on which we must draw for the purpose are so remote from everyday human experience. The chemicals leaking into our living spaces have long laboratory names that defy pronunciation and sound as sanitary as the ingredients in toothpaste. Their power to do harm is often expressed in fractions so minute (one part per billion, say, can be a dangerous dosage) that the mind does not know what to make of them. They have been deposited in so many dump sites throughout the country that a map identifying their locations would look like an explosion of dots. How, then, is one to convey the nature of the problem? How is one

to organize all of those odd statistics, all of those technical details, into a story?*

The obstacles facing anyone writing about the hazards of toxic chemical wastes are indeed great—the audience's lack of personal experience, the formidable scientific vocabulary, the similarity between the names of the wastes and of wonder-working ingredients in toothpastes, and the mind-boggling statistics. Obstacles of this sort arise from the subject and from the rhetor's purpose.

SUBJECT-RELATED OBSTACLES

There are two major obstacles created by subjects or topics: resistance created by *complexity* and resistance created by the *cultural history* of the issue.

Complexity

Some subjects are complex or, more to the point, the audience sees them as complex. In such cases, you will meet a special kind of audience resistance that is definitely an obstacle to joint rhetorical action. (Of course, there might also be an obstacle in your own capability to handle certain kinds of complex subjects. Even if you were speaking from personal experience, the preparation time would be far longer. But let's assume you can handle the subject.)

Subjects are complex or seem so (1) when they are remote from the audience's personal experience, (2) when they require technical knowledge or some other kind of special expertise, and (3) when they are bound up with many other difficult issues. That is, audiences resist participation in rhetorical acts for which they have no touchstone in their ordinary lives. They are uncomfortable with subjects demanding decisions that they do not feel competent to make, and they are often overwhelmed by subjects with broad ramifications.

Subjects that are outside the personal experiences of the audience create special difficulties. The audience feels incompetent to make judgments. This is the case with most foreign policy decisions. De-

---

* Kai T. Erickson, "Contaminating the Countryside," a review of M. H. Brown, *Laying Waste: The Poisoning of America by Toxic Chemicals.* © 1980 by The New York Times Company. Reprinted by permission.

spite a great increase in world travel by Americans, few of us were in Vietnam or have had experiences that would make us feel comfortable about deciding military or economic policies for that area. By contrast, farmers have considerable experience with acreage allotments, storage facilities, insecticides, crop failure, and the like, and bring a good deal of familiarity to decisions on such issues. Women who have delivered children in hospitals have experience they bring to proposals for birthing rooms; parents have had personal experiences with teachers relevant to educational decisions; and so forth. But when a subject is outside our personal experience, we are at the mercy of others. We have to rely on data gathered by others and on interpretations made by experts. Because experts rarely agree, we face trying to decide who is more reliable. And since we have to rely on others, we are more vulnerable to manipulation: it is easier to fool those without personal experience, because they have no basis on which to test the data or claims of others. That is one reason we feel helpless about foreign policy decisions and why we can be deceived more easily about what is really happening in Vietnam or Iran or Afghanistan.

Subjects are also complex when they require technical knowledge or a special kind of expertise. Subjects that demand a lot of scientific knowledge from the audience are particularly dangerous. The subject of nuclear safety, for example, demands many kinds of knowledge from an audience if that audience is to respond intelligently to a discussion of it. People must know something about the effects of radiation on humans, the meaning of certain units of radiation (millirems, for example), the procedures and rationale for setting up limits of exposure, the actual danger from various kinds of nuclear plants, the half-lives of various wastes, the geology of areas proposed for waste disposal, the odds on hijacking and sabotage, the nature and costs of safeguards against both, the truth about nuclear accidents in the past, and so forth. Audiences faced with such demands are likely to resist participation because basic information is outside their personal competence. In such a situation, the rhetor must become an educator, and under such circumstances, he or she is likely to use the entire range of rhetorical purposes in a persuasive campaign. Rhetors will begin by creating virtual experience, including altering the audience's perception of its own competence. This will be followed by efforts to explain that link and interpret the data. Only then can rhetors try to formulate beliefs in the audience about such things as nuclear power plants, the disposal of nuclear wastes, and the dangers of breeder reactors.

Subjects like nuclear power are also complex because they are bound up with many other difficult issues with broad ramifications.

Decisions on nuclear power cannot be separated from issues of unemployment, inflation, the cost and amount of uranium available, and the comparative costs of nuclear and other energy sources. The result is a sense that the problem is so large and its implications so extensive that no one can understand it or begin to solve it.

The history of the civil rights movement illustrates the complexity of the problem with broad ramifications. Initial efforts to solve the problem involved eliminating clearly defined evidences of oppression—segregated waiting rooms, water fountains, and bathrooms, and barriers to voter registration, for example. But when these basic battles were won, other issues arose that were not so easy to define or solve: providing quality education, decent housing, and decent jobs. Housing cannot be separated from employment nor employment from education. Hence, in order to solve one problem, all the problems apparently have to be solved. Such efforts take time and involve cultural dislocations (reflected, for example, in disputes over school busing and integration plans), and clear evidence of progress may be hard to see.

In summary, a subject may create obstacles because of its real or its perceived complexity. A subject is complex when the audience has no firsthand experience with it, when technical knowledge or special expertise is required, and when the subject is part of an interrelated set of problems or issues.

Cultural History

The second set of obstacles arising from the subject has its roots in events that happened long before you take the stage. Let us call them the subject's cultural history to indicate that the obstacles come from ideas or concepts about the subject formed during past discussions in your culture. Obstacles arising from cultural history include: (1) boredom or indifference due to familiarity with existing arguments, (2) closed minds about public discussion of some taboo topics, (3) conditioned responses to emotionally loaded subjects, and (4) conflict with cultural values.

No subject exists in a void. Every subject has a context and meaning consisting of past experience with the subject and the issues surrounding it. This context is the residue of past rhetorical action. It is the subject's cultural history. If your topic has a long and rich cultural history, beware.

Take, for example, the subject of capital punishment. (The word *capital* refers to losing one's head, from the Latin word for head, *caput*.)

The death penalty for certain crimes (usually murders) has been defended and attacked so often in American culture that the arguments on both sides have almost become clichés. Virtually any possible audience will have heard them all before. Everyone knows the argument that capital punishment deters people from murdering each other (the deterrence argument). And everyone also knows the counterargument that most murders are committed in the heat of passion when the part of the mind affected by deterrents is simply not in control. On go the arguments and counterarguments—from cruel and unusual punishment, unequal protection of the law (many more blacks and poor people executed than whites and wealthy people), the likelihood of rehabilitation, to the haunting possibility of executing the innocent. Death, as one anti-capital punishment argument reminds us, is so final.

Since everyone knows these arguments, the first obstacle you face may be *boredom*. Thus, unless you can find a fresh approach to the subject, you might be better off avoiding it.

Another rhetorical obstacle that may lurk in a subject's history is a *taboo* against discussing it. Consider, for example, almost any subject having to do with sexuality in the United States. Contraception and abortion are obvious and important examples. Others are pornography, venereal disease, homosexuality, prostitution, rape, incest, and spouse-beating. Several of these taboos are beginning to break down, the subjects are beginning to be aired, and the victims are beginning to get help. But if you talk about these subjects, you must choose your audiences and your words carefully, or their minds will be so tightly closed against you that no rhetorical action can occur, not even the sharing of basic data.

The cultural history of a subject may also include *highly charged emotional reactions*. Most taboo subjects have such emotional loads. Protestant-Catholic and Anglo-Irish relations are loaded subjects in Northern Ireland; racism, business ethics, abortion, and homosexual rights are loaded subjects in the United States. These subjects produce intense emotional reactions in audiences. If you choose such a subject, you can expect to face several obstacles falling under the general headings of *conditioned responses* and *closed minds*.

One sure sign of an emotionally loaded subject is to have a loaded slogan associated with it. In recent debates over legalized abortion in the United States and the use of Medicaid funds to provide abortions, the opponents of legalization have chanted "right to life." This slogan not only provokes a strong conditioned response and effectively closes minds to any discussion, but in any debate it puts the opponents in the position of defenders of life and the proponents of legalization in the position of murderers. Thus, proponents have been forced to come up with a slogan of their own, "pro-choice," which moves the debate to different ground. (More recently, some proponents have hit back harder, starting to call the right-to-lifers "forced pregnancy" groups.)

With any such emotionally loaded subject, your problem is to structure the discussion so issues can be dealt with apart from predictable and intense emotional responses—in short, to open closed minds, if only a little way.

Closely related to highly charged emotional reactions is the intense resistance created by subjects that are in *conflict with revered cultural values.* Anyone who chooses conservation or ecology as a subject will have to contend, for example, with the American cultural value of growth (usually expressed as "progress"). Growth has been an ultimate good in our culture for many decades, that is, its value is part of our history. Bigger was better, expansion showed health and strength, greater consumption equaled the better life. Faced with rising populations and dropping resource levels, voices are now suggesting that small is beautiful, the steady state can be a healthy state, and the good life means more than consumption. But until such steady-state values establish themselves, efforts to persuade people to limit their energy consumption, pollute less, and protect the environment will run head on into the growth value. And if minds are not actually closed to antigrowth purposes, they are certainly resistant.

The second major set of rhetorical obstacles arising from your subject and purpose, then, lie in what I have called cultural history. Specifically, they are boredom, taboos and emotional loads and the closed minds that can result, and conflicts with cultural values.

PURPOSE-RELATED OBSTACLES

As a rhetor, you will not just be dealing with a subject, you will also be trying to induce a certain kind of participation from the audience. The kind of response that you seek may create obstacles. The two kinds of obstacles that arise from rhetorical purposes are resistance to the *cost* of responding and audience perception that it has no *control* over the issue in question (audience members do not see themselves as *agents of change*).

Cost

Just what is the audience expected to do, and what is the cost in time, energy, money, irritation, or ridicule? The greater such costs to the audience, the smaller the chance that they will do what you ask. If you are a typical college audience, many of you smoke, few of you exercise enough, and some of you are already overweight and many more of you will be by the age of 40. In the face of medical evidence, no one argues that smoking is good for your health, that exercise is unnecessary, or that obesity makes you live longer. Why, then, do so many Americans smoke, live sedentary lives, and overeat? The answer is that doing otherwise would cost them too much—too much *agony* or at least *considerable discomfort* to quit smoking, and too much *sustained thought and effort* to fit a good diet and exercise into the American way of life. Thus, if your purpose is to change any one of these habits, you will meet solid obstacles in the form of the costs the audience sees in what you are suggesting. In fact, no single rhetorical act is likely to achieve this kind of purpose. Smoking clinics and diet groups that do succeed have long-term contact with participants and supply consistent support from people struggling with similar problems.

Time is another cost that may obstruct your rhetorical purpose. For example, it is much faster (and easier) to write a check to a political candidate than to telephone all the Democrats in a precinct; this telephoning, in turn, is easier than going door to door to distribute literature and discuss a candidate. The greater the time, the energy, or the commitment demanded by your purpose, the greater the resistance you will meet.

Still other costs may be involved in your purpose—costs in *money* and *expertise*. Your audience may not have to contribute either one directly, but may feel the burden in other ways. Recently, for example, complaints have surfaced in the mass media about the large amounts of money and scientific expertise spent on finding a cure for cancer. In spite of years of research by thousands of people and with billions of dollars spent, no cure is in sight. If you are calling for more federal support for medical research, you may meet strong audience resistance. Your audience may feel that the researchers should be doing something more productive, and that the money, which comes from their taxes, could be better spent. For example, they might want better benefits for Vietnam veterans, federally supported day care for their children, or better enforcement of federal laws against discrimination in education and employment. The present property tax revolt, which began with proposition 13 in California, shows how strong this feeling can be.

Finally, cost is closely related to cultural values; these are the social costs of some subjects and purposes. Some beliefs bring down ridicule and other *social sanctions* on the believers. Since all of us want to be liked and respected by our friends, neighbors, and family, a subject or purpose that would separate us exacts a cost that few are willing to pay, and then, only if the rewards are substantial. For example, nineteenth-century feminists recognized that what came to be called the "bloomer" costume was both healthy and comfortable. Its loose harem-style pants under knee-length skirts were far better than long dresses whose skirts trailed in the dirt and weighed up to twenty pounds and whose narrow waists, cinched by stays, cut off breath and circulation. Yet even the most stalwart feminists gave up bloomers because the ridicule heaped on them was so consistent and so great that it threatened their cause. Similarly, it is hard for a Roman Catholic to espouse abortion, a car manufacturer to support rapid transit, or a devout Christian to favor the Supreme Court decision outlawing prayer in public schools. There are exceptions, of course, but those who take such stances often pay a high social price.

The rhetorical problem of cost, then, measures the price the audience must pay in time, energy and commitment, money and expertise, or social pressure for going along with your purpose. The more your purpose demands from the audience in such costs, the greater will be your rhetorical problem.

Control

The second obstacle arising from purpose I shall call *control*. This concerns whether or not the audience thinks it *can* act to produce changes. Obstacles arise when members of the audience cannot see what they as individuals can do, or do not believe that their actions will have any appreciable effect—in short, when they feel they have no control. For example, many Americans fail to vote because they think their votes make no difference—all politicians are alike, no one vote counts, they don't know how to get elected officials who will do what they want, and so forth. Such feelings illustrate the rhetorical problem of control.

Problems of control are closely related to problems of the audience—specifically, the audience as agents of change and as created through rhetorical action (see Chapter 4). If rhetors are to overcome obstacles to control, they must ensure that rhetorical action engages those who are agents of change. But the obstacles to control that exist in the perceptions of the audience are difficult to overcome. How does one convince women who are socialized to passivity and deference that they should take the initiative? How does one counteract generations of social influence that has taught blacks they are inferior and inadequate and ugly? How do you convince members of Congress to cut off funding for the war in Vietnam, for sending troops to Angola, or for mounting a mission to rescue hostages in Iran? The rhetorical efforts of feminists, of black nationalists such as Malcolm X, and of politicians, protesters, and columnists writing and speaking on Vietnam, Angola, and Iran are examples of successful and unsuccessful attempts to overcome the obstacle of control.

Obstacles related to control—and also to cost—exist for all audiences. It is easier to act once and be done with it than to commit yourself to a long-term course of action. If an audience feels unable to make a long-term commitment, it may refuse to act at all. Usually, it is easier to act alone than to organize a group. If a rhetorical act demands group action, individual audience members may not believe that others will join them in the effort. It is also easier to act if a problem is relatively limited and sharply defined than if the problem is complex and calls for various actions.

Rhetorical obstacles arising from control are partly a function of the characteristics of the audience. If rhetors are to overcome problems of control, they must not only target the audience carefully, but they must see that the target audience includes agents of change or those who can influence agents' decisions.

Obstacles arising from purpose are related to obstacles arising from the subject. For example, the problem of control will be greater if the issue is diffuse and complex, and if its ramifications are so great that achieving results requires the concerted and varied efforts of a large group of people over a long period of time.

ANALYSIS OF OBSTACLES

These four obstacles embedded in the subject (complexity, cultural history) and purpose (cost, control) can be illustrated by the topics of capital punishment, nuclear power, and teen-age pregnancy.

Capital Punishment

Many students, in spite of the advice given in Chapter 3, speak on capital punishment. Considering only the obstacles arising from subject and purpose, advocating or rejecting the death penalty for capital crimes seems safe enough. First, the subject does not seem terribly complex. Statistical evidence about the death penalty's deterrent value is complicated, but no more so than most statistical evidence. Most states today have few capital crimes, and most of these can be easily defined. The statements of psychological authorities are somewhat complex, but psychological terms and concepts are familiar in much of our society. Most audiences strongly oppose crime, and a rhetor can channel whatever sympathies they might have for murderers away from those who commit particularly loathsome premeditated crimes. American cultural values support both positions—on the one hand, a strong belief in just retribution (or vengeance); on the other hand, a strong belief in the sanctity of life and the fear of a wrong that can never be righted. There is little cost to the audience—little time or energy is required, there is no audience discomfort or inconvenience, there is community support for either belief, the actual execution or incarceration is remote from the audience—hence there is little resistance. The action required is political pressure of a moderate kind. As a result, the subject makes few demands on the audience.

The price rhetors pay for avoiding these obstacles is that the subject usually is not very significant for members of the audience. They feel no strong need to know or understand; they do not wish to disturb prior values and beliefs. Unless a dramatic event intervenes, such as the 1978 "Son of Sam" killings in New York City (a series of murders committed by one man), capital punishment will have the advantage of being a subject that produces few highly charged emotional responses. If, however, such an event does occur, passions may be aroused, as shown by outbursts in the courtroom when the killer was sentenced and by pressure on the New York State Legislature to reenact the death penalty. In such cases, if you seek a response that does not reflect the passions of the moment, the rhetorical problem will be acute.

Nuclear Power*

Nuclear power, as already mentioned, creates many problems as a subject, chiefly because of its complexity. There is some relevant cultural history—the horrors reported from Hiroshima and Nagasaki, the dramatization of potential accidents by the near-meltdown at Three Mile Island, the progress and development implied by the phrase, "the peaceful uses of atomic energy," the Linus Pauling–Edward Teller debates. The costs seem to be balanced. Those opposing nuclear

---

* For general sources cited here, see the end of the chapter.

power are impelled by the dangers of radioactive wastes; those favoring nuclear power point to the need for energy and note its relation to jobs. Those who oppose nuclear power have had to fight a long, slow campaign to delay construction of specific plants and to prevent development; those favoring it have had to mount similar campaigns. The antinuclear efforts have forced utilities to pay greater costs and have lowered the profits from building nuclear facilities.* The problems of control are also balanced. Organized action is necessary, the desired actions are specific, and effects are evident—plants are abandoned, built, or delayed. But as a subject, nuclear power poses severe problems because of its complexity. These problems are slightly greater for those who oppose it, but both sides face formidable obstacles.

The issue of nuclear power is complex because it is part of the overall issue of possible energy sources—hydroelectric, geothermal, fossil (coal, gas, and oil), and solar—and their risks and benefits. It also involves the relationships between energy consumption and the nature of the U.S. economy and our style of life. However, exclude these wider issues and implications, and consider only the economics of nuclear power.

Proponents of nuclear power argue that it is inexpensive—cheaper, in fact, than coal or oil. Representative Mike McCormack said that consumers saved about $750 million in 1974, mainly because of the lower fuel and operation costs of nuclear power plants, and the Intertechnology Corporation reported to Congress that the breeder reactor would save the American economy around $1 trillion. In addition, proponents argued, sales of enriched uranium produced by nuclear plants were half a billion dollars in 1974 and should reach $5 billion in 1980.† Finally, proponents point out that a moratorium on the use and construction of nuclear plants would wipe out some 5 1/2 million jobs.

Opponents paint a different picture. They argue that nuclear power is not cost-competitive and that cost estimates are based on out-of-date information. More recent cost studies find nuclear energy less economical than coal. They argue that a moratorium on building nuclear plants would cost nowhere near 5 1/2 million jobs, and per-

---

* Charles Mohr, "Antinuclear Drives: Diffuse but Effective," *New York Times*, 24 June 1978, city ed., p. 6.

† According to information in *Statistical Data of the Uranium Industry*, January 1, 1980, domestic sales in 1979 were $846,720,000 and foreign sales were $112,320,000 for a total of $959,140,000 or just under $1 billion (pp. 81–83).

haps as few as 50,000. Opponents also say that nuclear power is not practical because uranium will eventually get scarce, as the Economic Research and Development Administration, the U.S. Geological Survey, the *Bulletin of Atomic Scientists*, and the utilities themselves all admit.

Opponents also point to a shortage of the plants needed to transform raw uranium into the enriched form in which it is used as fuel. If more of these plants are not built, there will be a severe shortage of enriched uranium by 1983 or 1984. Because it takes at least 8 years to build such plants, shortages are inevitable unless we start building now. Similarly, there is a lag in building reprocessing plants that will allow us to reuse nuclear fuel, and there is such a lag in providing facilities to store spent fuel that some existing plants may be forced to close. Importing uranium from abroad is possible but dangerous, and might be more hazardous to U.S. economic security than importing oil.*

Finally, opponents of nuclear power argue that the amount of energy required to mine, process, and produce electricity from nuclear material is actually greater than the energy produced, a conclusion reached by several analysts and researchers.

However, proponents have answers to these economic arguments. They have concrete proposals for eliminating bottlenecks in refining, reprocessing, and creating storage facilities. They cite the statements of 32 eminent scientists and a Ford Foundation Study that indicate that supplies of uranium are adequate.

This brief survey of the arguments and evidence should make it clear that it is very hard to assess the practicality of nuclear power. Each side publishes evidence supporting its position. The validity of the evidence depends on assumptions that are hard to test. Take, for example, the question of uranium supplies. The supply depends partly on how much uranium can be mined. That amount can only be estimated and the estimates depend on complex geological questions. The supply depends also on the availability of plants; how fast these plants can be built depends on the number of labor problems that arise, the weather, the availability of materials, and so on. In addition, the price of uranium will determine whether or not a given technology is profitable: at one price it may be; at another it may not.

---

* Domestic U_3O_8 procurement from foreign sources was 1,700 metric tons in 1979 (*Statistical Data*, January 1, 1980, p. 84).

If you are a typical layperson, you've found the preceding material somewhat complicated. You may have found yourself skimming it quickly to avoid all the detail. If so, you illustrate the rhetorical problem and its effect on an audience. Even the relatively limited question of whether or not nuclear power is economically feasible is so complex that it is hard to talk about to an average audience. Note that complexity arises because you lack firsthand experience with the data, and that considerable expertise is required to evaluate the evidence and determine the assumptions on which it rests. The problem is compounded by conflicting pieces of evidence. Finally, the issue is complex because it is related to so many other issues—to geology, price, jobs, the speed with which plants can be built, and so on.

Events, of course, may overcome an audience's resistance to such complexity. If a nuclear plant is about to be built in your backyard you can learn a great deal in a very short time. Members of the Clamshell Alliance, which opposes building a nuclear facility in Seabrook, New Hampshire, are directly involved in these economic questions, and can tolerate complex discussions of them. Similarly, the people fighting the breeder reactor in Clinch River, Tennessee, find the economic questions directly relevant to them, and they, too, are more tolerant of complexity.

Teen-age Pregnancy

The subject of teen-age pregnancy introduces other problems, particularly those related to cultural history, such as the beliefs, values, and attitudes held by many typical American audiences. Basically, many people think it improper to discuss sexuality in public. People with this attitude consider sex education of children a private matter to be handled at home by parents. Discussion of this subject, therefore, demands that an audience with such attitudes put them and any resulting embarrassment aside. This is a lot to ask of an audience.

In addition, many people in this culture are not comfortable with their own sexuality and tend to pretend that people with strong sex drives are abnormal, particularly if they are women. This particular part of the double standard harks back to a Victorian view that nice women (normal women) don't really enjoy sex and tolerate it only to please their husbands and in order to have children. Conversely, women who have strong sexual needs and enjoy sexual activity aren't normal or nice; they are nymphomaniacs or prostitutes. In other words, teen-agers who get pregnant are clearly "bad" girls. Giving such people contraceptives only encourages them in their abnormality and vice; providing abortions simply compounds the evil. They should be punished for their abnormal desires and evil deeds by pregnancy.

If one believes sexual activity is normal and natural, conception seems appropriate whenever the partners would probably not raise a happy and healthy child. The issue of teen-age pregnancy arouses a whole flock of attitudes, and a rhetorical stance like Konner's (see Chapter 2) requires that the audience see sexual activity, even among teen-agers, as normal and natural so precautions for the health and well-being of all concerned become appropriate. As you will recognize, it is hard to change such beliefs even in a long persuasive campaign; it is virtually impossible in one short rhetorical encounter.

Once again, however, circumstances may alter such resistance. A community that has chosen to ignore this problem may be shaken into awareness by a tragic event—a girl's suicide or death from a backroom abortion. Such events create a need for information and understanding and a desire for action to prevent more tragedies. In addition, the very number of pregnant teen-agers may influence attitudes toward public investigation and discussion.

SUMMARY

These three short analyses illustrate the four major obstacles—complexity, cultural history, cost, and control—and their relationship to the demands of subject and purpose on the audience. In preparing for rhetorical action, you too will need to analyze your subject and purpose to consider the demands you will make on the audience. In this way you will be able to see in advance the obstacles you must overcome to achieve your goal.

All the problems I have described are directly related to the progression of rhetorical purposes presented in Chapter 1. In terms of that progression, the complexity of a problem like nuclear power interferes with altering perception or providing an explanation the audience will consider. Cultural history—the beliefs, values, and attitudes of the culture and community—influences all the rhetorical purposes. Opening your mind to information that may force you to reconsider "how things really are" demands setting aside your past experience and preparing for new experience. Obviously, explanations and new beliefs may conflict with prior values, opinions, and attitudes, and disrupt a settled pattern of beliefs. Thus, all rhetorical action exacts some price from the audience. The kinds of costs I have detailed, however, arise particularly from attempts to formulate or alter belief and channel it into specific action. The problems of control arise most forcefully when an audience is asked to make a commitment that will inevitably lead to action. Audience members must believe that it matters whether they act; without such belief no reader or listener can be a member of the target audience or an agent of change.

To summarize the ideas in this chapter, here is an outline of the obstacles that arise out of subject and purpose. You can use it as a checklist when trying to choose a subject and an approach to it.

Summary Outline: Obstacles Arising from the Subject or Purpose

I. What sorts of demands does the subject make on the audience?
   A. Does the complexity of the subject make special demands on the audience?
      1. Do members of the audience have access to firsthand experience or must all data come indirectly from others?
      2. Is special expertise required to interpret basic information on this subject?
      3. Is an evaluation of the credibility and authority of secondary sources an inevitable part of this topic?
   B. How does cultural history create resistance?
      1. Do cultural values inhibit public discussion of this subject?
      2. What problems are created by traditional, familiar arguments and by famous pieces of evidence?
      3. Have past discussions created slogans or concepts that must be refuted or reformulated?
      4. What beliefs, attitudes, or values held by the audience will conflict with the specific purpose?
II. What sorts of demands does the purpose make on the audience?
   A. What special costs are exacted from the audience by the response desired?
      1. How much inconvenience and discomfort must the audience undergo in order to believe or act as the rhetor desires?
      2. How much time, energy, and commitment is required to achieve the desired goal?
      3. How much money and expertise must be expended to achieve the goal?
      4. How much social resistance from family, friends, and neighbors will the audience encounter in accepting the rhetor's claims?

    B. How much control does the audience have in achieving the
desired outcome; how much control does the audience perceive itself as having?

      1. Is the audience that is exposed to the rhetorical act the
group most directly involved in the issue or purpose?

      2. Are those exposed either the actual agents of change or do
they have an influence on these agents?

      3. Can one act alone or is concerted action required?

      4. Is a single act enough or must one commit oneself to a series
of actions to achieve the goal?

      5. Is the needed action simple, obvious, and likely to produce
an immediate reward or is it complex, difficult to discern,
and hard to evaluate?

You may use this summary to analyze your own topic and thesis.

SOURCES

A particularly detailed analysis of the cost of nuclear power is Saun-
ders Miller, *The Economics of Nuclear and Coal Power* (New York:
Praeger, 1976).

    Material cited from the *Congressional Record* includes Committee
for Nuclear Responsibility, "The Nuclear Fuel Scandal," 122 (26
April 1976), p. S5917; Mike McCormack, "Report of the Subcommit-
tee to Review the Liquid Metal Fast Breeder Reactor," 121 (7 May
1975), p. E2228; T. A. Nemzak, "Nuclear Power: Myths and Reality,"
121 (16 December 1975), p. S22370; "Statement of 32 Eminent Scientists," 121 (31 January 1975), p. E316.

    Other sources cited are C. Sharp Cook, "The High Cost of Nuclear
Power," *Bulletin of Atomic Scientists* 32 (December 1976); "Ford
Motor Study," *Science* 195 (1 April 1977), p. 41; Intertechnology Cor-
poration, *The U.S. Energy Problem* (Washington, D.C.: National Tech-
nical Information Service, November 1972); and Alvin Weinberg,
"Nuclear Moratorium," *Science* 195 (14 January 1977).

    A general source for information on ecological issues is *Living in the
Environment* by G. Tyler Miller (Belmont, Calif.: Wadsworth Publishing, 1982).

    The *Monthly Energy Review* published by the U.S. Department of
Energy, Energy Information Administration, provides data on all
facets of the energy industries in the U.S. See also annual issues of

Statistical Data of the Uranium Industry, published by the U.S. government.

MATERIAL FOR ANALYSIS

In 1979 an attempt was made to unify the movement against the use and development of nuclear power. On May 6, 1979, in reaction to a near-meltdown at Three Mile Island nuclear plant, a rally was held in Washington, D.C., to bring together diverse, regional groups and to kick off a national effort. There was little agreement on goals, however, and purposes were ill defined. There were several reasons for this. The subject of nuclear power is complex, and is tied to our cultural history since World War II. Also, the cost of limiting or eliminating nuclear power is steep for a highly industrialized society such as ours. In addition, the fledgling movement was arrayed against powerful forces in government, business, and the military. In such a situation, it would be easy to despair, to believe that one's acts could have no effect.

The rally is a special kind of rhetorical occasion that limits rhetorical action severely. The speaker faces a huge crowd spread over a large area. In this case, some 65,000 to 125,000 were assembled on the mall. The rally began with an invocation delivered by Father Paul Mayer of New York Theological Seminary that was labeled an "Indian Prayer." Here is what he said:

The Rally Invocation: An "Indian Prayer"
offered by Father Paul Mayer of New York
Theological Seminary*

1   Sisters and brothers, I thought that the one religious tradition we could all unite around is the religion of this continent, of this earth, which is that of the native peoples to whom the soul of this continent still belongs. Let us open our hearts to the Great Spirit, the maker of all things, who gave us the gift of our mother, the earth.

2   We ask You this day to give us the light and wisdom to love her, to help her to grow, to remember that we are the relatives of all things, the four-leggeds, the winged ones, the things that swim in the water, the grasses that grow, the flowers that bloom. Only by this understanding will we remember to protect our mother, the

---

* Transcribed from a tape recording by the author. Reprinted by permission.

earth, against the violations of nuclear radiation, of nuclear power plants, of nuclear weapons. Great Spirit, give us strength for the struggle ahead and above all to remember that we are brothers and sisters united in this struggle.

3   So be it!

A prayer is a special kind of rhetorical act, illustrating an unusual relationship between participants: an inferior addressing a superior. The prayer is also meant to be overheard by the speaker's peers for whom he is the representative.

This prayer is uniquely adapted to the setting, a rally, and the issue, nuclear power. After reading it carefully, consider these questions:

1.   Why would antinuclear protestors choose to begin a national rally with an invocation? How does it work strategically in terms of the issue and the audience?

2.   Compare the language of this invocation with another invocation, such as a prayer that opens a session of Congress or a political convention. How does this prayer differ from one of those in tone, persona, references to a higher being, introduction, and conclusion? Would you agree that Mayer "fulfills the requirements for an invocation creatively"?

3.   Consider how this short rhetorical act attempts to overcome problems of complexity, cultural history, cost, and control.

4.   What are the rhetorical implications of calling the invocation an "Indian Prayer"?

5.   What is the significance of having an ordained priest deliver this invocation?

EXERCISE

Coping with Boredom and Hostility

The class is divided into two groups. One group should prepare a list of topics that they consider most of their classmates would find uninteresting. The other group should prepare a list of topics that they think will arouse intense hostility from two or more class members. Each group should compose three or four introductions for their list of topics to be presented by speakers designated by the group.

The introductions for the uninteresting topics should seek to arouse interest, perhaps by presenting a novel point of view, a startling fact, or the like. However, the subject of the speech should be clear to the audience from the introduction.

The introductions for the highly controversial topics should seek to gain a fair and open hearing for a disliked point of view, perhaps by an appeal to self-interest or to the threat of biased or limited exposure, or the like. The controversial point of view should be clear to the audience from the introduction.

Present the introductions from each group. Discuss the strategies that were used, and suggest other possibilities. Discuss which approaches seemed to be more effective, and why.

CHAPTER 6

OBSTACLES TO SOURCE CREDIBILITY

Ideas do not walk by themselves; they must be carried—expressed and articulated—by someone. As a result, we do not encounter ideas neutrally, objectively, apart from a context; we meet them as *someone's* ideas. The relationship between people and ideas is reflected in the way we talk. We speak of Marxism, by which we mean the ideas associated with Karl Marx, ideas he expressed and explained. We speak of Jeffersonian democracy to refer to Jefferson's concept of what a democracy is. When the House Judiciary Committee debated articles of impeachment, we heard its members discuss the Madisonian theory of executive responsibility. Similar phrases are used to refer to scientific ideas, even though science is popularly regarded as impersonal. It's Darwin's theory of evolution, Einstein's theory of relativity, Heisenberg's uncertainty principle, and Watson and Crick's model of the DNA molecule. Such language reflects what we all know—that an idea as carried by one person is not the same idea when it is interpreted and defined by another.

The importance of the rhetor in the persuasive process has been recognized since people first began to think and write about the discipline of rhetoric. In the treatise on rhetoric he wrote in the fourth century B.C.E., Aristotle described three paths through which ideas were made persuasive for an audience. One of these he called *ethos,* the character of the rhetor:

Persuasion is achieved by the speaker's personal character when the speech is so spoken as to make us think him credible. We believe good men more fully and more readily than others: this is true generally whatever the question is, and absolutely true where exact certainty is impossible and opinions are divided. . . . his character may almost be called the most effective means of persuasion he possesses. (Rhetoric. *1. 2. 1356a. 4–12.*)

In other words, one way in which we are influenced is through the character of the rhetor—we accept the idea because we trust the person who presents it. Moreover, says Aristotle, this is particularly true of rhetoric because it deals with social truths, where certainty is impossible and where there is often controversy. Aristotle suggests, in fact, that the character of the rhetor may be the most potent source of influence, even more powerful than the arguments and evidence or the needs and motives of the audience.

The power of the speaker's character or *ethos* becomes more understandable if we comprehend the meaning of the ancient term. The word *ethos* is a Greek word that is closely related to our terms *ethical* and *ethnic*. In its widest modern usage, ethos refers not to the character or personality of an individual but to "the disposition, character, or attitude peculiar to a specific people, culture, or group that distinguishes it from other peoples or groups."* When understood this way, its relationship to the word *ethnic* is obvious, for ethnic means "characteristic of a religious, racial, national, or cultural group." In other words, ethos does not refer to your peculiarities as an individual but to the ways in which you reflect the characteristics and qualities that are valued by your culture or group. Similarly, ethics is "the study of the . . . specific moral choices to be made by the individual in his relationship with others." In other words, we judge the character of another by the choices that person makes about how she or he will live with other members of the community. What is ethical is right conduct in relation to other persons, the persons in our community or society. Ethical principles are the norms or values in a culture that describe what its members believe are the right relationships between persons. The ethos of a rhetor refers to the relationship between the rhetor and the community as reflected in rhetorical action.

When he described what contributed to the ethos of a rhetor in a rhetorical act, Aristotle wrote that it arose from demonstrated wisdom about social truths (*phronesis*), from moral excellence (*arete*),

---

* The definitions used in this chapter are taken from *The American Heritage Dictionary of the English Language* (Boston: Houghton Mifflin, 1969).

and from demonstrations that the rhetor was well intentioned toward her or his community (*eunoia*). In other words, he believed that members of the community were influenced by evidence of good sense on practical matters, by evidence of the rhetor's ethical principles, and by indications that the rhetor had the best interests of the community in mind. In more contemporary terms, your good sense is a measure of your expertise or competence on an issue, your moral excellence is a measure of your trustworthiness, and your goodwill is a measure of your concern for the community's interests.

Modern research has demonstrated that Aristotle's views of ethos were remarkably apt.* In contemporary research, *ethos* is usually defined as the attitude a member of the audience has toward the rhetor (the source of the message) at any given moment. Experimental studies demonstrate that the source of the message has a remarkable effect on its impact. The earliest studies compared the effects of messages attributed to different sources. For example, similar audiences listened to identical tape-recorded speeches attributed to different sources. These studies demonstrated that sources with high prestige for an audience had a significantly greater effect. Thus, for example, similar audiences were more favorable toward a message supporting group health care when it came from the Surgeon-General of the United States than when it was attributed to the Secretary of the Communist Party in America or to a Northwestern University sophomore. Studies like these are interested in prior ethos, or the attitude that members of the audience have toward the rhetor (the source) prior to the rhetorical act.

PRIOR ETHOS

Attitudes toward the rhetor prior to the rhetorical act originate in (1) the rhetor's reputation or track record, (2) the rhetor's appearance, (3) how the rhetor is introduced to the audience, and (4) the context in which the rhetorical act is presented. Because the attitude of the audience toward the source is so important, it is worth noting how each of these can create problems.

Reputation

Although you may not be famous, you have a reputation and a track record that can be as troublesome as that of a famous athlete, politi-

---

* See the list of sources at the end of the chapter.

cian, or scholar. Two stories about the problems that Jesus had in his hometown of Nazareth are illustrative. On one occasion, Jesus went home and preached in his local synagogue. According to the reports in three gospels, he did a superb job, but the members of his local community were not impressed. In effect, his neighbors asked how a local boy could know and do such things—wasn't this the carpenter's son, the son of Mary, whose brothers and sisters they knew? They were offended that an ordinary person whom they knew well should preach and teach so. When Jesus heard what they said, he responded, "A prophet is not without honor, except in his own country, and in his own house." (Matthew 13:54–58; Mark 6:1–6; Luke 4:16–24)

It is quite likely that, as in this story, you will initiate rhetorical action in your local community or in a place in which you are personally known very well. One of my students reported a difficult and embarrassing experience he had when he returned from a year of study abroad and was asked to speak at a convocation in his high school. As he walked to the podium, his friends laughed. This was little Andy Smith with whom they had grown up. What could he know about the world? The student described his struggle to gain attention and to be taken seriously, and he admitted that he never quite succeeded. As his story illustrates, you face a serious rhetorical problem when you try to establish your competence to speak to an audience in your local community, club, place of work, or neighborhood.

The second story is similar. The Gospel of John describes the process by which Jesus chooses his disciples. One of them, Phillip, tells another man, Nathaniel, how wonderful Jesus is. But Nathaniel responds, "Can any good thing come out of Nazareth?" And Phillip answers, "Come and see." (John 1:46). Many of us come from places that, like Nazareth, are unknown and undistinguished. (I grew up on a small farm near Blomkest, Minnesota, a metropolis of 147 residents.) Audiences may well ask, How can someone from a little town in Minnesota know anything about rhetoric or criticism or the analysis of discourse? In other words, when you are outside your local community you will have the problem of establishing your credentials and of convincing audiences that people from unusual places or small places or unknown places or places with bad reputations do have the knowledge to discuss an important subject.

Both ordinary and famous persons encounter another problem— the difficulties that arise from inconsistent behavior. We trust those whose behavior demonstrates a systematic commitment to principles, and we are wary of those who make dramatic shifts of position. For example, some persons doubted Charles Colson's conversion to

Christianity because of his record of highly pragmatic, even ruthless actions as a member of the Nixon administration. Such skeptics saw his conversion (a word that literally means a turnaround) as a calculated decision to appear repentant and to facilitate his return to society from prison. But as he continues to behave as a Christian would, he begins to confound the skeptics and to convince some, at least, that this was a sincere change of heart. Your track record as a rhetor (what you have said in the past) and as a citizen (what you have done on social issues) are analogous to your driving record or credit record. Just as you will pay higher insurance premiums if you've had accidents, or have difficulties getting credit if you have not paid your bills in the past, as a rhetor you must make a greater effort if your past statements or your past actions cast doubt on your sincerity or commitment. If what you urge appears to conflict with your past record, you will encounter a serious rhetorical problem.

In rare instances, however, deviation from the past can be an asset. David Shoup and James A. Donovan wrote an essay attacking the military that appeared in 1969 in the *Atlantic* entitled "The New American Militarism."* If you do not know who the authors are, you may assume that this is simply another essay by antiwar activists. But when you learn that Shoup was Commandant of the United States Marine Corps and served on the Joint Chiefs of Staff with the rank of general until 1963, and that Donovan is another retired Marine officer, you know that this is an unusual essay. And because of the consistent commitment to the American military represented by their backgrounds, you would probably listen to their criticisms with far more interest and consideration. When a person deviates from a lifetime of commitments, his or her message is important and becomes an informed criticism by an insider. Such evidence is called "reluctant evidence" because it is given reluctantly, against one's interests. In such a case, inconsistency can create positive ethos.

Appearance

Research that has been done on how humans form impressions of others indicates that we make initial decisions about an individual in a matter of seconds based on clothing, movement, posture, and facial expressions. Obviously, if the appearance of the rhetor creates negative impressions in the audience, an obstacle has been created that

---

* *Atlantic* 223 (April 1969), pp. 51–56.

the rhetor must overcome to be heard, much less to influence. As a result, I believe that rhetors need to make careful choices about appearance. Like you, I am many different people or, if you will, I play many different roles. As a feminist, I try to be the "me" that will create the least resistance in an audience. When I talk to students in a dormitory lounge about the film, "The Emerging Woman," on a weekday evening, I wear my favorite pair of jeans and a comfortable shirt, sit casually on the floor, and talk informally. When I give a speech at a scholarship dinner at a sorority, I put on a favorite fashionable outfit that I feel particularly attractive wearing, I stand straight, and I speak more formally. When I moderate a debate before students, faculty, and townspeople between a local anti-ERA activist and a psychiatrist on the one hand and a gay rights leader and a psychologist on the other, I wear a neat, relatively unobtrusive dress, and I try to speak, stand, and move with an authority and formality that bespeaks my desire to be fair. Recognize that I am all of these people—these are not false fronts that I put on. But if I shift them around, I will have problems. If I go formally to the dorm lounge, students will not feel free to talk easily and ask questions. If I am casual at the sorority, I will not do honor to the occasion and will disappoint and offend. If I go casually to the debate, my dress will be taken as a visual sign that I favor one side, and I shall be suspected of bias and expected to be unfair.

As an alert and sensitive rhetor, you must consider the demands of the situation, the subject, and the audience. You must consider which "you" is most appropriate and choose from your repertoire of selves so that you will not create unnecessary obstacles that prevent your message from reaching the audience or that violate the occasion. Unless you are making a rhetorical point, you should choose a style of dress, posture, and speech that is appropriate to the occasion and the subject, and one that will not prevent the audience from approaching your speech with interest and a willingness to listen.*

Your Introduction

The famous French philosopher Jean-Paul Sartre commented that one of the terrifying things about human life is that when we die our lives become the property of others to do with as they will. If you have listened to the eulogies given at funerals you will understand how

---

* See Chapter 12 for further discussion of the nonverbal dimensions of rhetorical action.

frightening that can be. In a less permanent but no less terrifying way, the rhetor's ethos becomes the property of the person who introduces her or him to the audience, and a potential rhetorical problem is in the making. The person who introduces you creates the climate in which you will begin to speak and can be significant in determining the initial attitude of the audience. Consider carefully what you would like to have said about yourself, and if the introducer asks you, be sure to tell her or him. Similarly, when you introduce someone else, think about the climate you will create. A really thoughtful introducer tells the rhetor what she or he plans to say and asks if the speaker would like any changes or additions. You, as a rhetor, will not be able to control all the possible problems that may arise, but you need to be aware of them.

The Context

Our initial impressions of a rhetor are influenced by context. We are likely to assume, until contrary evidence appears, that persons whose articles appear on the Op-Ed page of the *New York Times* are knowledgeable and interesting and that persons who write for the *Farm Journal* come from rural areas and are expert about some aspect of farming or ranching. In such cases, and in many others, audiences will form initial impressions from the process by which you came to be speaking or writing at this time or in this place. Although you may be totally unknown, you will have positive prior ethos if you participate in the DePauw University Undergraduate Symposium in Speech Communication because participants are selected competitively. If one of my students who is a well-liked member of a sorority invites me to speak at a scholarship dinner, the audience, to whom I am unknown, will probably assume that I am a professor who is often dynamic and interesting and who may be so on this occasion.

The context can also create a significant problem, however. Perhaps the most famous example of this involves the circumstances under which Henry Grady made a speech entitled "The New South" at a dinner of the New England society in New York City in 1886. Grady was a newspaper editor from Georgia, and he was the first Southerner to speak before this group after the Civil War. He wanted to convince his audience that there was a new South developing with which New Englanders and Northerners generally could form an economic partnership. But imagine his rhetorical problem when it turned out that the speaker who preceded him was none other than General William Tecumseh Sherman, the very person who was famous for his ruthless march through Georgia and who gave a speech that was most unsympathetic to the South. Here is what Henry Grady said in his introduction:

The New South

"There was a South of slavery and secession—that South is dead. There is a South of union and freedom—that South, thank God, is living, breathing, growing every hour." These words delivered from the immortal lips of Benjamin H. Hill,* at Tammany Hall in 1866, true then, and truer now, I shall make my text to-night.

Mr. President and Gentlemen: Let me express to you my appreciation of the kindness by which I am permitted to address you. I make this abrupt acknowledgment advisedly, for I feel that if, when I raise my provincial voice in this ancient and august presence, I could find courage for no more than the opening sentence, it would be well if, in that sentence, I had met in a rough sense my obligation as a guest, and had perished, so to speak, with courtesy on my lips and grace in my heart. (*Laughter*) Permitted through your kindness to catch my second wind, let me say that I appreciate the significance of being the first Southerner to speak at this board, which bears the substance, if it surpasses the semblance, of original New England hospitality (*Applause*), and honors a sentiment that in turn honors you, but in which my personality is lost, and the compliment to my people made plain. (*Laughter*)

I bespeak the utmost stretch of your courtesy to-night. I am not troubled about those from whom I come. You remember the man whose wife sent him to a neighbor with a pitcher of milk, and who, tripping on the top step, fell, with such casual interruptions as the landing afforded, into the basement; and while picking himself up had the pleasure of hearing his wife call out: "John, did you break the pitcher?"

"No, I didn't," said John, "but I be dinged if I don't." (*Laughter*)

So, while those who call to me from behind may inspire me with energy if not with courage, I ask an indulgent hearing from you. I beg that you will bring your full faith in American fairness and frankness to judgment upon what I shall say. There was an old preacher once who told some boys of the Bible lesson he was going

---

* Hill, like Grady, was a Georgian. Originally he opposed secession but accepted his state's decision and sat in the Confederate Senate. After the war he supported Reconstruction policies, but championed Southern causes in the U.S. Congress.

to read in the morning. The boys finding the place, glued together the connecting pages. (*Laughter*) The next morning he read on the bottom of one page: "When Noah was one hundred and twenty years old he took unto himself a wife, who was"—then turning the page—"one hundred and forty cubits long (*Laughter*), forty cubits wide, built of gopher-wood (*Laughter*), and covered with pitch inside and out." (*Loud and continued laughter*) He was naturally puzzled at this. He read it again, verified it, and then said: "My friends, this is the first time I ever met this in the Bible, but I accept it as an evidence of the assertion that we are fearfully and wonderfully made." (*Immense laughter*) If I could get you to hold such faith to-night I could proceed cheerfully to the task I otherwise approach with a sense of consecration.

Pardon me one word, Mr. President, spoken for the sole purpose of getting into the volumes that go out annually freighted with the rich eloquence of your speakers—the fact that the Cavalier as well as the Puritan was on the continent in its early days, and that he was "up and able to be about." (*Laughter*) I have read your books carefully and I find no mention of that fact, which seems to me an important one for preserving a sort of historical equilibrium if for nothing else.

Let me remind you that the Virginia Cavalier first challenged France on this continent—that Cavalier John Smith gave New England its very name, and was so pleased with the job that he has been handing his own name around ever since—and that while Miles Standish was cutting off men's ears for courting a girl without her parents' consent, and forbade men to kiss their wives on Sunday, the Cavalier was courting everything in sight, and that the Almighty had vouchsafed great increase to the Cavalier colonies, the huts in the wilderness being full as the nests in the woods.

But having incorporated the Cavalier as a fact in your charming little books I shall let him work out his own salvation, as he has always done with engaging gallantry, and we will hold no controversy as to his merits. Why should we? Neither Puritan nor Cavalier long survived as such. The virtues and traditions of both happily still live for the inspiration of their sons and the saving of the old fashion. (*Applause*) But both Puritan and Cavalier were lost in the storm of the first Revolution; and the American citizen, supplanting both and stronger than either, took possession of the Republic bought by their common blood and fashioned to wisdom, and charged himself with teaching men government and establishing the voice of the people as the voice of God. (*Applause*)

My friend Dr. Talmadge has told you that the typical American has yet to come. Let me tell you that he has already come.

(*Applause*) Great types like valuable plants are slow to flower and fruit. But from the union of these colonist Puritans and Cavaliers, from the straightening of their purposes and the crossing of their blood, slow perfecting through a century, came he who stands as the first typical American, the first who comprehended within himself all the strength and gentleness, all the majesty and grace of this Republic—Abraham Lincoln. (*Loud and continued applause*) He was the sum of Puritan and Cavalier, for in his ardent nature were fused the virtues of both, and in the depths of his great soul the faults of both were lost. (*Renewed applause*) He was greater than Puritan, greater than Cavalier, in that he was American (*Renewed applause*) and that in his homely form were first gathered the vast and thrilling forces of his ideal government—charging it with such tremendous meaning and so elevating it above human suffering that martyrdom, though infamously aimed, came as a fitting crown to a life consecrated from the cradle to human liberty. (*Loud and prolonged cheering*) Let us, each cherishing the traditions and honoring his fathers, build with reverent hands to the type of this simple but sublime life, in which all types are honored; and in our common glory as Americans there will be plenty and to spare for your forefathers and for mine. (*Renewed cheering*)

In speaking to the toast with which you have honored me, I accept the term, "The New South," as in no sense disparaging to the Old. Dear to me, sir, is the home of my childhood and the traditions of my people. I would not, if I could, dim the glory they won in peace and war, or by word or deed take aught from the splendor and grace of their civilization—never equaled and, perhaps, never to be equaled in its chivalric strength and grace. There is a New South, not through protest against the Old, but because of new conditions, new adjustments, and, if you please, new ideas and aspirations. It is to this that I address myself, and to the consideration of which I hasten lest it become the Old South before I get to it. Age does not endow all things with strength and virtue, nor are all new things to be despised. The shoemaker who put over his door "John Smith's shop. Founded in 1760," was more than matched by his young rival across the street who hung out this sign: "Bill Jones. Established 1886. No old stock kept in this shop."

Dr. Talmadge has drawn for you, with a master's hand, the picture of your returning armies. He has told you how in the pomp and circumstance of war, they came back to you, marching with proud and victorious tread, reading their glory in a nation's eyes! Will you bear with me while I tell you of another army that sought its home at the close of the late war—an army that marched home in defeat and not in victory—in pathos and not in splendor, but in glory that equaled yours, and to hearts as loving as ever welcomed heroes home. Let me picture to you the footsore Confederate soldier, as, buttoning up in his faded gray jacket the parole which was to bear testimony to his children of his fidelity and faith, he turned his face southward from Appomattox in April, 1865. Think of him as ragged, half-starved, heavy-hearted, enfeebled by want and wounds; having fought to exhaustion, he surrenders his gun, wrings the hands of his comrades in silence, and lifting his tear-stained and pallid face for the last time to the graves that dot the old Virginia hills, pulls his gray cap over his brow and begins the slow and painful journey. What does he find—let me ask you, who went to your homes eager to find in the welcome you had justly earned, full payment for four years' sacrifice—what does he find when, having followed the battle-stained cross against overwhelming odds, dreading death not half so much as surrender, he reaches the home he left so prosperous and beautiful? He finds his house in ruins, his farm devastated, his slaves free, his stock killed, his barns empty, his trade destroyed, his money worthless; his social system, feudal in its magnificence, swept away; his people without law or legal status, his comrades slain, and the burdens of others heavy on his shoulders. Crushed by defeat, his very traditions are gone; without money, credit, employment, material or training; and, besides all this, confronted with the gravest problem that ever met human intelligence—the establishing of a status for the vast body of his liberated slaves.

What does he do—this hero in gray with a heart of gold? Does he sit down in sullenness and despair? Not for a day. Surely God, who had stripped him of his prosperity, inspired him in his adversity. As ruin was never before so overwhelming, never was restoration swifter. The soldier stepped from the trenches into the furrow; horses that had charged Federal guns march before the plow, and fields that ran red with human blood in April were green with the harvest in June; women reared in luxury cut up their dresses and made breeches for their husbands and, with a patience and heroism that fit women always as a garment, gave their hands to work. There was little bitterness in all this. Cheerfulness and frankness prevailed. "Bill Arp" struck the keynote when he said: "Well, I killed as many of them as they did of me, and now I am going to work." (*Laughter and applause*) Or the soldier returning home after defeat and roasting some corn on the roadside, who made the remark to his comrades: "You may leave the South if you want to, but I am going to Sandersville, kiss my wife and raise a crop, and if the Yankees fool with me any more I will whip 'em again." (*Renewed applause*) I want to say to General Sherman—who is considered an able man in our hearts, though some people think he is a kind of careless man about fire—that from the ashes he left us in 1864 we have raised a brave and beautiful city; that somehow or other we have caught the sunshine in the bricks and mortar of our homes, and have builded therein not one ignoble prejudice or memory. (*Applause*)

But in all this what have we accomplished? What is the sum of our work? We have found out that in the general summary the free Negro counts more than he did as a slave. We have planted the schoolhouse on the hilltop and made it free to white and black. We have sowed towns and cities in the place of theories and put business above politics. (*Applause*) We have challenged your spinners in Massachusetts and your iron-makers in Pennsylvania. We have learned that the $400,000,000 annually received from our cotton crop will make us rich, when the supplies that make it are home-raised. We have reduced the commercial rate of interest from twenty-four to six per cent, and are floating four per cent bonds. We have learned that one Northern immigrant is worth fifty foreigners, and have smoothed the path to southward, wiped out the place where Mason and Dixon's line used to be, and hung our latch-string out to you and yours. (*Prolonged cheers*)*

Grady begins dramatically with a quotation from a converted fellow Georgian. The quotation is his thesis; its clear statement at the outset helps to gain him a hearing because it establishes that he and the audience share the desire to put the Old South of secession and war into the past.

Grady's statement of thanks to the New England society fulfills the demands of courtesy; implicitly it asks his audience to be courteous to him. He compliments the food, then tells jokes that change the mood markedly, creating warmth and informality. Both seek a tolerant hearing from his audience.

Grady shifts to a broad view of American history. He affirms the Cavalier tradition, which he represents, and the Puritan tradition, which his audience represents. In a moment of great emotional intensity and profound identification, he says that Lincoln is the culmination of both. Only a New Southerner could claim that Lincoln was "the first typical American"!

Grady accepts the concept of "The New South," but he also honors the Old, "the home of my childhood and the traditions of my people." Just as an earlier speaker vividly depicted the returning Union ar-

---

* Henry W. Grady, "The New South," in *American Public Addresses, 1740–1952*, ed. A. Craig Baird (New York: McGraw-Hill, 1956), pp. 180–188.

mies, he begs leave to do the same for the Confederate soldiers. Grady uses every resource of language to describe "ragged, half-starved, heavy-hearted, enfeebled" men who come home to devastation but who put the war behind them and set to work. Two examples bring them to life before our eyes. Then he jokes about General Sherman as "a kind of careless man about fire." This is indeed a New Southerner!

Grady's introduction glides imperceptibly into the body as he affirms his thesis in a resounding series of claims made more emphatic by parallelism: "We have found out . . . We have planted . . . We have sowed . . . We have challenged . . . We have learned . . ."

Grady's introduction is a masterpiece of strategic adaptation to a rhetorical problem. In the face of hostility, he creates identification and diminishes tension through humor. In the face of doubt, he demonstrates that he is indeed a New Southerner. In the face of audience resistance, he creates a willingness to listen.

The Occasion

Henry Grady's predicament illustrates the kind of problem that is created by the context of a preceding speaker. But other difficulties can arise. Every rhetorical act is limited by the occasion, by the kind of event or place in which it occurs. Effective rhetorical action, which reaches the audience, must be appropriate to its context. The problem of the rhetor is to select a purpose that is consistent both with her or his beliefs and desires and with the time and place in which it occurs. Think for a moment about inappropriate rhetorical acts you have experienced. I remember a long sermon at a cousin's wedding that no one could hear because they were angry that the clergyman could keep a nervous bride and groom standing in the front of a church for so long. I remember a highly partisan political speech given in a campus chapel that was so offensive that about half the students finally walked out. Just as audiences have purposes (the needs they wish to satisfy), occasions have purposes, and an effective rhetorical act must be consonant with that purpose. If the purpose of the occasion is entertainment, your rhetorical act must be entertaining—among other things, perhaps. If the purpose of the occasion is to do honor, your act must be consistent. For example, the scholarship dinner at a sorority is an occasion to honor women who have unusually fine academic records. As a feminist, I should like to have sorority members acutely aware of the problems of women and the injustices they suffer. But such a purpose is not entirely appropriate to a dinner of this kind. When I spoke on such an occasion, I tried to combine my purpose and theirs. I told the women that in 1776, exactly 200 years earlier, no women had scholarship dinners, and none of them had an opportunity for higher education that was comparable to that of males. I told them about the struggle of women to gain the right to an equal education, but I ended by honoring them and the University of Kansas where they were students by telling them that from the day it opened, their university had admitted women and that its first freshman class was composed almost equally of men and women. As a feminist, I accomplished my purpose by raising consciousness about the history of women's education; as a rhetor, I was heard because my purpose was consistent with the purpose of the occasion.

The rhetor is limited by the context of the occasion, and a rhetorical problem arises if the rhetor's purpose is not consistent with that of the occasion.

Rhetorical problems may arise even before the rhetor begins to produce a message. These may arise from your past, from your appearance or the role you choose to play, from the way in which you are introduced to the audience, and from a conflict between your purpose and the purpose of the occasion.

ETHOS FROM THE RHETORICAL ACT

Ethos is an attitude—the impressions or images persons have of the source of a message. Like all attitudes, those about the credibility of a rhetor (or the source of the message, whether it is an individual or a medium or an institution) are general and evaluative. Unlike most other attitudes, which are unidimensional (that is, determined by only one factor), ethos is multidimensional, affected by at least two distinct factors. One of these is authoritativeness and the other is trustworthiness.* For a rhetor to be authoritative for an audience means that he or she is perceived as informed, expert, qualified, intelligent, and reliable. This cluster of attributes is similar to those characterizing a person who, in the classical sense, showed wisdom on practical matters. For a rhetor to be trustworthy means that he or she is perceived as honest, friendly, pleasant, and selfless. This second factor seems to combine the Aristotelian view that a rhetor must be perceived as having moral excellence and as being well intentioned

---

* Admittedly this is an oversimplification. Using factor analysis as a technique, a number of other factors have been found, but these two are the most stable and generalized across studies.

toward the community. A third factor appears in some studies: dynamism. This means that, in some cases, the attitude toward the rhetor is affected by the degree to which he or she is emphatic, aggressive, forceful, bold, active, and energetic, but this factor functions less predictably and uniformly in diverse situations.

Additional studies of ethos have uncovered what is dubbed a "sleeper effect," a phrase used to describe the fact that if members of an audience are not exposed to materials that remind them of who said what, the influence of sources with high prestige diminishes and the influence of sources with low prestige increases.* One possible explanation for this effect is that members of the audience forget the source but remember the evidence and arguments. Another possible interpretation is that the ethos developed through and by the message itself is far more significant than that produced by prior events. Aristotle wrote that "this kind of persuasion [ethos] . . . should be achieved by what the speaker says, not by what people think of his character before he begins to speak." In fact, there is some basis for the view that the ethos developed by and through the rhetorical act is inseparable from the message.

The results of research on the "sleeper effect" may lead to a mistaken view that concern with ethos is unnecessary. Such a view rests on the notion that the rhetor's ethos and the message each has a fixed, unchanging meaning for the audience. It was once presumed that only the evaluation of the message is influenced by the prestige of the source from which it supposedly comes. S. E. Asch did an important criticism of this kind of resarch, and he argued that authorship did not function as a source of prestige but as a context that influenced the meaning statements had for members of the audience. Such a perspective holds that meaning is in people, and that when the context of a message is changed, its meaning will be interpreted differently.† In other words, you, as rhetor, as the source of an act, are the context that influences how the audience decides what the message means. The "sleeper effect" indicates that persuasion is a process in which the message is a major determinant of effects, but that the nature of the message itself will be influenced significantly by the rhetor, who provides a major part of its context.

---

* Carl Hovland and Walter Weiss, "The Influence of Source Credibility on Communication Effectiveness," *Public Opinion Quarterly* 16 (1951):635–650.

† S. E. Asch, "The Doctrine of Suggestion, Prestige, and Imitation in Social Psychology," *Psychological Review* 55 (1948):250–278; see Wallace Fotheringham, *Perspectives on Persuasion* (Boston: Allyn and Bacon, 1966), pp. 90–92, for a discussion of this research.

Identification

The importance of the rhetor for the determination of meaning is related to two processes with special significance for persuasion: identification and participation. *To identify* means "to establish the identity of; to consider as identical, equate; to associate or affiliate (oneself) closely with a person or group." The word is related to *identity* —"the characteristics by which a thing is definitively recognized or known" or "the quality or condition of being exactly the same as something else." If you look closely at these definitions, you will notice that they are apparently contradictory or at least ambiguous. On the one hand, these words refer to the set of characteristics that make something or someone unique, distinctive. On the other hand, these words refer to what is alike, even identical, about two or more things or persons. In other words, they are terms about the relationship between similarities and differences. Identification is possible because of general similarities—we are both women, married, over 40, widows, childless, for example—and because an individual embodies these characteristics so that their meaning is evident, they are seen and felt by the audience.

The characters in highly successful television dramas are illustrative. Kojak is a representative of order, a police lieutenant, but his appeal arises from ethnicity (he is Greek), baldness, and penchants for eating suckers, wearing hats, and being sentimental as well as principled. Similarly, Archie Bunker represents blue-collar Americans, but he has a wholly distinctive vocabulary and specific likes and dislikes that make him seem a real individual. Put differently, we do not identify with generalities, but with general characteristics as embodied in an individual. *Persons* identify with each other, and it is as an individual that the audience will respond to you, specifically as an individual who illustrates and represents general qualities and characteristics you and they hold in common.

Research that has been done on the development of trust helps explain this further. Trust arises out of a reciprocal pattern of interrelationships. We learn to trust by sharing, by mutual exchange, and by sensitivity to the other person. Trusting and risk-taking are two sides of the same coin, because a trusting relationship requires a willingness to engage in trusting acts of self-disclosure. Thus, within limits, others trust us to the degree that they know details about us; we are trusted as we emerge for them as unique individuals. There are limits, of course, but they are often broader than you may think.

For example, a story in the *New York Times Magazine* reported that when Truman Capote did research for *In Cold Blood* in western Kansas, he continued to look and behave as eccentrically as ever—wearing fancy brocade vests, talking in a high-pitched voice, making theatrical gestures—but he was able to gain the confidence not only of the two murderers but also of the lawmen and farmers whom he needed to interview. They probably laughed at him sometimes and thought him odd, but his book attests to the fact that they trusted him enough to tell him the minute details of the murders and of the events that led up to them and to the arrests.* In other words, the rhetor needs to emerge as a real and distinctive individual. The rhetorical problem is not to become a bland amalgam of the attitudes of the audience; the rhetorical problem is the risks involved in disclosing yourself as an individual to the audience.

Similarity is important in persuasion. Kenneth Burke, a contemporary rhetorical theorist, wrote: "Only those voices from without are effective which can speak in the language of a voice within."† At its simplest, this statement recognizes that we are most influenced by those whose voices are most like the voices we use in talking to ourselves, and the more the rhetor shares with the audience, the greater the chance he or she will have of being able to speak in ways the audience will hear and understand and feel. Empirical studies show that a rhetor's influence increases markedly when he or she announces at the outset that her or his personal views are similar to those of the audience, that members of the audience more readily accept the rhetor's view of an issue if common ground has already been established on previous issues, and that the audience is more susceptible to influence if its members decide that the intentions of the rhetor are consistent with their own self interests.‡

A cynical view of such findings would suggest that the rhetor should lie—tell the audience what they want to hear in order to gain the effects desired. That is good advice for only one kind of rhetorical situation: the one-shot effort at a quick payoff. The unscrupulous seller of, say, encyclopedias who plans to hit town once, then take the money and run, may use this effectively. But most of us act as rhetors in quite different circumstances. You will be in a class for a quarter or

---

* Anne Taylor Fleming, "The Private World of Truman Capote," *New York Times Magazine,* 9 July 1978, pp. 22–25.

† Kenneth Burke, *A Rhetoric of Motives* (1950; reprint ed., Berkeley: University of California Press, 1969), p. 39.

‡ J. Mills and J. M. Ellison, "Effect on Opinion Change of Similarity Between the Communicator and the Audience He Addressed," *Journal of Personality and Social Psychology* 9 (1968):153–156.

a semester, and some of your classmates will know you in other contexts; so, even as nomadic students it is difficult to wear a false face easily. It becomes even more difficult in a community in which you live and work over a period of time—the consistency of your behavior will be a test of your trustworthiness. In addition, most rhetorical acts are parts of persuasive campaigns. In such cases, you will be judged, over time, in different rhetorical actions with different audiences. In such cases, it is not only difficult, but most unwise to try "to fool all of the people all of the time."

The moral of the story is to find real areas of similarity that you share with the audience. Do not try to be what you are not, but make sure that they know what you share with them. If you are to be effective, you must find common grounds—yet you must also disclose yourself as a unique individual who is, in fact, different from anyone else.

Social Power

Ethos is also influenced by the relationship between the rhetor and the audience. In a rhetorical context, "power" refers to the rhetor's potential for social influence, that is, influence that arises from the degree to which the audience depends on the rhetor and the rhetor depends on the audience. The classroom is a good example. As students, you depend on your instructor in significant ways; your instructor has power, and your relationship is between unequals. Your ability to graduate and your grade point average, in part, depend on your teacher, and this additional power may increase her or his ability to influence your attitudes—at least for the duration of the class. However, an instructor also depends on the students. Any one of you can disrupt the class so that it cannot continue, and the course continues period after period because you as a group permit it to do so. Because of this power, you have the ability to influence your instructor or, at least, limit her or his behavior. The rhetorical acts of students and professors are influenced and limited by their relative power. These limits are evident in any relationship involving the potential for social influence—husband and wife, employer and employee, homeowner and plumber, department head and dean, coach and player, sorority member and pledge, parent and child, and so on.

Obviously, such interdependent relationships are a facet of identification. As employees we may dislike the boss but recognize that our livelihood depends on the health of the business. As students we may dislike the teacher but recognize that the class must continue if we are to learn what we need and get essential credits.

Participation

The ethos of the rhetor is also related to participation. To understand this process, we must return once again to the wisdom of Aristotle. In his *Rhetoric* he described a species of argument that he called the *enthymeme*, a form of argument he believed was peculiar to rhetorical acts. This form of argument is unusual because it requires a joint effort by the rhetor and audience for it to be completed and effective. The audience fills in the blanks, makes connections, or draws conclusions from material that is not stated explicitly. Sometimes they do that because of context, from what they know of a particular time or place. Sometimes they do it because of assumptions they make or values they hold. The ethos of the rhetor influences whether or not audience members will participate and complete the argument.

An enthymeme is difficult to define but easy to illustrate. For example, in 1979, the well-known British actor David Niven appeared in a series of advertisements for National City Bank Traveler's Checks. In each we see him driving a Jaguar in a foreign country. In one, he pauses to talk to us because sheep are crossing the road; in another, a parade delays him. He tells us that he loves to travel but hates to wait, even for sheep or parades; imagine how much more he would hate to wait for his money if he lost his traveler's checks! That's why he buys National City Bank Traveler's Checks. They have what he calls a "pre-authorized refund," he tells us. "And the others?" he asks, and shrugs his shoulders. At this point, the viewer was expected to provide the answer, based on the suggestion that this kind of traveler's check has a special gimmick, implying that others do not. No explicit claim of this sort was made (and none could be; all traveler's checks are alike in this respect), but the advertiser hoped we would draw this conclusion. They paid David Niven a tidy sum to make these ads because they hoped we would mistake him, the actor, for the sophisticated, jet-set characters he plays in films. After all, wasn't David Niven (as Phineas Fogg) the man who went "Around the World in Eighty Days"?

The process by which the ethos of the source increases our participation is most evident in commercials made by well-known actors.* Because we know little about them as individuals, we tend to believe they are like the characters they play. For instance, Lorne Greene is probably best known for his role in the television series "Bonanza." In

---

* For more details about the use of celebrities in television commercials, see Andrew Feinberg, "Madison Avenue's Cast of Famous Faces," *New York Times*, 16 November 1980, p. F 7.

1980 he appeared in a series of commercials for dog food. Dressed casually and shown in an outdoor setting, he tells us that dogs, like the large, frisky, shiny-coated one beside him, need lots of meat to stay healthy. That's why he feeds his dog Alpo. The advertiser hopes that we will confuse the actor Lorne Greene with the character he played on "Bonanza," the authoritative, powerful, decisive rancher, pioneer, and father. If so, we are more likely to accept his advice on what is good for our dogs.

In sum, the character of the rhetor is directly related to two important rhetorical processes: identification and participation. Both of these influence the ways audience members interpret messages and are willing to fill in the blanks or draw conclusions implied by statements in the rhetorical act.

These, then, are the kinds of problems that may arise in rhetorical action. Some of these problems arise out of the rhetor's background, appearance, the ways she or he is introduced, and the context or occasion. More important problems arise out of the relationship between the rhetor and the message. For an act to be effective, a rhetor must be perceived by the audience as competent and trustworthy. This is particularly significant because the rhetor is a context that affects how audience members will translate and interpret a message. Specifically, ethos influences audience identification—that is, the degree to which they see the rhetor as an individual is closely related to trust. In addition, as the rhetor emerges as a unique person, there is an association with, an affinity for those qualities, attitudes, and characteristics that form a common ground between rhetor and audience. This process is central to ensuring that the audience will hear the message and translate it with the greatest possible fidelity. In addition, ethos influences participation, the degree to which the audience is willing to involve itself in rhetorical action, to draw conclusions, or to assume relationships unstated or implicit in the message.

THE RHETORICAL
PROBLEM: INTERRELATIONSHIPS

By this time the interrelationships among the facets of the rhetorical problem should be apparent. For example, the decisions made by an audience member about the competence of the rhetor result from decisions that the rhetor makes about the treatment of the subject and the purpose selected. The problems the rhetor has in establishing credibility arise from the characteristics of a specific audience. The rhetorical problem on a given occasion will be a function of the interaction among these three elements: audience, subject/purpose, and rhetor. In the chapters that follow, I shall suggest ways to overcome these obstacles. Chapter 7 provides tools for analysis so the resources used by other rhetors to overcome rhetorical problems will be available to you. Part III explores the resources of evidence, argument, organization, language, and nonverbal action.

SOURCES

Andersen, Kenneth, and Clevenger, Theodore, Jr. "A Summary of Experimental Research in Ethos." *Speech Monographs* 30 (1963):59–78.

Delia, Jesse G. "A Constructivist Analysis of the Concept of Credibility." *Quarterly Journal of Speech* 62 (1976):361–375.

Greenberg, Bradley S., and Miller, Gerald R. "The Effects of Low-Credible Sources on Message Acceptance." *Speech Monographs* 33 (1966): 127–136.

MATERIAL FOR ANALYSIS

On December 9, 1978, Senator Edward M. Kennedy (D-Mass) made a speech to the midterm Democratic convention held in Memphis, Tennessee. While then-president Jimmy Carter and his supporters were trying to calm discontent among the delegates, Kennedy's speech intensified differences of opinion about the party's approach to health care. Newspaper articles described the speech as "impassioned," a "dramatic dissent," and "political theatre," and they reported that he "excited a lethargic group of Democratic delegates" and "brought the crowd to its feet cheering and clapping."* The speech is a plea for national health insurance, and it is an unusually powerful example of the use of personal experience and personal commitment in urging a course of action.

---

* See, for example, "Kennedy Wows 'em As Carter Tries to Cool 'em," *San Francisco Examiner and Chronicle,* 10 December 1978, p. A 20; "Kennedy Big Hit at Mini-Convention," *St. Louis Times,* 11–12 December 1978, p. 10; "Conference Delegates Lecture Carter and Aides, Who Stoutly Defend Policies," *Los Angeles Times,* 10 December 1978, p. A 8; James Reston, "Why Kennedy Endures," *New York Times,* 13 December 1978, p. A 27.

Speech to the Midterm
Democratic Convention*

1   Thank you very much. Thank you very much. Mr. Chairman and our fellow members of the panel, I am delighted to be here this afternoon. I am often invited to address Democratic Conventions, but it's always the wrong year. A Democratic Convention, whether it's a mini or a maxi, midterm or fullterm, means one important thing to me. It means that there is hope for millions of men and women and families across this country and around the world.

2   Since the time of Jefferson and Jackson, the Democratic Party has always held its standards high. And as a party we've stood for action, hope and progress, meeting the basic needs of human beings. We are not a party of reaction or retreat. We're not the party of McKinley or Harding. We're not the party of Coolidge or Hoover. At our best, we have had leaders with both vision to see the path and the skill to guide the nation forward to bring us closer to our historic goals. Woodrow Wilson saw a world at peace. Franklin Roosevelt lit a candle in the darkness of the depression. Harry Truman raised Europe to its feet after the devastation of war. John Kennedy touched the hearts of youth and launched the longest period of economic growth and price stability in the history of our country. (*Applause*) Lyndon Johnson and Hubert Humphrey brought the dream of equality closer to reality. (*Applause*) And Jimmy Carter has led us to the threshhold of peace in the Middle East and given America world leadership in the cause for human rights. (*Applause*)

3   We meet, however, at a time of caution and uncertainty in this land. The hopes and dreams of millions of citizens are riding on our leadership. Sometimes a party must sail against the wind. We cannot afford to drift or lie at anchor. We cannot heed the call of those who say it is time to furl the sails. We know that sometimes in America, today, some things are wrong. It is wrong that prices are rising as rapidly as they are. But it is also wrong that millions of our fellow citizens are out of work. And it is wrong that cities are struggling against decay. And it is wrong that women and minorities are denied their equal rights. (*Applause*) And it is wrong that millions who are sick cannot afford the care they need. (*Applause*) Inflation is a clear and present danger for this nation, and I support the fight against inflation. But no such fight can be effective or successful unless the fight is fair. (*Applause*)

---

* The text is a transcription by the author of the speech as delivered. Reprinted by permission.

4 The party that tore itself apart over Vietnam in the 1960s cannot afford to tear itself apart today over budget cuts in basic social programs. (*Applause*) There could be few more divisive issues for America and for our party than a Democratic policy of drastic slashes in the federal budget at the expense of the elderly, the poor, the black, the sick, the cities, and the unemployed. (*Applause*) There must be sacrifice if we are to bring the economy back to health. But the burden must be fairly shared by all. We cannot accept a policy that asks greater sacrifices from labor than from business. (*Applause*) We cannot accept a policy that cuts spending to the bone in areas like jobs and health but allows billions of dollars in wasteful spending for tax subsidies to continue and adds even greater fat and waste through inflationary spending for defense. (*Applause*)

5 Our workshop on health care will clarify this crucial point about priorities in spending federal dollars. One of the shameful things about modern America, [is] that it is an unbelievably rich land, [and that] the quality of health care available to many of our people is unbelievably poor, and the cost is unbelievably high. That is why national health insurance is the great unfinished business on the agenda of the Democratic Party. Our party gave Social Security to the nation in the 1930s. We gave Medicare to the nation in the 1960s. And we can bring national health insurance to the nation in the 1970s. (*Applause*)

6 One of the saddest ironies in the worldwide movement for social justice in the 20th century is that America now stands virtually alone in the international community on national health insurance. With the sole exception of South Africa, no other industrial nation in the world leaves its citizens in fear of financial ruin because of illness. A generation after Franklin Roosevelt set the noble goals of freedom from want and freedom from fear, large numbers of Americans are deprived of decent health care and are fearful of the bills they may be forced to pay to a very few for whom the need is least.

7 We have already made a start on national health insurance. We've got national health insurance for the rich who deduct the cost of major illness on their income tax returns, and the richer you are, the higher the percentage of your health bill you can charge to the I.R.S. (*Applause*) And we've got national health insurance for members of the Senate of the United States and House of Representatives. They give their speeches and cast their votes in Congress, and then they go out to Walter Reed Army Hospital or Bethesda Naval Hospital for the free medical and dental care that Uncle Sam provides. (*Applause*) And I say if it's good enough for the members of Congress, it's good enough for the Democratic Party and the people of Massachusetts and all over the place. (*Applause*)

8   There are some who say we cannot afford national health insurance. They say it has become an early casualty of the war against inflation. But the truth is, we cannot afford not to have national health insurance. (*Applause*) Health care in 1978 has become the fastest growing failing business in America. Costs are out of control. If we do nothing, as Joe Califano* pointed out, figures here by the Congressional Budget Office show if we do nothing at all, the explosions of health care costs are going to bankrupt all Americans, bankrupt the American people. The average worker is lucky if his paycheck barely holds its own against inflation, and yet the cost of health in recent years has been rising twice as rapidly as the Consumer Price Index. And there is not enough money to go around. Something has to give, and it's often the family's budget for health that is the first to go. Every day parents are deciding whether they can afford the $25 office charge and the $25 laboratory bill when the child is sick. (*Applause*) Elderly citizens are deciding whether to spend for food or rent or health. Young Americans are gambling on their health, signing up for cut-rate, fly-by-night insurance schemes, because their budgets cannot afford the premium for a decent health insurance policy. Only through national health insurance can we achieve the effective controls on cost that will bring inflation down and bring adequate health care within the financial reach of every citizen.

9   Together we can provide a decent health care system for the benefit of the people of this land. We can make health care a basic right for all, not just an expensive privilege for the few. But to achieve the reform we need, we must have genuine leadership by the Democratic Party. We are the heirs of a great tradition in American public life. Our party took up the cause of jobs for the unemployed in the great depression. Our party took up the cause of civil rights for black and brown Americans and the cause of equal rights for women in America and the people of the District of Columbia. (*Applause*) And in that same tradition of leadership it time for the Democratic Party to take up the cause of health.

10   There probably has not been a family in this country that has been touched by sickness, illness, and disease like my own family. I had a father that was touched by stroke and sick for seven years. We were able to get the very best in terms of health care because we were able to afford it. It would have bankrupted any average family in this nation, any average family that is represented in this hall this afternoon, and the millions of people you represent all over this nation of ours. I had a son that was

---

* Secretary of Health, Education, and Welfare.

touched by cancer, extraordinary health bills that we were able to afford, and we received the very best. It would have obliterated and wiped out the savings of any family, mortgaged their savings, and mortgaged the education of their children into the future. Seven months in the hospital I was with a broken back and received the very best of health care. I've been able to receive it for myself and for my family, just like all of us who are on the tip of the iceberg, way up high in the health care services. We've got the very best, all of us at the tip of the iceberg. But I want every delegate at this convention to understand that as long as I'm a vote, and as long as I have a voice in the United States Senate, it's going to be for that Democratic Platform plank that provides decent quality health care north and south, east and west, for all Americans as a matter of right and not of privilege. (*Applause*)

After making a descriptive analysis of the speech, discuss these questions:

1. In what ways does the ethos of the speaker make the speech effective? Specifically, consider the use of authority and position, personal experience, personal commitment, and identification with the history of the party.

2. What role does Kennedy want the audience to play? How does he seek to create his audience?

3. How does Kennedy use resentment against the rich, privileged, and powerful to his advantage?

4. How does Kennedy try to refute the charge that we cannot afford national health insurance?

5. Kennedy tries to persuade his audience that national health insurance is the inevitable next step for the Democratic Party. What obstacle is he trying to overcome?

6. Kennedy's delivery was strident, impassioned, and emphatic, and he shouted and pounded the podium during the conclusion. How might that sort of delivery enhance his ethos?

7. What paragraphs form the introduction? Discuss how the introduction prepares the audience for the thesis and makes them more likely to respond positively.

CHAPTER 7

UNDERSTANDING
THE RHETORICAL PROBLEM:
THE RESOURCES OF
ANALYSIS

The efforts of past rhetors are a resource that can be tapped both to understand rhetorical obstacles and to discover ways of overcoming them. Speeches and essays appearing in the mass media are excellent models of strategies designed in recognition of and in response to specific barriers. You must become an analyst and critic if you are to learn from the rhetorical efforts of others, including experts, political figures, and your classmates and friends.

Two methods of analysis have already been presented: descriptive analysis, outlined in Chapter 2, and the rhetorical problem, outlined in Chapters 4, 5, and 6.

Descriptive analysis is basic to the study of all rhetoric. As a critic, your first task is to understand a discourse as fully as possible. That requires a close reading of the act. Here is an outline of descriptive analysis specifically devised for your use as a critic:

Descriptive Analysis*

I. What is the rhetor's purpose?
  A. What is the thesis?
  B. How is the subject limited or narrowed?
  C. What response is desired?

II. Who compose the target audience?
  A. What must you know, believe, or value to participate in this act?
  B. Who are relevant agents of change?

III. What role does the rhetor assume?

IV. What is the rhetor's tone?
  A. What is the rhetor's attitude toward the subject?
  B. What is the rhetor's attitude toward the audience?
    1. Is the rhetor a subordinate of those addressed?
    2. Is the rhetor a peer of those addressed?
    3. Is the rhetor a superior of those addressed?

V. How is the discourse structured?
  A. What does the introduction do?
  B. What kind of organization is used to develop ideas?
  C. What does the conclusion do?
  D. What efforts are made to create relationships among ideas?

VI. What kinds of supporting materials are used?
  A. How is evidence adapted to the audience?
  B. How is the selection of evidence adapted to the purpose?
  C. What evidence is evoked from the audience?

VII. What strategies are used?
  A. What is the rhetor's style?
    1. How does language reflect the rhetor's role?
    2. How does language reflect the relationship between rhetor and audience?
    3. How is language adapted to the complexity of the subject?

---

* Some rhetors use ghostwriters. As part of your analysis, you may need to determine what persons played a major role in the creation of the rhetorical act and how they affect the character of the text.

B. How does the rhetor appeal to the needs, drives, desires, and and cultural values of the audience?

C. What strategies are used to assist in proof?

D. What strategies are used to animate ideas?

E. What strategies are used to alter associations and attitudes?

These categories apply equally to speeches or essays by classmates and to statements by public figures.

The rhetorical problem is the second method of analysis. It goes beyond the text to look at a discourse in relation to its context. The obstacles that may arise can be outlined this way:

The Rhetorical Problem

I. What demands do subject and purpose make on the audience?

   A. Is the subject's complexity an obstacle?

      1. Do audience members have firsthand experience of the subject?

      2. Is special expertise required to interpret essential information?

      3. Is evaluation of the credibility and authority of secondary sources inevitable?

   B. Is the subject's cultural history an obstacle?

      1. Is there a taboo against public discussion?

      2. Are available arguments familiar and boring?

      3. Has past discussion created slogans and symbols that have to be refuted and reformulated?

      4. Does the purpose conflict with beliefs, attitudes, and cultural values of the audience?

   C. What will it cost the audience to participate?

      1. How much inconvenience and discomfort are involved?

      2. How much time, energy, and commitment are needed?

      3. How much of our resources, money, and expertise must be expended?

      4. How much social resistance can be expected from family, friends, and neighbors?

   D. What control does the audience have over the outcome?

      1. Are the agents of change in the exposed audience?

      2. Is concerted action required?

3. Is a series of actions needed?

4. Is needed action simple, obvious, and likely to produce immediate rewards, or complex and difficult to evaluate?

II. What kinds of obstacles arise from the audience?

   A. Can the rhetor reach the target audience?

   B. Are misinterpretation and misperception likely?

   C. Is the subject salient for the audience?

   D. Does the audience believe that it can take effective action?

III. What obstacles are created by the rhetor's character?

   A. What obstacles exist prior to rhetorical action?

      1. What is the rhetor's reputation and track record?

      2. How was the rhetor introduced?

      3. How do the setting and occasion limit the rhetor's choices?

         a. What expectations are created by the occasion?

         b. What expectations are created by setting or environment?

         c. What preceding or subsequent events affect audience response?

         d. Who are the competing persuaders?

         e. How do the media of transmission select the audience and create expectations?

   B. How can the rhetor demonstrate competence, trustworthiness, and dynamism?

   C. What is the rhetor's relation to the audience?

      1. Are there bases for identification?

      2. What is the social power of the rhetor?

The rhetorical problem is a critical device to set up a fair basis for evaluation. For example, a novice tennis player probably cannot beat Bjorn Borg, and we would be most unfair if we judged him a failure merely because he lost. We have to weigh his efforts in terms of the obstacles he must overcome.

Applying these questions to the essay on adolescent pregnancy in Chapter 2 illustrates how the rhetorical problem can be used as an analytical device to locate the obstacles a rhetor faced and discover the strategies she or he used to overcome them.

The subjects of Konner's essay are the problem, increasing pregnancies among teen-agers, and the solutions, abortion and contraception. These subjects are *complex* and *controversial*. As these are usually discussed, the complexity and controversy are moral: What are the causes of teen-age pregnancy—family breakdown? a decline in morals? a cultural decline? How can we decide whether abortion and contraception are moral responses to this problem?

The author, Konner, reduces this kind of complexity and controversy by avoiding moral issues altogether. He argues, instead, that the cause is biological, a physical change produced by the better food and medical care found in developed societies. This simplifies the problem; it has a single, definable cause. And it lessens the controversy; morality (behavior) has remained the same; only the physical conditions have changed.

The decision to take a biological perspective is also a response to obstacles created by *cultural history*. Although he violates a taboo in talking about sexuality (and the title, "Adolescent Pregnancy," in bold, black letters may turn some readers away), the choice of a biological perspective means that his arguments are fresh and different, not the old familiar ones that may bore us. However, in response to the slogans and labels from past discussion, such as "right to life," he does create a powerful label, "pregnant children." That phrase addresses the moral issue, because it suggests that it is not right to hold these "children" responsible for biological changes outside their control. Konner also recognizes conflicting beliefs when he limits his audience to those morally willing to consider the solutions that he proposes.

These proposed solutions will require concerted and sustained action to produce legislative change. Unless his audience becomes deeply concerned about the issue, it is unlikely that such solutions will occur. Konner does little to lessen the *cost*. His only effort is to try to convince the reader how serious the problem is and what a potential threat it poses for society in the future (the cost of inaction).

The audience he has selected (the target audience) is chosen in recognition of the problem of *control*. Although teen-agers are surely as concerned about this problem, only adults have the political and economic power to do what he asks. Hence, he addresses those who can vote, influence school boards to provide contraceptive information, and the like.

The actual audience, those exposed, are readers of the *New York Times*. That is a most appropriate channel, given the audience he wants to reach. The *Times* is a newspaper for politically interested and better-educated adults. It has no comics to tempt children or adults, and it is the national paper "of record" with unusually thorough coverage of national and international events. It is read by opinion leaders in government and the mass media, those most likely to be influential (agents of change).

However, there are some disadvantages in writing an editorial for the Op-Ed page. The argument must be very brief, and there is little space for detailed evidence. The author is identified by a single line reporting that he teaches at Harvard (a sign of status) and that his field is biological anthropology (a sign of expertise; he is writing in the area of his specialty). These are limited bases for credibility, trust, or identification. In addition, an editorial that appears on this page is, by definition, persuasive; thus, readers expect these authors to try to persuade them. As a result, their guard is up, and they may be more resistant to appeals.

This analysis reveals that complexity, cultural history, and control were Konner's chief concerns. He made two strategic choices: to take a fresh perspective toward a familiar set of issues and to address a better-educated, politically interested adult audience capable of producing change and willing to consider these solutions as moral. These choices have disadvantages: moral reservations are not addressed, and the editorial format limits the development of the argument, the presentation of evidence, and the establishment of grounds for identification. It is also possible that he has limited his audience to such an extent that, unless they can influence others, change cannot occur.

Identifying these obstacles and choices provides sound grounds for evaluating how well Konner recognized the barriers he faced and how well he chose his strategies. However, neither descriptive analysis nor the rhetorical problem are, in and of themselves, methods of evaluation. In order to evaluate rhetorical action, you must consider the criteria or standards you can apply, and you must be aware of special pressures created by context and occasion.

STANDARDS FOR EVALUATION

10-5-92

Four general standards or criteria can be used, alone or in combination, to judge rhetorical discourses. They are (1) achieving desired effects, (2) presenting a truthful account of the issue, (3) producing an aesthetically satisfying discourse, and (4) advancing ethically desirable ends for society and for rhetorical practice. Each is relevant to rhetorical action. Each has important strengths and limitations.

1) The Effects Criterion

The effects criterion, the evaluation of a rhetorical act in terms of the response that it evokes, reflects the demand that every rhetorical act communicate, induce participation from an audience, and affect perceptions, beliefs, and attitudes. Unless some form of reaction occurs, the act initiated by a rhetor must be judged a failure.

But effects are difficult to isolate and verify. It is difficult to separate response to one act from response to actions that precede and follow it. Most influence is the result of a campaign or of a series of experiences. Similarly, it is hard to measure just what the audience response was. Clapping may be a matter of relieved courtesy; questionnaires report only what people *say* occurred; the size and nature of the response may be greatly affected by the medium in which an act is presented. For these reasons, it is usually difficult to determine accurately the effects of a given rhetorical act.

The effects criterion also raises ethical problems. Applied strictly and in isolation, it would applaud rhetoric without regard for truth or social consequences. By such a measure, the finest rhetorical works would be the speeches of Adolph Hitler, advertising that persuades teen-agers to smoke despite serious health hazards, and the come-ons of particularly savvy con men. Clearly, the effects criterion cannot be used alone. Other criteria have to be used with it.

2.) The Truth Criterion

The truth criterion is a measure of the similarity between the "reality" presented in a speech or essay and "reality" as presented in other sources. In this case, the critic tests the accuracy and typicality of evidence in the discourse against other sources, and compares the arguments selected against the pool of arguments available. Rhetoric is a part of social decision-making. If we are to make good decisions, we need the best evidence available, and we need to examine all the relevant arguments. For this reason, considerations of truth are always important.

But this criterion also has limitations. As noted in Chapter 1, the truths of rhetoric are social truths, truths created and validated by people. There is no simple way to verify rhetorical claims or to validate rhetorical arguments. The occasion for deliberation is one in which well-intentioned, informed persons disagree. A good critic has to acknowledge conflicting evidence, varying interpretations, and competing perspectives, and recognize that no simple judgment about the truth of an act can ever be made. In addition, no discourse is ever long enough to tell the whole truth, and the constraints of space and time, which are inherent to rhetoric, complicate strict application of this standard.

In one respect, this criterion conflicts with concerns for effects. Discourses that tell the whole truth, as far as that is possible, and adhere to strict, technical accuracy, are likely to be suitable only for experts. In fact, if the truth criterion were applied strictly, nearly all rhetorical acts would be judged inadequate, and the finest pieces of rhetoric would be those directed to an elite group of specialists. Given its popular character and its role in social decision-making, this criterion alone would not be an appropriate basis for evaluating rhetorical action.

3.) The Aesthetic Criterion

The aesthetic or artistic criterion focuses on means, on *how* effects are produced. The word *aesthetic* comes from the Greek word *aisthetikos* which means "pertaining to sense perception." This original meaning is retained in the word *anaesthetic*, which refers to a substance like ether or novocaine that creates total or partial loss of sensation. The aesthetic criterion is a measure of how well a rhetorical act succeeds in altering perception, creating virtual experience, and inducing participation and identification. It is a measure of *how well* an act achieves its purpose, of how creatively a rhetor responds to the obstacles faced, of how inventively a rhetor fulfills the requirements of a form. For example, I rate Benjamin Hooks's speech (see Chapter 4) high on artistic grounds because I think he was quite creative in responding to a difficult situation. In his case, there is little evidence of effects. Television commentators said little about his speech; no text was printed; no commentary appeared in the *New York Times*. In this case, the critic must recognize how many obstacles existed and anticipate limited response. Despite that obstacle-filled situation, however, one can applaud the skill with which Hooks tried to overcome his rhetorical problem.

The Mondale eulogy of Hubert Humphrey, reprinted at the end of this chapter, also deserves high artistic ratings. Mondale not only fulfills the requirements of the eulogy, discussed on pages 161–162, but he tailors this form to his subject and to himself, and he produces a moving speech that has the capacity to endure as a model of its type. In this case, however, there is some evidence of effect. The text of his speech (along with the text of President Jimmy Carter's eulogy) was printed in the *New York Times*, and a major clip from the speech was shown on CBS Evening News (by contrast, no clip from Carter's speech was shown). But even without such evidence a critic can judge

Mondale's skills as a rhetor. The aesthetic criterion demands analysis of techniques, means, strategies. These can be assessed whether or not there is external evidence that a discourse achieved its goal. The aesthetic criterion also reveals those works that have the capacity to endure through time as models of rhetorical action.

The limitations of the aesthetic criterion are evident when we turn our attention to advertising and admire the skills of those who produce commercials in exploiting the strategic resources of verbal and nonverbal language. Examples such as the Daisy spot (a political commercial; see pages 205–207) are aesthetic masterpieces, but their effect on political decision-making is troubling. The aesthetic criterion does not provide standards to judge the purposes or ends of rhetorical action.

4.) The Ethical Criterion

The ethical criterion judges ends. It evaluates the social consequences of rhetorical action. It judges the long-term effects of rhetoric both for society (what happens to a political system in which voting decisions are made on the basis of 30-second television commercials?) and for future rhetorical action (how can we communicate about complex issues if norms for rhetorical action are limited to the 11-minute segments typical of commercial television programming?). Obviously, such judgments are highly controversial. In recent history, the conflict in government between deception and obfuscation on the one hand, and the requirements of national security on the other, illustrates this kind of problem. Ethical judgments require us to balance legitimate competing claims. There are limits on first amendment freedoms, for example, but we ought to fight to see that only absolutely essential limits are set. In this regard, the essay by Terry Markin (at the end of Chapter 12) is ideal for ethical evaluation. Similarly, C. D. B. Bryan's essay (at the end of Chapter 10) tries to take an ethical position without arousing controversy. In evaluating it, you might ask whether the principle he develops is defined clearly enough to be a good standard by which to judge the arguments for military intervention. The speeches by Edward Kennedy (at the end of Chapter 6) and Helen Caldicott (at the end of Chapter 9) take strong, even extreme positions. Ethical evaluation of these requires that you take a close look at opposing views and at the social consequences of the policies they advocate. You might contrast the ethical dimensions of these speeches with the more moderate and prudential policies advocated by Benjamin Hooks. Then, as a final exercise, ask yourself whether you have just defined as ethical only what is reformist or supports the status quo.*

CONTEXT AND OCCASION

Rhetorical evaluations must be modified in terms of the special pressures created by the context and the occasion. These special pressures or constraints (a constraint is something that limits, restricts, or regulates) include: (1) competing rhetorical action, (2) preceding or subsequent events, (3) the media of transmission, and (4) expectations and requirements created by the occasion. Each of these should be examined to see if it leads us to qualify or refine our judgments about effects, truth, aesthetics, and ethics.

Competing Rhetorical Action

Very few rhetorical acts occur in isolation, and many are part of campaigns and movements. But campaigns include competition from other persuaders—political candidates or advertisers—and movements are protests against the status quo, which will be defended by advocates of the establishment. In other words, much rhetoric occurs in a competitive environment, and it has to be judged in relation to its competition. For example, it's nice to receive a Clio (an award for excellence in advertising), but it's equally important to know how well you did against competing products.

Political campaigns illustrate how competition modifies judgments. For example, advertising agencies considered the advertisements created for Ronald Reagan in the 1980 campaign rather dull,† but when the ads are compared to Carter campaign ads, they must be evaluated more favorably. Similarly, John Kennedy's performance in 1960 has to be assessed in comparison to that of Richard Nixon, just as Jimmy Carter's has to be compared to Ford's in 1976 and to Reagan's in 1980. Effective rhetoric is responsive to the specific con-

---

* For a discussion of this thorny problem, see Robert L. Scott and Donald K. Smith, "The Rhetoric of Confrontation," *Quarterly Journal of Speech* 55 (February 1969):1–8.
† Philip H. Dougherty, "Campaign Shop Ran Tight Ship," *New York Times*, 18 November 1980, p. D 16.

text: it refutes precisely those charges made by the opposition; it reacts to issues of concern to this audience; it takes account of the stands of competing advocates. And what might be highly praised in one situation might be inappropriate for another. For example, Benjamin Hooks is a skilled preacher, but he was wise to reject that rhetorical style and persona and adopt the role of nonpartisan representative of blacks at the Republican National Convention.

Comparison is an integral part of assessing rhetorical acts. As you evaluate, consider the choices available and then examine the ways in which those choices were limited by opponents, competing positions, or by events and issues. Ask yourself what was possible, given the situation. Given the opposition, what was the best strategy? Given competing persuaders, what role was possible, what purpose was reasonable? Pay special attention to attempts to respond to issues, charges, and opponents. These should help you notice one kind of constraint that limits rhetorical action.

Preceding or Subsequent Events

A rhetorical act is always one in a series of events. The meaning of a rhetorical act is not an absolute or a given; it is always, in part, a function of the context in which it occurs. Evaluation needs to include an awareness of events that preceded and followed it, for these may explain the act and modify its meaning.

The speech by Henry Grady, "The New South," discussed in Chapter 6, illustrates the significance of preceding events. If you did not know what preceded it, you might, as a contemporary reader, think that this was a somewhat wordy introduction that would not hold the audience's attention. There are many other examples. What has come to be called Richard Nixon's "Checkers Speech" (named for his children's dog Checkers, who was mentioned in the speech) is one.* Unless you know that Nixon was being pressured to resign by the Republican National Committee, that Eisenhower withheld his support even after Nixon was cleared by an audit and a legal opinion, and that his entire political future hung on whether he could generate an extraordinarily massive response from the audience, you are likely to view the speech as highly emotional and sentimental, a tear-jerker.

---

* For a detailed discussion of the events leading up to this speech, see Garry Wills, *Nixon Agonistes* (New York: Signet, 1969), pp. 93–114.

But when you know the events that preceded it, the speech takes on a slightly different hue.

Political campaigns also illustrate the role of surrounding events in rhetorical evaluation. For example, it is often forgotten that the first Kennedy–Nixon debate in 1960 took place very early in the campaign, on September 26. Americans were highly interested in the 1960 presidential race, and the first debate, *given its date,* was able to define issues and create impressions because very little of the campaign (which traditionally begins on Labor Day) had preceded it.* By contrast, because the debate between Jimmy Carter and Ronald Reagan occurred so late in the 1980 campaign (the Thursday night before the election), it was the culmination of the campaign and cannot be understood or assessed apart from what preceded it. Similarly, disappointed Carter supporters pointed to preceding events as a way of explaining his defeat, particularly to events just prior to the election that raised and then dashed hopes that the hostages held by Iran would be released. Even the most skillful rhetorical efforts might be ineffective in such a context.

As discussed earlier, the obstacle of cultural history is a long-term view of the problem of preceding events. In light of the past, a rhetor may be expected to develop a new argument, take a new perspective, develop a new role, or respond to unforeseen events. The problem of long-term cultural history, as well as that of immediate happenings, needs to be considered in making assessments.

Subsequent events can have a variety of effects that complicate assessment. As I note in the materials for analysis at the end of Chapter 11, it is difficult to assess the final speech of Dr. Martin Luther King, Jr., without being affected by what now seem to be his prophetic statements about his own death. Similarly, the Thanksgiving Day Proclamation prepared by President John Kennedy before he traveled to Dallas took on special poignancy after his assassination. Subsequent events transformed these statements into "last words," which we treat with special significance.

Subsequent happenings can also become a truth criterion against which to measure the claims of speakers, and the passage of time is the ultimate determinant of ethical judgments. Similarly, the ability of some rhetoric to withstand the test of time is clear evidence of aesthetic excellence. Thus, Lincoln's Gettysburg Address is no longer

---

* See *The Great Debates, Kennedy vs. Nixon, 1960,* ed. Sidney Kraus (Bloomington: Indiana University Press, 1962), pp. 224–231, 319–329.

merely a speech made to honor those who died in the battle of Gettysburg; it remains an enduring commemoration of all those who have given their lives in battle for this nation. As time passes, you may be forced to take account of two different judgments: that of the immediate audience and that of history.

Media of Transmission

Rhetoric is disseminated in many different ways: by direct mail, newspaper, radio, television, in face-to-face encounters, and through a microphone system in an auditorium or rally. Like all elements in rhetoric, these media create opportunities and generate constraints.

The great opportunity provided by the mass media is, of course, the chance to reach large audiences quickly and simultaneously. The ability of President Franklin Roosevelt to reach millions of Americans through radio in his "Fireside Chats" and to explain policies and raise morale in periods of crisis illustrates this opportunity. His success reflects his understanding of the immediacy and intimacy of radio as a medium and his skill in adapting to it—he "chatted" with Americans as citizens, peers, and members of a common national family united in their efforts.

But the mass media also create problems. Gone are the days when public figures could speak privately to a part of the electorate; somehow, government leaders must find ways to speak to all of the nation all of the time. If you have understood the concept of the target audience, you will understand why this is a problem: it is nearly impossible to adapt to a truly heterogeneous audience. Inevitably, what pleases some will alienate others, and vice versa. In many cases, rhetors face a two-audience dilemma; that is, the immediate audience to whom they speak is composed of one group, while the larger, mediated audience is quite different. In such circumstances, it is possible to be a resounding success with one and a disastrous failure with the other. In assessing such efforts, you will need to consider several questions: (1) Did the speaker know when he or she spoke that the speech would be transmitted via the mass media? Not all rhetors know that a second, large, heterogeneous audience will develop.* (2) Is the

---

* See, for example, Ron Dorfman, "George Wald: But for the Grace of the *Boston Globe* . . . ," *Chicago Journalism Review* 2 (May 1969):4, for the story of how George Wald's address, "A Generation in Search of a Future," unexpectedly became available in print, on radio, and was made into a record. The speech is reprinted in K. K. Campbell,

rhetor a national leader who can reasonably be expected to speak to all of the people? Not all rhetors serve the same constituency; for example, one can argue that Benjamin Hooks must speak for blacks in the larger audience no matter what the ethnic background or ideology of the immediate audience of Republican convention delegates. (3) What discrepancies, if any, exist between the act as delivered and the act as transmitted via the mass media? Most rhetorical acts are transmitted only in excerpts, usually as part of 99-second segments on the network news. Such snippets can give a most deceptive impression of the entire act, and critics need to assess the degree to which rhetors can be held responsible for what reporters pick up and pass on in newspapers, magazines, and radio and television newscasts.

As these questions indicate, radio and television are often used to transmit rhetorical acts that occur in other settings—at conventions or rallies, for example. So, for instance, we watch Edward Kennedy or Ronald Reagan speak to the national party conventions or we listen to Helen Caldicott addressing supporters at the May 6 Anti-Nuclear Moratorium rally. In such cases, the medium itself makes no special demands, other than limits of time. We expect to hear someone pound on a podium in a dramatic convention speech or shout at an audience spread out over the Washington, D.C., mall. But rhetorical acts created for television are quite different, whether they are a speech by the president from the oval office, a debate between presidential candidates, a documentary, or an advertisement. Then, additional constraints arise. Like radio, television is an intimate medium. We watch it in our living rooms and bedrooms; we look at close-up shots of people's faces most of the time; we witness domestic dramas on soap operas and in prime time programming, and we hear the news from a "family" of local reporters who chat together informally. As a result, delivery that was effective at a convention or rally may be unpleasant on television—too loud, too strident, too formal, an irritating intrusion into the intimacy of our homes. In the 1960 debates between Kennedy and Nixon and the 1980 debate between Carter and Reagan, commentators suggested that the successes of Kennedy and Reagan were linked to the fact that their delivery and personalities

---

Critiques of Contemporary Rhetoric (Belmont, Calif.: Wadsworth, 1972), pp. 60– 68. For an illustration of a critique that holds a speaker responsible for material excerpted in the media, see Robert L. Scott and Wayne Brockriede "Hubert Humphrey Faces the Black Power Issue," *Speaker and Gavel* 4 (November 1966):11– 17.

were more suited to the medium of television.* Once again, evaluations of such rhetorical acts need to take account of the demands made by electronic, as well as print, media.

Expectations and
Requirements Created by the Occasion

In his *Rhetoric*, Aristotle described three types or genres of rhetoric: deliberative rhetoric dealing with policy that occurred in legislatures; forensic rhetoric dealing with justice that occurred in the law courts; and epideictic (from *epideixis*, to show forth or display) rhetoric dealing with praise and blame, honor and dishonor, that occurred on special occasions. Epideictic rhetoric, tied to specific occasions, demands special evaluation because of the requirements and expectations created by these occasions.

Typical examples of epideictic rhetoric are inaugural addresses, Fourth of July speeches, commencement addresses, and eulogies. Such speeches appear on occasions that recur at regular intervals, and our experience with such rhetoric, and the traditions that have developed around them, create special constraints on rhetorical action. For each kind of occasional address, distinct requirements exist.

In general, however, epideictic rhetoric is closer to the nondiscursive than to the discursive ends of the continua of rhetorical action (see Chapter 9). Its very name, meaning to display or show forth, suggests its consummatory purpose; that is, we are to celebrate or commemorate the occasion. The language of such rhetoric tends to be more formal, poetic, and figurative. Structurally, it is likely to explore topically all aspects of a feeling or attitude. The occasions themselves suggest that supporting materials are likely to emphasize what is psychologically appealing and what reflects cultural values. Finally, such addresses are more likely to develop ritualistically than to provide logical arguments.

The eulogy (*eu* = well, *logos* = to speak; in short, to praise) is one kind of epideictic rhetoric. It appears on the occasion of death. The death of any person forces us to confront our own mortality, and it disrupts the human community of which the deceased was a part. The eulogy meets certain very basic human needs: it acknowledges

---

* *The Great Debates*, ed. Kraus, pp. 280–283.

death; it reunites the sundered community; it shifts the relationship between the living and the deceased and suggests that although dead in the flesh, the deceased lives on in spirit—in children, good deeds, or in principles—reassuring the living that a kind of immortality exists for all of us. The tone of the eulogy is personal (death is an intimate matter) and somber, and it frequently uses metaphors of rebirth to express the idea of immortality. If a eulogy is to be judged satisfactory, it must do these things.*

Eulogies fail when they do not meet these expectations. For example, eulogies cannot arouse controversy because controversy prevents the reunification of the community. As a result, when Senator Charles Percy bluntly advocates gun control and an end to the war in Vietnam in a eulogy to Senator Robert F. Kennedy, he violates our expectations and fails to perform the eulogistic function of unification. In short, the characteristics of the eulogy become bases for evaluating this particular kind of occasional rhetoric.

The presidential inaugural is another example of epideictic rhetoric, although the requirements for such a speech are less rigid. Because we have just completed a long and divisive political campaign, we expect the newly elected president to reunify the nation. Because this is an occasion tied to fundamental national values (the speech is given after the presidential oath of office has been administered), we expect the president to rehearse our fundamental values. Because we fear the power of the executive, we expect the president to be humble, to admit his limitations, and to ask for the help of Congress, of the people, and of God in his efforts to govern. Finally, because this is the beginning of a new administration, we expect the president to indicate the philosophy and tone that he and his appointees will follow in the future, to suggest in broad terms the foreign and domestic policies that are of particular importance.† Presidential inaugural addresses vary greatly, but these four expectations are criteria that can be used to evaluate how well a president satisfies the needs of the audience.

They are also bases for distinguishing competent from outstanding inaugurals. Jimmy Carter, for example, did an outstanding job of unifying the country after what was not only a long and divisive campaign but a period of national disgrace in which we were gov-

---

* See Kathleen M. Jamieson, *Critical Anthology of Public Speeches* (Chicago: Science Research Associates, 1978), pp. 40–42. The eulogy by Senator Percy (referred to in the next paragraph of this text) is on p. 42.

† Jamieson, *Critical Anthology*, p. 28.

erned by our first unelected president, Gerald Ford. Here is one report of the opening of Carter's Address:

> *The Inaugural speech began with a moving gesture. "For myself and for our nation," said Carter, "I want to thank my predecessor for all he has done to heal our land." There was a swell of cheers; Ford blinked back tears and stood for a moment. "God bless you, sir," said Carter, "I'm proud of you." He extended his hand to Ford, who accepted it in a warm two-handed clasp – and the era of Jimmy Carter began.**

By contrast, he did only an adequate job of rehearsing fundamental values. He recalled most of our traditional values, but in a rather jumbled list of clichés. Carter showed no ability to breathe new life into old values so that they would still seem right for us. He asked for our help and that of Congress and God, but the request was not in a form that made us eager to cooperate. He told us nothing of his plans for the new administration. He indicated only his concerns for human rights and disarmament, and these were already well known from the campaign. In other words, if you look at Carter's inaugural in light of these expectations, you can begin to explain why his speech will not be memorable.

Requirements and expectations are also a basis for recognizing outstanding rhetorical acts—ones that continue to express the kinds of feelings we have on such occasions. For example, use these criteria to compare Carter's inaugural to that of John Kennedy, or to Franklin Roosevelt's first. In these cases, you will discover speeches that not only meet these expectations, but meet them in ways that are deeply moving, adapted to the occasion, and highly original.

SUMMARY

As an analyst or critic, your first task is one of descriptive analysis — full and detailed understanding of the rhetorical act. Your second task concerns the rhetorical problem: what obstacles did the rhetor face and what resources were used to overcome them? Your third task is evaluative. There are four criteria that can be used. You can assess the

---

* "A New Spirit," *Newsweek*, 31 January 1977, p. 15.

capacity of the act to achieve its end (effects). You can evaluate the consistency between the picture presented in the discourse and that presented in other works (truth). You can weigh the long-term consequences of both the ideas advocated for the society and the method of presentation for the future of rhetorical action (ethics). You can judge the appeal and force of the strategies or means used to achieve the ends (aesthetics). Finally, you can refine your judgments by considering the constraints created by the context (competition, surrounding events, media of transmission) and by the occasion. The expectations and requirements for some occasions provide special criteria for evaluation, as in the case of eulogies and inaugurals.

Models of critical analysis are suggested in the list of readings that follows.

SOURCES

Black, Edwin. *Rhetorical Criticism: A Study in Method.* New York: Macmillan, 1965, pp. 78–90. These pages include a speech and a critique based on the aesthetic criterion.

Bormann, Ernest. "Fetching Good Out of Evil: The Rhetorical Use of Calamity." *Quarterly Journal of Speech* 63 (April 1977):130–139. This essay looks at the same strategy used in different periods.

Campbell, Karlyn Kohrs. *Critiques of Contemporary Rhetoric.* Belmont, Calif.: Wadsworth, 1972. This book contains a number of criticisms that illustrate principles developed in this chapter.

Halloran, Michael. "Doing Public Business in Public." *Form and Genre: Shaping Rhetorical Action,* ed. Karlyn Kohrs Campbell and Kathleen Hall Jamieson. Falls Church, Va.: Speech Communication Association, 1978, pp. 118–138. This is an analysis of the rhetorical action of the impeachment debates of the House Committee on the Judiciary.

Hart, Roderick P. "The Rhetoric of the True Believer." *Speech Monographs* 38 (November 1971):249–261. The characteristics of doctrinaire rhetoric are specified.

Hill, Forbes. "Conventional Wisdom—Traditional Form: The President's Message of November 3, 1969." *Quarterly Journal of Speech* 58 (December 1972):373–386. This is a critique of Nixon's Vietnamization Address that emphasizes the aesthetic and effects criteria.

Jamieson, Kathleen M. Hall. "Generic Constraints and the Rhetorical Situation." *Philosophy & Rhetoric* 6 (Summer 1973):162–170, and "Interpretation of Natural Law in the Conflict over *Humanae Vitae.*" *Quarterly Journal of Speech* 60 (April 1974):201–211. These essays analyze the rhetoric of the papal encyclical.

Leff, Michael C., and Mohrmann, G. P. "Lincoln at Cooper Union: A Rhetorical Analysis of the Text." *Quarterly Journal of Speech* 60 (October 1974):346–358. A close reading of the text reclassifies this famous speech and illuminates its purpose.

Ling, David. "A Pentadic Analysis of Senator Edward Kennedy's Address to the People of Massachusetts, July 25, 1969." *Central States Speech Journal* 21 (Summer 1970):81–86. A close textual reading of Kennedy's *apologia* for Chappaquiddick contrasts explicit statement and implicit argument.

Stelzner, Hermann G. " 'War Message,' December 8, 1941: An Approach to Language." *Speech Monographs* 33 (November 1966):419–437. A close analysis of the style of F.D.R.'s declaration of war.

Windt, Theodore Otto, Jr. "The Diatribe: Last Resort for Protest." *Quarterly Journal of Speech* 58 (February 1972):1–14. This essay examines the effects of ideology on rhetorical form and compares the rhetoric of ancient cynics with that of modern yippies.

Zyskind, Harold. "A Rhetorical Analysis of the Gettysburg Address." *Journal of General Education* 4 (April 1950):202–212. This is a detailed generic analysis that argues that Lincoln's speech is primarily deliberative rather than epideictic.

MATERIAL FOR ANALYSIS

On Sunday, January 15, 1978, then-vice president Walter F. Mondale delivered a eulogy for his friend and mentor, Senator Hubert H. Humphrey, at the Memorial Service held at the U.S. Capitol. Here is what he said.*

1   Dear Muriel, the Humphrey family, and guests: There is a natural impulse at a time like this to dwell on the many accomplishments of Hubert Humphrey's remarkable life, by

---

* This is a copy of the text as released to the press and corrected to reflect the transcript printed in the *New York Times,* 16 January 1978, p. A 25. Reprinted by permission.

listing a catalogue of past events as though there were some way to quantify what he was all about. But I don't want to do that because Hubert didn't want it and neither does Muriel.

2   Even though this is one of the saddest moments of my life and I feel as great a loss as I've ever known, we must remind ourselves of Hubert's last great wish: that this be a time to celebrate life and the future, not to mourn the past, and his death.

3   But, Muriel, I hope you will forgive me if I don't entirely succeed in looking forward and not backward, because I must, for a moment. Two days ago as I flew back from the West over the land that Hubert loved to this city that he loved, I thought back over his life and its meaning. And I tried to understand what it was about this unique person that made him such an uplifting symbol of hope and joy for all people.

4   And I thought of the letter that he wrote to Muriel over 40 years ago when he first visited Washington. He said in that letter, "Maybe I seem foolish to have such vain hopes and plans. But, Bucky, I can see how, someday, if you and I just apply ourselves and make up our minds to work for bigger things, how we can someday live here in Washington and probably be in government, politics or service. I intend to set my aim at Congress."

5   Hubert was wrong only in thinking that his hopes and plans might be in vain. They were not, as we all know. Not only did he succeed with his beloved wife at his side, he succeeded gloriously and beyond even his most optimistic dreams.

6   Hubert will be remembered by all of us who served with him as one of the greatest legislators in our history. He will be remembered as one of the most loved men of his times. And even though he failed to realize his greatest goal, he achieved something much more rare and valuable than the nation's highest office. He became his country's conscience.

7   Today the love that flows from everywhere, enveloping Hubert, flows also to you, Muriel. And the presence today, here, where America bids farewell to her heroes, of President and Mrs. Carter, of former Presidents Ford and Nixon, and your special friend and former first lady, Mrs. Johnson, attest to the love and respect that the nation holds for both of you.

8   That letter to Bucky, his Muriel, also noted three principles by which Hubert defined his life: work, determination, and high goals. They were a part of his life's pattern when I first met him 31 years ago. I was only 18, fresh out of high school, and he was the Mayor of Minneapolis. He had then all the other sparkling qualities he maintained throughout his life; boundless good humor, endless optimism and hope, infinite interest, intense concern for people and their problems, compassion without being patronizing, energy beyond belief, and a spirit so filled with love there was no room at all for hate or bitterness.

9   He was simply incredible. When he said that life was not meant to be endured but rather to be enjoyed, you knew what he meant. You could see it simply by watching him and listening to him. When Hubert looked at the lives of black Americans in the 40's, he saw endurance but not enjoyment, and his heart insisted that it was time for Americans to walk forthrightly into the bright sunshine of human rights.

10   When Hubert looked at the young, who could not get a good education, he saw endurance and not enjoyment. When Hubert saw old people in ill health he saw endurance and not enjoyment. When Hubert saw middle class working people striving to survive and working people without jobs and decent homes, he saw endurance and not enjoyment.

11   Hubert was criticized for proclaiming the politics of joy, but he knew that joy was essential to us and is not frivolous. He loved to point out that ours is the only nation in the world to officially declare the pursuit of happiness as a national goal.

12   But he was also a sentimental man, and that was part of his life, too. He cried in public and without embarrassment. In his last major speech in his beloved Minnesota, he wiped tears from his eyes and said: "A man without tears is a man without a heart." If he cried often, it was not for himself but for others.

13   Above all, Hubert was a man with a good heart. And on this sad day it would be good for us to recall Shakespeare's words: "A good leg will fall; a straight back will stoop; a black beard will turn white; a curled pate will grow bald; a fair face will wither; a full eye will wax hollow; but a good heart is the sun and the moon; or rather, the sun, and not the moon,—for it shines bright and never changes, but keeps its course truly."* Hubert's heart kept its course truly.

14   He taught us all how to hope and how to love, how to win and how to lose; he taught us how to live, and, finally, he taught us how to die.

After you have made a descriptive analysis, answer these questions:

1.   How does Mondale's speech fulfill the requirements of a eulogy?

Henry V, act 5, sc. 2.

a.   Is the tone personal, somber?

b.   Is death acknowledged explicitly?

c.   How is the community unified? Assess the significance of the fact that this was Nixon's first public appearance after his resignation.

d.   What principle establishes Humphrey's immortality? Discuss how refutation is used to deal with the "politics of joy," the unfortunate slogan associated with the 1968 campaign that followed the Chicago convention and bitter controversy over the Vietnam War.

2.   Humphrey had a form of cancer and knew he was going to die. He chose to speak publicly about his condition. How do these facts affect the conclusion?

3.   What is the function of the quotation from *Henry V* in the speech?

4.   Use the requirements of the eulogy to evaluate this speech. Can you make a case that this is a superior eulogy, one that not only meets the expectations discussed but goes beyond them to become a masterpiece?

5.   Compare this speech with "Memorial Day at Stony Creek, Conn." by C. D. B. Bryan at the end of Chapter 10. In what ways are both commemorative? eulogistic? How do they differ?

EXERCISE

A GROUP RHETORICAL ANALYSIS

The class is divided into groups of four to six students, and each group is asked to do this exercise.

Select a rhetorical act for analysis. You might analyze a television series (e.g., whether or not "All in the Family" contributed to or lessened bigotry, based on empirical research, attacks by writers such as Laura Hobson, author of *Gentleman's Agreement*, and defenses made by its producer, Norman Lear; why M*A*S*H is such a hit with college students), a book (why *Rubyfruit Jungle* is unobjectionable to most readers despite the controversial life style presented by its author, Rita Mae Brown; what made *Jonathan Livingston Seagull* such a commercial success), a speech (why Alexander Solzhenitsyn's Harvard Commencement Address produced such varied reactions), a movie (why people "act out" at the "Rocky Horror Picture Show" and return to view it over and over), a presidential campaign debate or a debate on "Firing Line," or news coverage of an event (e.g., the riots in Miami).

There are four requirements:

1.   You must turn in a prospectus at least two weeks before your oral presentation in which you indicate the act you have chosen, the general approach you will take (what issues you will consider, what questions you will raise), and the way in which you plan to divide your responsibilities (e.g., Dick will talk about Harvard Commencement Addresses—who has given them and how speakers are chosen; Sam will develop a biography of Solzhenitsyn to explain his ethos and authority; Tanya will outline Solzhenitsyn's political-religious philosophy; Maria will describe the varied responses; then we will all suggest reasons why these different reactions occurred). Turn in only one prospectus from each group; one page should be adequate. The instructor will return these with comments and suggestions.

2.   The rhetorical act you analyze must be accessible to all class members (this is presumed to be the case for a regular television series or a major news event, but forewarning is needed to allow us to pay special attention). If you are treating something that has been published, you need only tell us where it can be found (you can probably arrange with the instructor to have copies made of a speech). If you select a movie, be sure it is reasonably available for viewing before your presentation.

3.   An oral presentation by the group to the rest of the class should take not more than 30 minutes, leaving time for questions and discussion by the class and the instructor.

4.   You must turn in an essay summarizing your individual presentation; it should include a list of the sources you used in gathering information, analyzing the work, and developing an interpretation. The essay should not be identical to what you present orally as a member of the group, but it should describe your special contribution to the group analysis and the sources you used to develop it.

Use descriptive analysis in doing a close reading of the act itself. Use the rhetorical problem as a way of looking at the act strategically. Use the four evaluative criteria and special evaluations drawn from context, occasion, and medium of transmission to assess how and why and whether the rhetorical act achieves its ends and for whom.

PART THREE

RESOURCES FOR RHETORICAL ACTION

CHAPTER 8

THE RESOURCES OF
EVIDENCE

Alison sits quietly in a corner of the hospital reception room, waiting to be called for her weekly examination. She is 16, and her slender face looks healthy, but fatigued. Five months ago, she dropped out of her ninth-grade class. Any day now she is going to have a baby.

Alison is scared. Any 16-year-old girl who is about to become a mother might be. But she says that she is happy, too. There is a child inside her; to Alison, this means that she's a woman. Now people will have to see that she's a grown-up, and respect her.

The father of the child doesn't come to the hospital with Alison. He is 18, and has no job. He can't support himself or her, let alone support a child. Besides, Alison doesn't like him "that much anymore," she says. It is the baby that she wants. The baby will be someone she will care for and play with, someone who will be sure to love her in return.*

That is how a different essay on adolescent pregnancy begins. It was written by Eunice Kennedy Shriver. This part of the essay, the opening paragraphs, is an introduction, the part of a rhetorical act designed to attract our attention and lead us into its subject and give us a hint of the rhetor's purpose. It is also a piece of evidence, an *example*. And supporting materials like this one are one of the most im-

---

* Eunice Kennedy Shriver, "A Surprising View of Teen-Age Pregnancy." © 1978 LHJ Publishing, Inc. Reprinted with permission of *Ladies' Home Journal.*

portant resources available to rhetors in overcoming the rhetorical problem.

After reading Chapters 4, 5, and 6, you may feel that the situation is a nearly hopeless one, that rhetors face obstacles so great that there is little they can do. That is not the case. There are many obstacles; there are also many resources for overcoming them. One of the most important is evidence. Along with the arguments used and the structure of the rhetorical act, these are resources that exist in our ability to use and respond to reasoning and data.

Writing long ago in his *Rhetoric*, Aristotle said: "A speech has two parts. You must state your case, and you must prove it" (1414a.30–1). His statement emphasizes the role of a thesis, logical arguments, and facts in persuasion. However, as Aristotle also noted in the *Rhetoric*, proof comes in different *forms*. He wrote about three *modes* of persuasion arising from the discursive or rational qualities of language (*logos*), from the feelings, attitudes, or state of mind of the audience (*pathos*), and from the audience's perceptions of the rhetor (*ethos*). Aristotle was also concerned with the resources in language, particularly in metaphor. Aristotle's ideas are valid today. We cannot discuss evidence solely in logical or empirical terms. We must also consider its psychological impact on the audience—whether evidence makes ideas vivid and clear or affects attitudes toward the rhetor.

In practical terms, every piece of evidence must be judged by two criteria: (1) what are its logical or empirical strengths and limitations? (2) what are its psychological powers? Ideally, good supporting materials show the truth of a claim; they are clear, vivid, and concrete; and they present the rhetor as competent and trustworthy.

EXAMPLES

The piece of evidence that opens this chapter is an *example*. An example is a case or an instance, real or hypothetical, detailed or undetailed, used to illustrate an idea or to prove that a particular kind of event has happened or could happen. Alison is an example of a teen-age girl who is pregnant. Her story is a real example (it is the story of an actual person and its details are factual). The example is fairly detailed: we know Alison's age, many of her feelings, where she is and some of the events of her life (she is a ninth-grader, she has dropped out of school, she is near delivery, she is receiving regular medical care). We also know something about the father of her child. Alison's case illustrates a situation in which a pregnant teen-ager might find herself.

What does Alison's case prove or demonstrate? That one 16-year-old girl became pregnant in 197?, wanted to have her baby, did not want to marry its father, and dropped out of school because of her pregnancy. It does *not* prove that all or many teen-agers who become pregnant are like Alison. As proof, it simply shows us that this particular situation has happened once.

As you will have realized by now, the example is a weak form of evidence when judged logically or empirically. It merely shows that something happened once, and if the example is hypothetical or imaginary, it does not even do that. In order to illustrate the weakness of the example as proof, I tell my students the true story of a woman who was killed instantly while asleep in her bed by the fall of a large meteor. No matter how dramatically I tell the story or how detailed I make it, they are never frightened. From their personal experience, from the experience of others, and from news reports and astronomical data, they know that meteors rarely fall all the way to the ground on our planet, especially in sizes that would be harmful, and that they rarely strike people or animals. The students' reaction is, "Okay, it happened once. The odds are that it won't ever happen again, and the chances of its happening to me are infinitesimal."

Just like the story of the death from a meteor, the story of Alison *by itself* proves very little. As good critics, we ask, appropriately, Does this happen often? Is this a typical case? Is Alison's situation common enough so that we can draw conclusions from it? Without other evidence, without a different kind of evidence, such questions cannot be answered.

But Alison's story is a strong piece of evidence on psychological grounds. As human beings, we have trouble imagining hundreds or thousands or millions of anything—including pregnant teen-agers. But we can imagine one teen-age girl who is frightened by what is happening to her, whose life will be made more difficult by maternal responsibilities and who, with less than a ninth-grade education, is ill-equipped to handle such responsibilities, especially if they include earning a living. We imagine the immature relationships that might result in such a pregnancy, and we feel the need for love and closeness that might prompt a girl like Alison to want a baby—someone of her very own to love and to love her. In other words, the rhetorical force of the example lies in its capacity to make us imagine a scene, imagine ourselves in it, and identify with the people and events. The more detailed the example—and the more skillfully the details are chosen—the more we identify with the problem or situation and participate in it. It is this capacity for stimulating identification that makes examples such extremely powerful pieces of evidence psychologically. They clarify through detail; they engage us by creating the bases for identification.

If you understand what an example can do at its best, you can also discriminate among examples that are more or less effective. In most cases, a real example of an actual event or person is better than a hypothetical or imaginary case. But real examples are not always available. We have not yet had a major ecological disaster, so the rhetor who seeks to describe vividly and in detail what would occur in such a case must resort to hypothetical example.* Similarly, no terrorist has acquired a nuclear device. If a rhetor is to describe such an event, it will be necessary to develop a hypothetical example, and events of this kind have already become the subjects of works of fiction. As proof, both logically and psychologically, a hypothetical example is strongest when it seems most plausible to the audience, when it has, in literary terms, the greatest verisimilitude, the appearance of truth or likelihood, when it creates virtual experience. In other words, the details of the example should conform to what is known—imaginary presidents must behave like their real-life counterparts; imaginary nuclear accidents must take account of all the levels of protection in real-life nuclear plants, and so forth. The similarity between the film *The China Syndrome* and the near-meltdown at Three Mile Island was a major reason why the film drew large audiences and became an important rhetorical event.

Real examples too—indeed all examples—are judged by their plausibility and verisimilitude. Although no example by itself can demonstrate its own representativeness, it should conform to common knowledge of what is plausible and likely. In addition, our willingness to accept examples is heightened by the amount of detail that is provided. The details we know about Alison conform to what we know about relationships among junior high school students. In addition, the sheer number of details helps us to believe that there is a real Alison who is in this situation and feels in just these ways.

Plausibility is not just a function of the example itself, it is a function of the similarity between what happens in the example and the experiences of the audience. You will recall that in Chapter 2 when I discussed the *New York Times* essay, "Adolescent Pregnancy," I commented on the author's views of religious advice as timid and negli-

---

* See, for instance, Paul Ehrlich, "Eco-Catastrophe!" *Ramparts*, September 1969, pp. 52–56. Note, however, that the events at Three Mile Island and the effects of toxic wastes in the Love Canal area of upstate New York provide real examples of highly dangerous ecological threats.

gent. I said then that your acceptance of his views depended on your own experience. If the religious people you knew had behaved timidly or refused to discuss sexual questions, then you would probably accept Konner's statement. But if you had known religious leaders who were concerned and forthright, you would probably reject his views. A similar process goes on with examples. If an example is to create identification and induce participation by the audience, it must fit their experience; otherwise you, as rhetor, must be prepared to show through other evidence that the case you provide is representative or relatively common.

In addition, you should note that a number of examples will strengthen an individual case so that, as a series, they suggest that each is typical or representative of a larger number of instances.

Examples also contribute to the ethos of the rhetor. They suggest that the rhetor is concerned with real people and events and imply that she or he has had firsthand experience with the situation. Very often, examples demonstrate the goodwill of the speaker and the expertise that comes from combining practical experience with theoretical knowledge. In the article that began with the story of Alison, Eunice Kennedy Shriver makes a deliberate attempt to connect her expertise, her experience with other women, and the story of Alison:

> As a social worker at the House of the Good Shepherd in Chicago and at the Federal Penitentiary for Women in Alderson, West Virginia, I worked with girls who were the victims of extreme poverty, broken families, uncaring communities. When they became pregnant, as they often did, it was not the result of too much love, but of too little love; not of caring too much, but of a life in which no one cared enough to offer guidance the girls could accept. Today I find that many other girls, less radically deprived, account for the greatest number of teen-age mothers; but their reasons for becoming and remaining pregnant are not very different. Like Alison, when they feel the fetus moving inside of them, they imagine a new life, serene and filled with love, for themselves and their expected babies.*

From this material, you cannot determine whether the author has actually met Alison, but Alison is like the young women she has worked with. Her concern for and interest in Alison show that she is a

---

* Shriver, "A Surprising View," p. 102. Reprinted by permission.

warm person who cares for others. If we care for Alison, as we have met her in the example, we are likely to trust an author who seems to care for her, too.

In summary, then, the example is psychologically a vivid evocation that clarifies the meaning of an idea or problem. When details are given, and when the audience finds an example plausible because of detail or conformity to their experience, it becomes highly effective in creating identification and in involving the audience with the problem. Real examples are stronger than hypothetical ones. To be effective, a hypothetical case must establish its similarity to real-life situations. Examples are stronger when they are relatively detailed and when a series of them is used. Examples are weak as proof because they are single instances that may be atypical and unrepresentative. They are also weak if they are undetailed and if they contradict the experiences of the audience.

STATISTICS

In many ways, the strengths and weaknesses of the example and the statistic are mirror images—where one is weak, the other is strong and vice versa. As a result, combining examples and statistics is often a very effective move. For instance, immediately after the introductory example of Alison, Shriver wrote:

> This year, *600,000* teen-age girls will become pregnant and, like Alison, will make the decision to have their babies. These girls belong to every ethnic, racial and economic group. *Most of them* will find no alternative but to go on welfare, and *many* will stay there. *One out of four* will be pregnant again within a year. The saddest fact of all, perhaps, is that *nearly 40,000* of the girls will not have *turned 15* when they become pregnant, and *the number* of these young mothers *is increasing* (emphasis added).*

A statistic is a numerical or quantitative measure of scope or of frequency of occurrence. In the paragraph above, I italicized all the actual statistics and some indications of relative numbers. Both the actual statistics ("This year, 600,000 teen-age girls will become pregnant," or "nearly 40,000 of the girls will not have turned 15") and the

---

* Shriver, "A Surprising View," p. 100. Reprinted by permission.

relative number phrases ("most of them," "many," "the number is increasing") are attempts to show that Alison's case is not atypical; rather, she is a representative example of the problem. Like her, hundreds of thousands of teen-age girls who become pregnant will decide to have their babies. Like her, most (a majority) will be unmarried when they conceive, and, like her, most will remain unmarried afterward. Like her, "many" will drop out of school. Many teen-age mothers like Alison will be forced to go on welfare. One quarter of them will be pregnant a second time within a year after the birth of their first child. Many teen-age mothers are even younger than Alison (she is not atypical in age).

Rhetorically, statistics are measures of the size or extent of something and of its location in a population. Statistics also document certain recurring characteristics. In this case, statistics tell us how many teen-age women keep their babies and present a profile of such women, their circumstances, and what happens to them. These numbers are cold; they give no personal details. As numbers, they may be hard to understand or remember. In this case, the author has tried to make the statistics easier to absorb. "One out of four" is a bit easier to grasp than "25 percent" or "150,000" (one-fourth of 600,000). "Most of them" is more intelligible than "302,345" (or whatever the actual number might be). In fact, the author is wise in presenting only two whole numbers in this paragraph. Many more, and the material would become too complex or dull for many readers.

Statistics are strong logically and empirically because they are careful measures of frequency. But as proof, they pose some problems you should know about. As the subtle cliché puts it, "Figures can't lie but liars can figure." In other words, numbers can be used to distort and misrepresent. At least two questions should be asked about every statistic: (1) what counts as an instance of what is being measured? and (2) how was the whole population sampled to obtain these data? The first question is not such a great problem here. Most of us can agree about the criteria for "pregnant teen-ager." Pregnancy is an objective state (as well as a joy or a sorrow or a frightening possibility) for which there are clear empirical measures. A teen-ager is a person between the ages of 13 and 19. But do we count the person who conceives at age 19 but gives birth at age 20? That is a relatively small problem here, perhaps, but it is a large problem in many statistical measures.

For another example, let us suppose that the state highway department reports speeding as the major cause in one-third of all fatal automobile accidents. It is not hard to determine what a fatal auto accident is, but it may be hard to decide just what "speeding" is. Is it exceeding the posted speed limit? If so, how do we know that was happening? Was someone clocking the speed? Is speeding traveling faster than is safe for the conditions? A fatal accident would seem to be proof that the driver exceeded the safe speed. In addition, how do we decide what is the major cause? Suppose we know that someone was driving faster than the speed limit but was also drunk. Which is the major cause? If you ask such questions, you will realize that this statistic is a rough approximation of what state troopers believe is a major factor in serious auto accidents based on their reading of the signs (skid marks, damage, distance traveled after impact) and on extensive experience.

For the data about pregnant teen-agers, the second question is also easy to answer. This set of statistics is not an extrapolation from a smaller population. Presumably, birth records show the ages of motherhood, and public agencies have gathered data on all the women who have found themselves pregnant before their twentieth birthday. However, other statistics are gathered through survey research, the kind of technique through which George Gallup, Louis Harris, Elmo Roper, and the Nielsen agency question a random sample whose views are then taken to be representative of the views of all Americans "with a margin of error of plus or minus 5 percent" or some similar figure. What is called a "sampling" error occurs when this smaller population—the group questioned—is unlike the larger population it is meant to represent. For example, in the 1948 election when pollsters predicted that Dewey would beat Truman, one major error seemed to come from sampling that included only people with telephones, people who were, at least in 1948, more affluent and more sympathetic to Republicans.

Many contemporary cigarette ads illustrate another kind of statistical distortion—the suggestion that a measurable difference makes a difference. Currently, brands of cigarettes are advertised as having 1 or 4 or 7 milligrams of "tars" or nicotine, and ads suggest that it is healthier to smoke these brands. However, there is no evidence of any medically significant advantage from smoking brands with lower measured levels of these ingredients. Smoking any cigarette is apparently bad for the health. The undesirable effects of smoking may even arise, not from the amount of "tars" or nicotine, but from the products of combustion—carbon dioxide nitrous oxide, sulfur dioxide, and others. But the statistic makes it seem "safer" and "better" to smoke some brands than others, and if we fear the effects of smoking but cannot bring ourselves to stop, we may go along with the pretext that a numerical difference makes a medical difference.

The willingness to make such an assumption calls attention to a psychological asset of statistics: the appearance of objectivity and precision that makes us treat them as factual and true. Our "scientific" society reveres the empirical and "objective" so much that, as members of audiences, we are likely to be particularly impressed by statistical evidence. This psychological strength is offset in part, however, by a psychological problem: statistics are dull and hard to understand and remember. An audience confronted with a series of statistics is likely to become confused and lost; special efforts must be made to translate large numbers remote from personal experience into more familiar terms. For example, instead of listing the number of teen-age pregnancies for a year, which is over one million, a rhetor might say 1 out of every 10 teen-age girls will become pregnant this year. One million anythings is probably beyond imagination, but 1 in 10 is a familiar and known proportion.

Because of this problem, you may want to use visual aids when you present statistics. Statistical evidence often makes better sense to both readers and listeners if it is in the form of charts and graphs that depict quantitative relationships in visual terms. For example, the Women's Campaign Fund created this chart to demonstrate the need for support for women candidates of both parties:

WHO RUNS GOVERNMENT?*

	Men %	Women %
U.S. POPULATION	48.7	51.3
U.S. Senate	98	2
U.S. House	96	4
U.S. Supreme Court	100	0
Federal Judges	99	1
Governors	96	4
State Representatives	90	10
State Senators	95	5
Statewide Elective/Appointive Offices	90	10
County Officials	95	5
Mayors and Councilors	96	4
School Board Members	75	25

*Figures compiled by The National Women's Education Fund and The Center for the American Woman in Politics.

Note that the chart simplifies a mass of information and puts it in a form that lets us make comparisons easily. One form the simplification takes is that it gives percentages not whole numbers.

The same group also printed this graph to dramatize the financial problems faced by women candidates:

WE NEED TO EVEN UP THE ODDS.

Campaign contributions in 1976 by political action committees

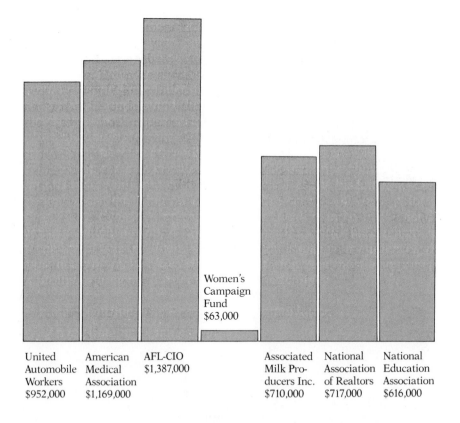

| Women's Campaign Fund $63,000 |

| United Automobile Workers $952,000 | American Medical Association $1,169,000 | AFL-CIO $1,387,000 | Associated Milk Producers Inc. $710,000 | National Association of Realtors $717,000 | National Education Association $616,000 |

In this case, because the black columns are so simple and vivid, it is possible to include the whole numbers. Note that the chart is laid out to dramatize the contrast in size between contributions from traditional political action and lobby groups and the size of the women's campaign fund. These are typical ways to present statistical evidence so that audiences can understand the data and absorb them.

You can also compensate for the weaknesses of statistical evidence by combining numbers with analogies, another kind of evidence. For example, Dr. Paul Erhlich, a population biologist, explained the rate of world population growth by combining statistics and analogies.* First, he said that the rate of growth was 1.9 percent per year at compound interest, an analogy to banking. He explained that, at this rate, the population of the earth doubles every 37 years, a comparison of growth to current population levels. He said that we actually add 70 million people to the planet every year, and that in 3 years, the number of babies born is equal to the population of the United States. Finally, he dramatized the growth rate by this comparison: in all the wars in which the United States has fought, 600,000 men have died in battle. World population growth now makes that up in just three days! Analogies like these compare numbers too large for comprehension with other, more familiar quantities (U.S. population, all U.S. battle casualties). Such comparisons fight boredom by dramatizing size and scope, and they translate statistics into terms that are better known and understood.

In summary, statistics are a strong form of evidence you can use to convey how often something happens or the size and scope of a problem. To interpret statistics, you need to know how the raw data were gathered, how measurements were made, what counted as an instance of this event, how sampling was done, and what kinds of error might be involved.

Psychologically, statistics are strong because of the empirical and scientific bias of our society and our respect for objectivity, for "hard cold facts." However, despite this general attitude, statistics are a difficult form of proof to use effectively. Lists of numbers are hard to understand and remember. Speakers and writers must make special efforts to translate numerical measures into more familiar terms, into proportions and relationships that are within our personal experience. Often this is done through analogies, the third major form of evidence used in rhetorical acts.

ANALOGIES

Analogies are likenings or comparisons between things, processes, persons, or events. They appear in two varieties: *literal* analogies (usually simply called comparisons) and *figurative* analogies.

---

* "Too Many People, Not Enough Stuff," an address given to students and faculty at San Diego State College on March 5, 1970.

Literal Analogies

Literal analogies focus on the similarities between items that are obviously alike in some ways: all schools of engineering, all criminal lawyers, all field hockey players, all rivers, and so on. Literal analogies are comparisons among items that are alike in detail and similar in explicit and obvious ways. The demands made on two professional quarterbacks are similar, for example, and you might compare their records of completions, touchdown passes, and yardage gained as evidence, in order to state that one is more skillful than another.

Such comparisons serve the purposes of *evaluation* and *prediction*. One compares in order to judge which player is better or to predict which will be more successful in a future situation. However, it is risky to predict a quarterback's success since his success also depends on the skill of his receivers and on the protection he receives from his offensive linemen. These complexities suggest the critical factor in the power of literal analogies as proof: the extent of relevant similarities and the presence of relevant differences. As a rule, the greater the number of relevant similarities between two cases, the better the basis for evaluation or prediction; the existence of relevant differences (differences directly related to the evaluation or prediction being made) lessens the strength and force of any claim. Football teams are just that—teams. The skill of a quarterback is only one element in its success, and the differences in talent and experience of other members of the teams being compared are significant for evaluating the performance and predicting the success of any one member.

Literal analogies enable us to go from what is known and tested and in operation to what is unknown, untested, and not yet working. For instance, in one high crime neighborhood traffic patterns are altered to prevent through traffic, and a crime control unit to report suspicious events is set up. The burglary rate drops 45 percent during the year after these changes are made. If we can replicate this success in other neighborhoods, people and property will be much safer. Careful analysis of such a project and determination of how similar—how analogous—any two neighborhoods really are should help us determine whether or not what worked in the one area will work in another.

Figurative Analogies

The process by which we go from what is known and familiar to what is unknown and unfamiliar is accentuated in the *figurative analogy,* a comparison of items that are unlike in obvious ways, that are apparently totally different if looked at with objective and practical eyes. The figurative analogy asserts a similarity that is metaphoric or that is a similarity in principle. For example, there are no obvious similarities between floods, famines, epidemics, and one million pregnant teen-agers. Literally, teen-age pregnancy involves no water, no starvation (though there may be some malnourishment from poverty), no contagious disease. No one alleges that hundreds or thousands are now dying, as they do in floods, famines, and epidemics. Konner makes these figurative comparisons (Chapter 2) on the basis of what he perceives as a common principle: all of these phenomena are the consequence of natural disasters; however unlike they may be in other ways, they share this common characteristic.

The figurative analogy is also a means by which this problem is made more vivid and dramatic. Through reading and other media, we have mental images of the devastation and disruption of a flood, of the helplessness and horror of massive starvation from drought, of the struggle to fight disastrous epidemics of, for example, smallpox or polio. If we think of teen-age pregnancy in these terms, we come to understand the extent of the disruption and pain that it causes. The scope of the problem has been translated into more human and familiar terms.

Note, however, that Konner's comparisons are controversial and harder to sustain before a hostile listener. Those whose views are different from Konner's will argue, perhaps, that this is a moral crisis, not a natural disaster, that the rise in teen-age pregnancy should be compared to other moral crises. Such disagreements are a weakness of the figurative analogy—it may work only for those who already agree. For this latter audience it clarifies and reinforces, makes a concept or problem vivid and dramatic, and puts the unknown and unfamiliar into terms that are within our personal or imaginative experience.

The main weakness of the figurative analogy, however, is that, in logical and empirical terms, it gives no proof, makes no demonstration. But figurative analogies are not all equivalent in rhetorical force; some are stronger and more persuasive than others. As a rule, a figurative analogy is more powerful when it is more comprehensive, that is, when there are many points of similarity. Consider Konner's comparison of teen-age pregnancy to an epidemic. The two are similar in size—a disease that struck one million persons each year would clearly be treated as epidemic. Like the rate at which a highly contagious disease spreads, the problem of teen-age pregnancy has risen abruptly and quickly. Like a disease, pregnancy in teen-agers threatens both mother and child with serious physical effects. Finally, one may argue that just as germs spread through a population, so do ideas. As social conditions have changed, teen-agers have "caught" the idea from popular entertainment that sex satisfies needs for love and affection, and they have come to believe that having a baby is one way to find the love they lack elsewhere. Because of all these similarities, Konner's analogy, although imaginative and metaphorical, is a relatively strong one. It is not a comparison that relies on a single principle, but on several.

Weaker figurative analogies rest on one or few similarities of principle—for example, the comparison between famine and teenage pregnancy. Both involve large numbers and affect certain populations. Both affect children more severely than adults. And that, I think, is all. The same limitation exists in the comparison to floods. All three analogies suggest a disaster from a natural (or partially natural) cause, but one is stronger than the others.

The strengths of the figurative analogy are, like the power of a metaphor or the force of a slogan, somewhat difficult to describe. When the analogy is a fresh comparison that strikes the audience as highly apt, it has enormous persuasive force. For example, during the black protest of the 1960s, Martin Luther King, Jr., said, "The ghetto is a colony."* Ghettoes are not, literally, colonies. (A *colony* is defined as "any region politically controlled by a distant country; dependency.") The sections of cities that have come to be called ghettoes are not ruled by a government from a distant country, but by the same municipal government that controls all parts of the same city. Ghettoes are not separate, dependent entities. But for many blacks (and some whites) that analogy captured the essence of the relationship between blacks who lived in congested and usually rundown areas of cities and the whites who held all or nearly all the political, economic, and social power that determined the details of their lives.

King's analogy is strong in the way I have detailed—it points out a number of similar principles (like a colony, a ghetto tends to lose its skilled labor and to have manufactured goods returned to it; like a colony, a ghetto tends to be run by people of a different ethnic or cultural group; like a colony, a ghetto tends to be populated by the poor and unskilled). The analogy is also strong because of what it did: it allied the struggle of American blacks with the struggles of all

---

* Dr. Martin Luther King, Jr., "The President's Address to the Tenth Anniversary Convention of the Southern Christian Leadership Conference," in R. L. Scott and W. Brockriede, *The Rhetoric of Black Power* (New York: Harper and Row, 1969), p. 152.

"third world" nations for independence, and it made their victory seem inevitable. When combined with others seeking independence, American blacks ceased to be a national minority and became an international majority. Finally, the analogy suggested that many of the blacks' problems were the result of actions taken by their oppressors, not the "fault" of blacks who should pull themselves up by their bootstraps. The right response to colonial oppression is independence, not the Puritan ethic! For these many reasons, the analogy is powerful. It summarizes in a single phrase the whole problematic relationship. It rests on a number of shared principles. It allies the struggles of blacks to those of others in ways that give blacks hope and self-esteem.

The figurative analogy derives its strength from its originality, its ability to make us see things from a new angle; from its aptness, its capacity to evoke an "aha" reaction; and from its brevity, its ability to crystallize a whole range of problems into a single phrase or image. That, too, is the power of the slogan, the brief phrase that expresses a position or idea in a vivid, unforgettable image. "Pro-Choice" and "Forced Pregnancy" struggle against the power of "Right to Life." "A Woman's Place is in the House—and Senate!" turns the stereotypic view of women ("a woman's place is in the home") on its head to express precisely the opposite point of view. This tactic of turning things around to express the opposite view is the best defense against a figurative analogy or slogan in argumentative terms. For example, opponents transformed the Goldwater campaign slogan of 1964, "In Your Heart You Know He's Right," into "In Your Heart You Know He Might." Every advertiser seeks to find a vivid catchphrase to express the essence of its product or business, a phrase that captures the attention but cannot be parodied or ridiculed. "Better Things for Better Living Through Chemistry," "Does She or Doesn't She?" and "You'll Wonder Where the Yellow Went" are examples. Each illustrates the summarizing power of a clever slogan. At their best, figurative analogies have the same power.

AUTHORITY

The final form of evidence, citation from authority, is also a way of translating complex and difficult material into a more intelligible form for nonexpert audiences. The contrast between a lay and an expert witness in a courtroom is a helpful way to define the special function of this kind of evidence. If you or I, as ordinary people or lay witnesses, testify in a court of law, we can testify only to what we have actually seen or heard or know from personal experience. (We give *testimony*, a form of the example.*) We are not allowed to draw conclusions and lawyers are not allowed to "lead" us, that is, to ask us to draw conclusions or interpret evidence. In contrast, the expert witness comes to court specifically to draw conclusions and make interpretations. A ballistics expert draws on her experience and training to conclude that two bullets were shot from the same gun; a psychiatrist draws on her experience with the defendant and on her training to interpret the defendant's mental capacity. The functions of the expert witness are the same functions performed by authority evidence.

For example, Eunice Kennedy Shriver cites an authority as evidence that even if contraceptives and abortions were freely available to teen-agers, many would choose to carry their pregnancies to term:

> Dr. James F. Jekel of Yale University, one of the nation's leading authorities on teen-age pregnancy, describes the reason for it [why these solutions will not affect this problem] this way: "Most of the teen-agers I have spoken to and heard about emphasize that they got pregnant because they wanted to have someone to love and to love them. Even if *all* clearly unwanted pregnancies were prevented," he says, "several hundred thousand infants would be born each year to teen-agers," even though a large proportion of the teen-age population is not engaging in sexual activity at all.†

The author is buttressing her own credibility (she describes herself as a social worker and notes her experiences in Chicago and West Virginia). The expert is a doctor, presumably a physician—perhaps a psychiatrist, perhaps a Ph.D. in psychology or social work. He is associated with a prestigious institution, Yale University. The author increases the expert's stature (if we respect her and her credentials) by describing him as "one of the nation's leading authorities on teen-age pregnancy." In turn, he supports his conclusions from his experiences with (presumably) large numbers of pregnant teen-agers whose views he has collected, and the typicality of this sample (recognize that it is only a long series of examples) is based on his authority as an expert who is familiar with the research of many others.

As I detail how authority evidence works, many of its weaknesses

---

* For a detailed analysis of the many problems with this form of evidence, see Elizabeth F. Loftus, *Eyewitness Testimony* (Cambridge, Mass.: Harvard University Press, 1980).

† Shriver, "A Surprising View," p. 102. Reprinted by permission.

become evident. We have no specific knowledge of Jekel's expertise. We have only the word of the author about his preeminence as an expert in this area. We have no reason, outside of his authority, to believe that this sample is typical of pregnant teen-agers, and we have no information about how these opinions were gathered (is this casual recollection or a systematic survey?). Yet the evidence indicates that a highly trained, widely experienced national authority interprets the data in the same way the author does, and his conclusions suggest that her interpretations are accurate readings of the situation.

Evidence from authority, like evidence from statistics, can be misused. The commonest sort of misuse is to cite experts in one area as if they were experts in another. For example, I listen closely when Joe Namath assesses the skills of quarterbacks and the relative strengths of two football teams. He is not only a skilled practitioner, he is also an articulate football analyst. However, when advertisers try to suggest that Joe Namath speaks as an expert on pantyhose or popcorn poppers, I am highly skeptical. Similarly, I doubt Robert Young on the benefits of decaffeinated coffee and David Niven on the best kind of traveler's checks. However, I would listen seriously to Young on television acting and to Niven on film acting—both have demonstrated their ability to perform successfully in these media. But neither is an expert in the areas in which they are presented in television advertisements. No one is an expert in all areas; the strength of authority evidence as proof is directly related to the authority's degree of expertise in the area in question.

Authoritative evidence is strongest (1) when we know the credentials of the authority—her or his training and experience, (2) when the relationship between the expertise of the authority and the subject is explicit, and (3) when we know details about the data used by the authority to make interpretations. Authority evidence is weakened when we do not know details about credentials, when the relationship of the authority to the subject is indirect or unclear, or when we do not know what data or principles were used in drawing conclusions or making interpretations.

SUMMARY

Knowing what you now know about the various forms of rhetorical evidence, what should you do to use evidence most effectively in your rhetoric? Combine the different forms of evidence so the limitations of one kind are compensated for by the strengths of another— compensate for the impersonality of statistics with the vivid, concrete drama of an example; compensate for the lonely example with statistical measures showing frequency of occurrence; compensate for the complexity of data with the analyses and interpretations of experts; predict specific cases, as you cannot with statistics, through detailed comparisons. Summarize an essential principle through the figurative analogy; contrast the generalizations of an expert with examples of testimony from people who have actually experienced the problem.

The functions of evidence are to prove, to make vivid, and to clarify. Each type of evidence has strengths and weaknesses, particular functions and limitations. Each enables you to do different things for an audience. Such data are the building blocks of rhetorical action. To fulfill their functions, they must be combined into larger units, into arguments and organizational patterns, which are the subjects of Chapters 9 and 10.

Summary Outline

I. Each form of evidence has particular strengths and weaknesses.
   A. An example is a case or instance, real or hypothetical, detailed or undetailed, used to illustrate an idea or prove that an event has happened or could happen.
      1. The example is weak logically and empirically because it demonstrates only that something could happen or occurred once.
      2. The example is very strong psychologically because it is specific and concrete, because it puts ideas into human terms, and because it creates bases for identification.
      3. The testimony of lay persons is a form of the example.
   B. A statistic is a numerical or quantitative measure of frequency of occurrence, size, or scope.
      1. A statistic is strong as demonstration of typicality or extent.
      2. The strength of a statistic as proof depends on knowledge of how the data were collected or computed.
      3. Statistics are strong psychologically because of the empirical and scientific bias of our society.
      4. Statistics are weak psychologically because they are impersonal and hard to understand and remember.
   C. Analogies are literal or figurative comparisons.
      1. A literal analogy compares things that are obviously alike.
         a. They are important as proof because comparisons are the bases for evaluations and predictions

      b. Their strength depends on the extent of relevant similarities and the absence of relevant differences.

      c. They are strong psychologically because they compare what is known and familiar with what is unknown and unfamiliar.

      d. They are vulnerable as proof because no two situations, processes, events, objects, or persons are ever identical.

  2. A figurative analogy compares things that are not obviously alike and alleges a similarity of principle.

      a. They are strong psychologically as vivid and dramatic comparisons of the familiar with the unfamiliar.

      b. Their strength depends on the number and kinds of similarities of principle that can be shown.

      c. Logically and empirically, they are not proof.

D. Authority evidence cites the interpretations and conclusions of experts.

  1. The strength of authority evidence as proof is directly related to the authority's degree of expertise on the subject.

  2. Psychologically, the force of authority evidence rests on the willingness of the audience to recognize the expert as an authority.

  3. Authority evidence is weakened when we do not know the expert's credentials, when we do not know how conclusions were drawn, and when the relationship between the subject and the expert is unclear.

  4. The testimony of lay persons, including celebrities, is a form of the example.

EXERCISES

Adapting Evidence and Language

Prepare a speech designed to explain or to create understanding about something unfamiliar to the audience. Plan the speech carefully to run not more than 5 minutes.

The audience is allowed to interrupt the speaker at any time to ask two kinds of questions: (1) what do you mean (a request for explanation, clarification, or definition) and (2) how do you know? (a request for data). No one should be allowed to argue with the speaker or to refute claims or challenge evidence. However, active audience participation is essential.

Discuss problems of clarity (vocabulary, explanation) and audience needs for evidence that speakers did not recognize. Discuss the problems of delivery created when your presentation is interrupted by questions from the audience. What factors seemed to make some speakers more effective than others in doing this assignment?

Using Audiovisual Aids

Prepare a speech on a subject that mandates the use of audiovisual aids, such as the styles of radio disc jockeys, methods of musical arrangement, a detailed statistical analysis, an explanation of a form or map. Ideally, students should seek to use the full range of audiovisual aids: graphs, charts, audio and videotapes, records, photos (shown on overhead projectors), slides, and films.

Discuss the physical (delivery, lights, eye contact, etc.), mechanical, and temporal (how much more time they take) difficulties they create. Discuss the kinds of data that they make available. Try to formulate some useful principles for deciding when to use them.

CHAPTER 9

THE RESOURCES
OF ARGUMENT

No fact has any meaning by itself. To be significant, to have impact, evidence must become part of an argument, and arguments, in turn, must be combined into larger rhetorical wholes (the subject of Chapter 10). My concern in this chapter is with arguments, the building blocks of rhetorical action. Just what is an argument?

Most commonly, an argument means a debate or a quarrel, because arguments usually express differing viewpoints or disagreements. In a very specialized sense, we can speak of the argument of a novel, referring to the principle or pattern of its development. This usage reflects the fact that arguments are structures, ways of organizing material. In this chapter, however, I want to use argument to refer to the process of giving reasons for or against some position. Thus, for rhetorical purposes, an argument is a claim or a conclusion backed by a reason.

Based on that definition, here are some arguments: Capital punishment should be legalized because it is an effective deterrent against rising murder rates. Teen-agers should be given contraceptive information and abortions on demand because they are not equipped to be good parents. Further development of nuclear power should be halted because there is no safe way to dispose of nuclear wastes. These are arguments because each makes a claim and provides a justification for it.

These examples also illustrate the role of evidence in argument. One appropriate response to these arguments is, how do you know—that capital punishment is an effective deterrent against rising murder rates? That teen-agers are not equipped to be good parents? That there is no safe way to dispose of nuclear wastes? And each question must be answered with evidence. Some arguments omit the evidence on which they are based, but all arguments are based on evidence. All imply that evidence exists and could be presented.

The most basic elements of an argument and their relationship can be illustrated this way:*

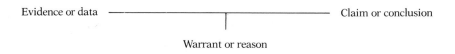

Since evidence was discussed in Chapter 8, let us now turn to the other two elements.

✓ CLAIMS

The shape or character of an argument is determined by the kind of claim that it makes. <u>A claim is a conclusion, an assertion</u>. Some examples are: That is a dog. You are in good health. Saccharin causes cancer. Medicaid funds should be used to provide abortions for poor women.

<u>Every claim is an assertion, and every assertion is a claim that goes beyond the facts, beyond what can actually be proved.</u> A claim involves a logical or inferential "leap." Even when you make a claim as simple as "That is a dog," you "jump" to a conclusion based on a few surface characteristics that seem to indicate that this creature is a kind of canine. When we make such a claim, few of us have either the necessary data or the biological expertise to back up our statement or to distinguish canines from other mammals or domestic dogs from coyotes, foxes, or wolves.

Even when the person who makes the claim is an expert who has lots of data, such a leap is present. During the summer of 1979, a St. Louis Cardinals football player died in the course of a practice session.† Before training began, all players had complete physicals and were pronounced fit. In each case, the physician made a leap from the

---

*This is a simplified version of the method of laying out arguments developed by Stephen Toulmin, *The Uses of Argument* (Cambridge, England: Cambridge University Press, 1958). See especially Chapter 3, "The Layout of Arguments," pp. 94–145.

† "Cause of Cain's Death Is Still Baffling Doctors," *New York Times*, 25 July 1979, p. A 19.

data gathered in the examination to a conclusion about the individual's health. Such a leap is informed by evidence, long training, and years of medical practice establishing just what are signs of health. The death of this player was a dramatic and tragic reminder that a physician's conclusion, like all argumentative claims, goes beyond the available evidence.

The special character of an argument is precisely this: that it makes a leap from data to a conclusion. That is why it is a fundamental building block in rhetorical action. That is also what gives an argument its force, and, as the example shows, it is what makes arguments risky and open to challenge.

✓WARRANTS

The leap made in an argument is not a blind leap made in ignorance. As indicated in the diagram, we go from evidence or data to a claim or conclusion *via* a warrant or reason. A warrant is an authorization or certification that legitimizes the leap made in an argument. In other words, warrants are grounds or bases for drawing conclusions.

To illustrate this process, let us return to the physical examination. In giving a physical, a doctor follows a procedure that gathers data: pulse and respiration rate, blood pressure, reflex action, blood sugar level, and so forth. When the results are in, they are measured against certain standards of normality established for people of different ages, circumstances, and of each sex. By comparing the data from the examination against these standards, a physician can decide whether an individual is healthy. Note that several warrants are involved: (1) all reliable tests of health have been made, (2) they were made by a competent physician using accurate instruments, and (3) the results were compared to standards for what is normal for similar persons. Each of these is a reason a physician might use to support a conclusion about an individual's health: all essential tests of health were made; these tests were made and interpreted by an expert; the results were compared to established standards of health for a given class of people. Warrants such as these are called *field dependent* because they belong to a particular field or area of expertise, and they rely on the authority of persons skilled in that field. (Recall that, in Chapter 8, an authority was defined as a person thought competent to interpret data and to decide what conclusions could be drawn from it.)

That warrants often arise out of the knowledge accumulated in a field means that the reasons appropriate for one subject may not be appropriate for another. It does not mean, however, that there is no way to categorize kinds of arguments.

An *issue* is a fundamental point in dispute, a question that is crucial in deciding what attitude or action is best. Issues are of three types: questions of *fact*, of *value*, and of *policy*.* Issues distinguish kinds of arguments and reveal the resources of each.

Question of Fact

A *question of fact* is a dispute about what evidence exists and how it should be interpreted. For example, several issues about capital punishment are really questions of fact: Does capital punishment deter others from committing murder? (What evidence of deterrence exists? What is reliable evidence of deterrence? How can it be gathered?) Are a disproportionate number of poor, nonwhite people executed? (What proportion of capital crimes are committed by poor nonwhite people? What kind of data exist about the socioeconomic status and race of executed persons?) What is the relative cost of execution as compared to life imprisonment? (How can such costs be computed? What costs should be included?) Such disputes are not simple, as the conflicting evidence about deterrence demonstrates. But they do reflect fundamental agreements: that deterrence is an important goal; that penalties should be applied without class or ethnic bias; that costs to taxpayers are a consideration.

In other words, when you address a question of fact, you agree on a common goal and proceed to examine the evidence to determine whether or not a specific policy, such as capital punishment, meets that goal. The dispute will focus on the evidence and its interpretation, and most of the warrants will be field dependent. Authoritative evidence will be particularly important.

Question of Value

A *question of value*, by contrast, is a dispute about goals, and it reflects a more fundamental disagreement. Some of the issues about capital punishment are questions of value: Is our goal to avenge murder or to

---

*Aristotle classified issues into four types: being (fact), quantity (scope), quality (value), and procedure (policy). See the *Rhetoric*. 1417b.21–28. Some contemporary analyses, following Cicero (see *De Inventione*.1.8.), add questions of definition to those of fact, value, and policy, but in this text such considerations are treated in Chapter 11 on language, because definitions are central elements in all rhetoric, in my view.

obey absolutely the injunction against killing? Is our goal to rehabili-
tate or to protect society from murderers? Is our moral standard
"better that ten guilty persons go free than that one innocent person
die"? Such issues reflect fundamental commitments, and no single
rhetorical action is likely to change them. Conflicts over values often
define target audiences (those who share a fundamental value). They
may serve as a measure of audience hostility, one facet of the rhetorical problem. Conflicts among the values held by individual members
of the audience may be a resource for initiating rhetorical action.
Such conflicts may be used to provoke individuals to reconsider their
priorities and to seek ways to reestablish internal consistency within
their value systems.

Values arise from our basic needs, from cultural norms, and from
our peculiarities as individuals (see Chapter 4). All of these values are
resources for arguments because each value is a reason or warrant.
Such warrants are not field dependent, they depend on cultural
norms and social mores. Warrants that rely on such values are sometimes called *motivational warrants* because they are grounded in our
motives as human beings, as members of a culture, or as unique
individuals.*

When we are urged to act to ensure our survival—for example,
when we are pressed to buy a year's supply of food to protect ourselves against the devastation of nuclear attack or against economic
depression—a motivational warrant is at work. Such warrants are
also present in many arguments that appeal to our need for esteem
(vote Jimmy Carter out of office because he has allowed the United
States to be humiliated by Iran on the hostage issue), for love (avoid
dandruff and be attractive to women by using Head and Shoulders
shampoo), and for self-actualization (buy *How to Make a Million Dollars in Real Estate*). When arguments appeal to basic needs, cultural
values, or to personal achievement, motivational warrants are being
used.

Question of Policy

The issues in *questions of policy* are so universal that they are known
as stock issues (they are commonplaces, always "in stock"). A policy

---

* For a discussion of the complex interrelationship between our basic biological needs
and their cultural modification through language, see Kenneth Burke, "Definition of
Man," *Language as Symbolic Action* (Berkeley: University of California Press, 1966), pp.
3–24.

is a course of action, a procedure that is systematically followed and applied. The issues arise from what a rhetor must do to make a good case for changing a policy. These issues can be stated as follows:

1. Is there a compelling need to change the current policy? To demonstrate this, show that:
    a. Someone is harmed or injured.
    b. The harm or injury is of sufficient scope to be of social concern.
    c. The harm or injury is a direct consequence of the policy presently in effect (inherency).
2. Is there an alternative policy? (More than one may need to be considered.)
3. Is the alternative policy practical and beneficial?

Each of these elements combines questions of fact and questions of value.

A policy is a way of doing something. It is a systematic way of dealing with a particular kind of situation or event. Because we do not assume that change is good in itself, when you advocate policy changes, you assume an argumentative responsibility that is called the *burden of proof*. However, if you fulfill its requirements, as described below, then supporters of current policies are obligated to respond to your arguments and evidence.

First, you must show that someone is *harmed* (a question of fact and of value). A fact by itself does not demonstrate harm. The fact must be measured against a standard (or value) to show that what exists is harmful. Consider, for example, the startling fact that approximately the same number of American soldiers were killed in Vietnam as are killed each year on our highways.* The former fact produced national concern and considerable social disruption. The latter fact seems to be an accepted part of our car-oriented culture. As these examples illustrate, a claim that some situation is harmful combines data with a warrant drawn from a value.

---

* According to "Health: United States, 1980," the annual report of the U.S. Public Health Service, there were 53,610 deaths from motor vehicle accidents in the United States in 1978. See the *New York Times*, 6 December 1980, p. 8. There were 57,692 casualties in Vietnam.

But demonstrating harm is not enough. The harm must have a certain *scope* or *magnitude*. This measurement moves from injuries to individual persons to harm affecting the well-being of society. For example, on 6 June 1980, CBS News reported that unemployment in the United States was 7.8 percent of the labor force in the month of May. Clearly, most of the 8.2 million persons this affects are harmed financially and psychologically (those least affected are changing jobs voluntarily). However, that same evening a commentator on the "MacNeil-Lehrer Report" claimed that unemployment needed to stay at 6 percent to prevent labor shortages from becoming inflationary. This commentator argued that, from a societal (not an individual) point of view, 6 percent unemployment was good for the economy because it prevented any inflationary pressure. His viewpoint emphasizes that justifying a change of policy requires that harm to society, not just to individuals, be demonstrated.

A student did this well in a speech arguing that measles vaccinations should be required of all children. She transformed that topic from triviality to significance by citing evidence to show how many unvaccinated children would get the measles, how many of those children would be permanently brain-damaged, and what the cost to society would be. Suddenly a rather unimportant childhood disease that had been quite remote from the class became a significant social problem with important financial implications for each of us.

As these examples suggest, scope or magnitude is usually demonstrated with statistics, but that is not always the case. A single innocent person who is executed through capital punishment is likely to raise serious questions, not only because of the importance of one human life, but also because that one instance is a sign that all the procedures designed to ensure justice were not sufficient to prevent its most serious miscarriage. Similarly, the accident at Three Mile Island in which radioactive materials were released into the air (something we were told could never happen) may be significant enough to call into question policies governing nuclear power plant constuction and inspection and employee training requirements.

But harm and scope are not enough by themselves. You must also demonstrate that these problems are the direct result of the present policy. In other words, you must prove that harm of this magnitude is *inherent* in, that is, an inevitable part of, the current procedure. As an illustration, suppose that, using your current method of study (the policy), you receive a D in nutrition. That grade, clearly harmful, does not automatically mean that you will conclude that your current method of study is at fault. Perhaps you were not adequately prepared for this kind of science course and are really proud that you passed it in spite of your handicap. Perhaps your teacher was unskilled at explaining ideas, inaccessible for conferences, and absentmindedly asked questions on the tests about material that wasn't covered in the text or lectures. Perhaps you were seriously ill during a major part of the semester, and any course you were able to pass was a victory over ill health. Note that, in these cases, the cause lies outside the policy. Change, if any, needs to occur somewhere else, in your preparation for the course, in the teacher's approach, in your health, but not in your mode of study.

Inherency is part of a question of policy because no policy is ever presumed to be perfect. All policies are carried out by imperfect humans who have bad days and who can create any number of problems for which the policy itself cannot be held responsible. As a result, the issue of inherency is a demand that you show that it is the policy itself, not the persons who carry it out or some special set of circumstances, that is generating the problem.

If you can prove harm, and inherency, you must still show that *an alternative* course of action exists. In most cases this is easy—several alternatives will seem obvious. But the issue exists because if we are to change, there must be something to change to. For instance, many students do not consider changing the way they study because they are not aware of any alternative. Most students are not taught how to study or exposed to various approaches, and so do not see any other way to do it. Conditions must exist that make change possible. After a certain number of heart attacks, for example, a person no longer has the opportunity to change life style. Given a certain amount of damage, exercises to improve heart action and circulation are no longer possible.

And if you demonstrate that an alternative exists, you must still show that the policy is *practical*. That is, you must show that the personnel, expertise, time, money, and materials are available to institute the new procedure. If the resources are not available, the policy is not a realistic alternative. If the cost of the policy is too high, we may decide to live with the current level of harm (what would it cost to reduce highway fatalities to fewer than 1,000 per year?). For example, many students consider the cost involved in following a method of study that would produce an A average too high. They place higher priorities on time spent in recreation and with friends.

Finally, you must demonstrate that the alternative policy is, on balance, *beneficial*. This issue reflects a recognition that all policies, no matter how wonderful, have undesirable as well as desirable effects. If we change our procedure, we want to be assured that we will come out ahead. For instance, the president, in the face of unacceptable rates of inflation (say, approaching 20 percent per year), may propose measures to Congress that will reduce inflation but induce a recession. Members of Congress will try to determine, to the extent they can, whether the benefits of lowered inflation outweigh the evils of recession (unemployment, for instance).

Each of these issues combines questions of fact and questions of value. Questions of harm and scope measure facts against values. Evaluation of the current policy depends on how clearly we can establish that it is responsible for the problem. That an alternative policy exists must be demonstrated before we can evaluate its practicality (what costs we will bear combines facts and values) or benefits (evaluation of predicted effects). Policy questions are treated separately here, not because they differ from questions of fact and value, but because certain demands must be met by any rhetor who advocates policy change. The values used to judge these questions may differ among persons or cultures, but these same issues are addressed whenever anyone evaluates policies.

INVENTION

The ancient Greek and Roman rhetoricians called the process of preparing for rhetorical action *invention* (from the Latin *invenire,* to come upon or find). The term reflects their understanding that, ordinarily, rhetors do not create new arguments from scratch, but rather discover arguments in their research—in evidence, in other speeches or essays, in cultural ideas. Invention also reflects the creative role of the rhetor in selecting and adapting arguments and evidence for the occasion and audience, and in organizing these into an effective whole. Recall the example analyzed in Chapter 2. Konner's essay on teen-age pregnancy is a good example of rhetorical invention. He does not create new arguments from scratch; instead, he applies the research findings from his field, biological anthropology, to a social problem. That turns out to be a particularly apt adaptation to his audience; because many people are weary of familiar moral arguments over abortion, his biological approach to this issue seems fresh and new.

Skillful invention requires that you know yourself and the role you will play, that you know just what audience you are trying to reach, and that you are familiar with the available evidence and arguments and with the cultural history of your subject. Once again, an understanding of your specific rhetorical problem is essential to making wise choices in preparing your materials.

Some clues about the importance of arguments in invention come from a body of research that is called persuasive arguments theory.* This research has been done on decision-making in small groups, and the results suggest that arguments have more to do with attitude change than peer pressure, the influence of the attitudes of others on the positions taken by individuals.

Persuasive arguments theory goes like this. It is assumed that there is a culturally given pool of arguments on an issue (what I have called the cultural history of the subject). In order to decide what position to take, an individual samples from this pool of arguments. Arguments vary in availability (the chance that they are known or will come to mind), direction (pro and con), and persuasiveness (impact on, salience for an individual). According to this research, people take positions on issues because of the balance of arguments; that is, they decide where they stand based on the number of pro or con arguments that have force for them that they know about or are exposed to. As a result, novel or unfamiliar arguments become very important because such arguments may tip the balance and change an individual's attitude. This research also demonstrates the significance of cultural history as part of the rhetorical problem, because in these studies attitude change was least likely to occur when all members of the group were familiar with the entire pool of arguments (that is, the entire cultural history of the subject was known to them).

One kind of evidence, citations from trusted and respected authorities, assumes special significance. When individuals encounter an unexpected position in a statement by an authority, they tend to think up arguments that would explain why the authority would take such an unexpected position. These potentially novel arguments, constructed by members of the audience, can also shift the balance and change attitudes. For example, imagine that you are a committed conservative with high regard for Ronald Reagan. You discover, to your surprise, that he opposes the draft. You then think up reasons why he might take that position (it is coercion by the federal government; the need for a draft is a symptom of our failure to pay military persons a wage adequate to their services; and so on). The arguments you construct will be good reasons for you—sensible, salient, forceful. Such arguments are ideally adapted to their audience (you) and have a unique capacity to influence you.

The research by persuasive arguments theorists indicates that

---

* See the list of sources on persuasive arguments theory at the end of the chapter.

evidence and argument play an important role in decision-making. Arguments that are novel to the audience are particularly potent because they can alter the balance of arguments to shift opinion. Audiences may construct highly potent novel arguments when confronted with an unexpected stance from a respected authority. The research underlines the rhetorical obstacles created by the cultural history of a subject; that is, attitude change is unlikely when the audience is familiar with the entire pool of arguments.

Some of the reasons that arguments are the building blocks of rhetorical action are now apparent. Arguments are essential units in rhetoric because they combine facts and values to advance claims that express our knowledge, understandings, and commitments. As such, they harness together the power of our knowledge and our values. Arguments are building blocks because they address the fundamental issues of fact and value that are part of all choices. They focus on essentials, the grounds for belief and attitude. They are structures that make sense of the world. For all of these reasons, arguments are *powerful* rhetorical resources.

Thus far, I have considered arguments as exclusively rational structures that make explicit claims backed by reasons and evidence. But arguments, even rational arguments, are often implicit, subtle, and incomplete, especially when they appear in the statements of real human beings in contrast to neat diagrams in logic textbooks. The special kind of arguments found in rhetoric are called enthymemes, and they illustrate resources of argument that lie outside the field of logic.

ENTHYMEMES*

An *enthymeme* is a rhetorical argument. Ordinarily, it draws a conclusion that is probable rather than certain, it is formally deficient in terms of strict logical standards,† and its subject matter is concrete and specific rather than abstract. However, what distinguishes the enthymeme is that it is constructed from the beliefs, attitudes, and values of the audience. An enthymeme is an argument jointly created by author and audience. It is an argument that gains its force from the

---

* See also pp. 139–140.

† Virtually all arguments that appear in ordinary discourse are formally deficient. See Ray Lynn Anderson and C. David Mortenson, "Logic and Marketplace Argumentation," *Quarterly Journal of Speech* 53 (April 1967):143–151.

fact that the audience fills in the evidence or supplies the warrant or draws the conclusion. A rhetor can plan such an argument, but the argument cannot be made unless the audience supplies essential parts of it.*

The concept of the enthymeme comes from the work of Aristotle, but some contemporary theorists refer to the interact or the transact as the minimal unit of communication.† This means that you cannot commit a rhetorical act alone. Rhetoric is a *trans*action (*trans* means across or over or through) or an *inter*action (*inter* means between or among). Each of us brings a store of experience, feelings, beliefs, values, and concepts to every encounter; these are the raw materials through which we participate in rhetorical action.

The sense in which rhetoric is a process that builds on prior experiences can be illustrated by a recent personal experience. I read an essay edited from letters written by a convict to Norman Mailer.‡ The essay is a vivid description of what it is like to be a prisoner today in a federal penitentiary in the United States. Because of the details provided and the personal experience on which it was based, the letters began to alter my perception of what it means to be punished by imprisonment; they created virtual experience. The day after I read the essay, I heard an item on the news that, with the exception of the Soviet Union and South Africa, the United States has the greatest proportion of its population in prisons. It was also reported that, particularly due to overcrowding, a number of state prison systems have been declared unconstitutional by the courts. If I had not read the essay, I don't think I would have "heard" or noticed these items. But the essay focused my attention and changed the context in which I encountered these facts. I began to construct arguments. Because I associate the repression of minorities and the suppression of dissent with the Soviet Union and South Africa, I began to ask whether the large prison population in the United States was also a symptom of repression. I assumed that prison systems were declared unconstitutional because they constituted "cruel and unusual punishment." I treated the judgments of the courts as confirmation that the essay by this convict was an accurate description of typical conditions of

* Lloyd F. Bitzer, "Aristotle's Enthymeme Revisited," *Quarterly Journal of Speech* 45 (December 1959):399–408.

† B. Aubrey Fisher and Leonard Hawes, "An Interact System Model: Generating a Grounded Theory of Small Groups," *Quarterly Journal of Speech* 57 (December 1971):444–453; C. David Mortenson, *Communication: The Study of Human Interaction* (New York: McGraw-Hill, 1972), especially pp. 14–21, 376–377.

‡ Jack Henry Abbott, "In Prison," *New York Review of Books,* 26 June 1980, pp. 34–37.

prison life. These moves are typical enthymematic behavior. In response to a few cues, I was supplying warrants, drawing conclusions, creating arguments. But participation in rhetorical action can take somewhat different, less logical forms.

The actor Robert Young, star of the long-running television series "Marcus Welby, M.D.," has made a series of commercials urging listeners to drink Sanka brand decaffeinated coffee. He is usually identified as the actor Robert Young. In each commercial he suggests that drinking Sanka is the solution to a problem of nervousness or sleeplessness, and he tells us that Sanka is real coffee and tastes good. A discursive or logical argument is implied saying that caffeine is a stimulant that contributes to nervousness or sleeplessness in some people. You can have the good taste of real coffee without the problems caused by caffeine if you drink Sanka. How do we know? We hear testimony about taste from persons who drink the coffee, and Robert Young asserts that Sanka is real coffee (presumably made from roasted coffee beans, not some other substance). Since Young is not an authority, the listener assumes the statement is true because of Federal Trade Commission rules governing advertising claims. The evidence is testimony, a form of the example, and is relatively weak— the tastes of these people may be atypical.

But there is a second argument, and its existence is the reason that Robert Young is paid large sums to make these commercials. For many people, Robert Young is virtually indistinguishable from the character of the wise, kind physician, Marcus Welby. Although nothing in the ad suggests it (Young wears an ordinary suit and is shown in nonmedical settings), it is assumed that many listeners hear not Young but Dr. Welby giving them medical advice on how to stay calm and sleep better. Such listeners transform the actor into a trusted and familiar medical authority who is as concerned for their well-being as Dr. Welby was for his patients and as Robert Young is for the troubled person in this particular advertisement. In this case, no claim is made that his advice is medical or that the speaker is an authority. But listeners draw these conclusions just the same.

A commercial made for the Lyndon Johnson presidential campaign of 1964 is a more famous and controversial example of these two levels of argument. It has come to be known as the Daisy spot, and as described by its maker, Tony Schwartz, it "shows a little girl in a field counting petals on a daisy. As her count reaches ten, the visual motion is frozen and the viewer hears a countdown. When the countdown reaches zero, we see a nuclear explosion and hear President Johnson say, 'These are the stakes, to make a world in which all God's children can live, or to go into the darkness. Either we must love each other or we must die.' As the screen goes black at the end, white lettering appears stating, 'on November 3rd, Vote for President Johnson'."*

There are, once again, two levels of argument. One is a rather simple and explicit logical or discursive argument. The claim: Vote for President Johnson. The reason: Because he prefers a world safe for God's children to darkness, and loving to dying. The evidence: The sound of Johnson's voice saying these words.

The second level of argument is subtle and implicit. It concerns the other presidential contender, Republican Barry Goldwater, although no mention is ever made of him, and no claims are made about him. This second argument is stimulated in the mind of the viewer by the nonverbal, visual cues. The values of life and of a world safe for children are made vivid and salient by the opening shots of the child in a meadow, holding a daisy and counting, somewhat inaccurately, as she pulls off its petals. The threat to life and to our children is presented in an instantly recognizable and highly charged symbol—the mushroom cloud. These are connected associatively: the ragged counting of the child leads to the countdown that signifies the power of advanced technology, which is associated with an atomic blast (not a space shot, for example). Johnson's statement ensures that we interpret these cues correctly, that we see the child as a symbol of life and innocence, that we take the mushroom cloud as signifying the threat of nuclear disaster. Given the context of an election in which candidates holding opposing positions compete to be elected, Johnson's statement implies, very indirectly, that since he favors life and love, Goldwater must be against them. Listeners accept such a suggestion and begin to construct an argument about Goldwater if they are somewhat nervous about the Republican candidate and not entirely sure just what he said about the use of nuclear weapons.

More explicitly, the subtle, nondiscursive argument goes something like this: It would be dangerous to vote for Goldwater. Why? Because he might start a nuclear war. How do we know? We saw a mushroom cloud symbolizing the threat of nuclear war, which reminded us of our fears about Goldwater.† We know that he is ideologically opposed to Johnson. Since Johnson favors life and love, Gold-

---

* Tony Schwartz, *The Responsive Chord* (Garden City, N.Y.: Anchor, 1974), p. 93. Still photographs from the ad are found on pp. 94–95.

† Fears about Goldwater were aroused early in the campaign by his nomination acceptance speech in which he said, "I would remind you that extremism in the defense of liberty is no vice! And let me remind you also that moderation in the pursuit of justice is no virtue!" Fears were also created by his position that use of tactical nuclear weapons should be considered as a military option in Vietnam.

water must oppose them. When spelled out in this way, the argument seems a little silly, but both Democrats and Republicans thought, inaccurately, that they heard a very direct attack on Goldwater suggesting that he was willing to start a nuclear war.*

The second level or nondiscursive argument not only illustrates how audiences construct the proofs by which they are persuaded, it shows us a case in which they construct an argument out of pictures, associations, and suggestions. The enthymeme, the process of rhetorical argument, involves creating nonlogical or nondiscursive arguments out of materials that are not related in any way, as well as completing an incomplete logical or discursive argument (providing the evidence or warrant or drawing the conclusion).

In other words, rhetorical arguments come into being in the minds of members of the audience through logical and nonlogical means. In fact, all rhetorical action combines elements that are discursive (logical, formed out of propositions and evidence) and nondiscursive (nonlogical, formed by association, frequently visual and nonverbal). In order to understand the nature of argument in rhetoric, we have to step back to take a broader view of rhetorical action.

DIMENSIONS OF RHETORICAL ACTION

As I wrote in Chapter 1, rhetoric is the study of all the processes by which people are influenced. Some of these processes are logical, some are not. The dimensions of rhetorical action reveal the mixture of qualities that are found in it. Each of these dimensions is a continuum; that is, each dimension is formed by a pair of qualities related in such a way that one of them gradually becomes the other. The ends of each continuum represent extreme forms of the same quality or characteristic.

	Discursive	**Nondiscursive**
Purpose	Instrumental	Consummatory
Argument	Justificatory	Ritualistic
Structure	Logical	Associative
Language	Literal	Figurative
Evidence	Factual	Psychological

---

* See Schwartz, *Responsive Chord*, pp. 93 and 96. He quotes an article in the *New York Times* in which a writer, Ted Venetoulis, alleged, incorrectly, that immediately after the mushroom cloud appeared, an announcer asked sternly, "Whose finger do you want on the trigger?" (p. 96).

Each dimension focuses on the mixture of qualities involved in every facet of rhetorical action: purpose or argumentation or structure or language or evidence.

Instrumental-Consummatory

Something that is instrumental functions as a tool; it is a means to an end. Something that is consummatory is its own purpose for being—the end is the act itself; the purpose is enactment. Most rhetoric is primarily instrumental because it seeks to achieve some goal outside itself: to share information or understanding, to change attitudes or induce action. But rhetoric is also consummatory. For example, Gerald Ford speaks at the 1980 Republican National Convention. The fact that a former president, highly respected by Republicans and Democrats, condemns the Carter Administration is as important, perhaps more important, than the specific charges he makes. Similarly, the boasts of victorious athletes during championship competitions are consummatory in celebrating their prowess. However, they are often instrumental in spurring their opponents to new efforts. These are instances in which instrumental and consummatory purposes are mixed and interrelated.

Some rhetorical acts are primarily consummatory. For example, if you should attend a football or basketball game at the University of Kansas, you would see the Kansas fans rise and begin to murmur what sounds like a Gregorian chant while waving their arms slowly over their heads. They repeat, at an ever-increasing speed, the words "Rock Chalk. Jayhawk. K.U." Unless you are a member of the University of Kansas community, the words and gestures are meaningless.* But if you belong to the community, you chant and wave to affirm and reaffirm your membership in it. There is also an instrumental component. The chant expresses, indirectly, support for the athletic team, which represents the community on this occasion. Since morale affects play, the chant may increase their likelihood of winning.

Most rhetorical acts are a combination of these purposes, with the emphasis on instrumental ends. Consummatory purposes are often

---

* They are also meaningless to many K.U. students who do not know that the waving arms symbolize waving wheat or that "rock chalk" refers to quarries in which skeletons of prehistoric animals were discovered by K.U. geologists, whose students originated the chant.

revealed in introductions and conclusions that express shared values and affirm membership in a community.*

Justificatory-Ritualistic

An act that is justificatory gives reasons; it explains why something is true or good or desirable. Ritual refers to the form of an act, to the way it is performed. For this reason, ritualistic elements are often nonverbal or involve the sheer repetition of verbal elements, as in a chant. Ritual involves formal practices, customs, and procedures. Rituals do not justify or explain, they affirm and express. Some common ritualistic acts are pledging allegiance to the flag, standing to sing the national anthem, taking communion, or participating in the "Rocky Horror Picture Show." Ritual requires behavior such as standing, putting your hand over your heart, kneeling, throwing rice, eating, or drinking. Rituals are performed by members of a community; they are repeated over and over again; the form of their performance is very important. By contrast, justificatory acts imply an absence of shared belief, which requires the presentation of arguments and evidence. Note that the enthymeme illustrates the degree to which rhetorical action falls between these two extremes.

A vivid example of the use of ritual to make a rhetorical argument occurred during the Olympic Games in 1968. Two black athletes, Tommie Smith and John Carlos, winners, respectively, of the gold and bronze medals in the 200-meter dash, violated the ritual of the award ceremony. Smith wore a black glove on his right hand, Carlos wore one on his left. As "The Star-Spangled Banner" was played and the American flag rose up the mast, each held a black-gloved fist aloft and bowed his head, refusing to look at the flag. By violating the ritual (one looks up at the flag rising, hand over heart, while the anthem is played), they made a dramatic protest, and their actions provoked intense disapproval.† Their behavior and its effect reveals the ritualistic dimension of rhetorical argumentation.

---

*For further discussion of the interrelationship between the instrumental and consummatory purposes, see Richard B. Gregg, "The Ego-Function of the Rhetoric of Protest," *Philosophy & Rhetoric* 4 (1971):71–91.

† John Kieran, Arthur Daley, and Pat Jordan, *The Story of the Olympic Games: 776 B.C. to 1976*, rev. ed. (Philadelphia: J.B. Lippincott, 1977), pp. 429–432. For a different view of this protest, see Harry Edwards, *The Struggle That Must Be* (New York: Macmillan, 1980).

Ritualistic arguments can also be made positively. For example, the conflict over school prayer is, in part, a conflict over the force of ritualistic appeal. Just how much pressure is put on a child when a teacher says, "Let us pray"?

Logical-Associative

Logical relationships are necessary relationships, such as cause and effect. Logical structures reflect such relationships; they express connections that are objective. By contrast, associative relationships are arbitrary (determined by whim or caprice) or idiosyncratic (peculiar to an individual). Associative relationships are based on personal experience and subjective reactions.

The structure of the opening shots in the Daisy spot is associative. The counting of a child reminds us of a countdown, which reminds us of an atomic blast. The verbal part of the spot is structured logically: if you share Johnson's values (as expressed in his statement), you should vote for him.

Logical structure is ordinarily explicit and overt. Claims are stated as propositions. The connections between ideas are made clear to us, and we can examine claims, evidence, and reasons, testing them against other evidence and the like. Associative structure is usually implicit and oblique. Relationships are suggested to us, indirectly, by juxtaposing ideas or events or pictures, and we test these connections against our personal experience and subjective response. The Daisy spot suggests a connection between Goldwater and nuclear war that is based on an association called up by a picture (the mushroom cloud) and that is implied, negatively, as the opposite of Johnson's statement.

Many of the strategies discussed in Chapter 11 use the resources of language to make associative connections. Repetitions of sounds, words, and phrases create structures based on association. Relationships based on logic are only one kind of form that appears in rhetorical action. Other forms are based on relationships that emulate patterns in nature and in our experience: repetition, crescendo and decrescendo, and the like.*

Rhetorical action combines forms based on logic and on associa-

---

* Kenneth Burke, "Psychology and Form," *Counter-Statement* (Chicago: Phoenix, 1957), pp. 29–44, discusses form as the psychology of the audience. Kinds of form and their appeal are discussed on pp. 124–149.

tion. Both kinds of form create arguments in the minds of listeners. Television advertising is an excellent source of examples of the use of associative form to support claims.

Literal-Figurative

Literal language is prosaic and factual; it informs us about the world. Figurative language is poetic and metaphorical, and it reveals the speaker. Literal language deals with external reality; it can be tested for its logical validity and its empirical verifiability. Figurative language reveals the experiences and feelings of the rhetor. One poet calls the moon "the North wind's cookie"; another calls it "a piece of angry candy rattling around in the box of the sky." These statements reveal the attitudes of the authors but give us little information about the moon. As critics, we look for metaphors to discover how a rhetor perceives the world. For example, Abraham Lincoln uses birth, death, and rebirth as the unifying metaphor in his Gettysburg Address, and the metaphor reflects his view of the nation as a living organism.

Rhetorical acts combine the literal language of factual statements with metaphors and other poetic devices. Ronald Reagan calls his campaign for the presidency a crusade; Benjamin Hooks tells the Republican National Convention that he remains committed to the American dream; Helen Caldicott describes the potential threat of nuclear power in terms of a rainbow snake that, if disturbed, will devour the world. Chapter 11 explores these and other dimensions of language and their role in rhetorical action.

Factual-Psychological

These qualities of evidence have already been explored in Chapter 8. The factual dimension of evidence can be verified to determine its accuracy or truthfulness. Psychologically, evidence appeals to our needs, drives, and desires. Evidence can be fictive or hypothetical, inducing us to imagine and speculate. Evidence can pander to our prejudices or reflect our opinions and beliefs, which may be wrong. Rhetorical evidence is both data about the world and our perception of the world in terms of ourselves, a process that transforms "facts" into instruments for our use and into obstacles that frustrate us.

These continua express the discursive and nondiscursive dimensions of rhetorical action. Although the concept of argument emphasizes discursive or logical processes, rhetorical argumentation includes all kinds of cues that stimulate us to treat our associations as evidence, to construct reasons, to draw conclusions. Many of these cues are nondiscursive. The characteristics of the enthymeme reflect the ways in which rhetorical action combines these dimensions.

SUMMARY

This chapter describes the resources of argument. They include:

1. Combining evidence (information, beliefs) and reasons (values, trust in authority) to draw conclusions

2. Addressing fundamental issues of fact and value (combined in issues of policy)

3. Structuring what is known and valued into ordered and meaningful units

4. Presenting novel perspectives or justifications that affect the balance of arguments on an issue

5. Using authority evidence to stimulate the construction of arguments

6. Selecting and adapting arguments for a particular audience

7. Stimulating the audience by using discursive and nondiscursive cues to participate in creating the proofs by which they are persuaded

The resources of argument, in turn, are combined into larger organizational units, which are the subject of the next chapter.

Summary Outline: The Resources of Argument

I. Arguments are composed of claims, warrants, and evidence.

A. A *claim* is an assertion that goes beyond what is known.

B. A *warrant* is a *reason* for drawing a conclusion (the claim) from what is known (the data).

C. *Evidence* consists of all forms of supporting materials.

II. Requirements for sound argumentation vary with the kind of *issue.*

    A. Questions of *fact* concern what data exist and how they are to be interpreted.

    B. Questions of *value* are disputes about goals.

    C. Questions of *policy* include both issues of fact and issues of value.

III. *Invention* is the process of selecting, ordering, and adapting arguments to the issue, audience, and rhetor.

    A. Rhetorical invention selects, orders, and adapts in both *discursive* (logical) and *nondiscursive* (nonlogical) ways:

        1. Rhetorical *purposes* range from the instrumental to the consummatory.

        2. Rhetorical *arguments* range from the justificatory to the ritualistic.

        3. Rhetorical *structures* range from the logical to the associative.

        4. Rhetorical *evidence* ranges from the empirically verifiable to the psychologically appealing.

        5. Rhetorical *language* ranges from the literal to the figurative.

SOURCES

Persuasive arguments theory is developed in the following articles: Eugene Burnstein and Amiram Vinokur, "Testing Two Classes of Theories about Group-Induced Shifts in Individual Choice," *Journal of Experimental Social Psychology* 9 (March 1973): 123–137, and "What a Person Thinks upon Learning He Has Chosen Differently from Others: Nice Evidence for the Persuasive-Arguments Explanation of Choice Shifts," *Journal of Experimental Social Psychology* 11 (September 1975): 412–426. Also see Amiram Vinokur and Eugene Burnstein, "Effects of Partially Shared Persuasive Arguments on Group-Induced Shifts: A Group-Problem-Solving Approach," *Journal of Personality and Social Psychology* 29 (March 1974): 305–315; and Amiram Vinokur, Yaacov Trope, and Eugene Burnstein, "A Decision-Making Analysis of Persuasive Argumentation and the Choice-Shift Effect," *Journal of Experimental Social Psychology* 11 (March 1975): 127–148.

A critique of this theory is found in: Glenn S. Sanders and Robert S. Baron, "Is Social Comparison Irrelevant for Producing Choice Shifts?" *Journal of Experimental Social Psychology* 13 (July 1977): 303–314.

MATERIAL FOR ANALYSIS

On May 6, 1979, an antinuclear rally was held on the mall in Washington, D.C. It began with an invocation by Father Paul Mayer, which is reprinted at the end of Chapter 5. The prayer was followed by some 30 speeches, one of which was given by Dr. Helen Caldicott, a pediatrician and long-time opponent of nuclear power.* Although an Australian, she now practices in Boston. George Wald, Nobel Prize-winning biologist and activist, says: "She is probably the most effective antinuclear speaker in the country. As a mother and pediatrician, she doesn't hesitate to raise moral questions or display intense emotions about these matters that are life-threatening in the extreme. She has a gift for making the hard scientific facts meaningful to the public."†

A rally is a special kind of rhetorical occasion in which setting and context limit the options of the rhetor severely. Estimates of the crowd in this case ranged from 65,000 to 125,000, and the audience was assembled outdoors near the Capitol. Distances between speaker and audience were great and microphones were essential.

A rally is a kind of ritual to build morale and reinforce commitment, and an ideal rally speech has certain characteristics. It provides parallel structure, repetition, and rhetorical questions that allow the audience to understand and to participate. In order to build commitment, it divides the world sharply between good and evil, and it describes the evil to be fought in simple, exaggerated terms and in grim, concrete detail. It must be structured to build to a dramatic, climactic call for action. The physical setting demands an extreme form of oral style. Sentences need to be short and simply structured. Tone needs to be personal and style informal. Evidence is simplified, and assertions abound. Rhetorical questions invite audience participation.

Here is the speech that Dr. Helen Caldicott made under these circumstances:‡

1   I speak to you from the steps of the most powerful place in the world. This place here is the most powerful place in the

---

* For an analysis of the entire rally, see Kathleen Hall Jamieson and Karlyn Kohrs Campbell, "The Anti-Nuclear Rally of the May 6 Coalition: The Inception of a National Movement?" *Exetasis* 5 (6 July 1979), pp. 3– 19. Caldicott is the author of *Nuclear Madness: What You Can Do!* (Brookline, Mass.: Autumn Press, 1979).

† Cited in Katie Leishman, "Helen Caldicott: The Voice the Nuclear Industry Fears," *Ms.* 8 (July 1979), pp. 50– 51.

‡ The text is a transcription by the author of the speech as delivered. Reprinted by permission.

world. It runs the world. We are here to save the world. America has led the arms race, it has led the nuclear reactor race, and we are here to save the world.

2   Last week I was in Grants, New Mexico, where Gulf Oil are drilling the deepest uranium mine in the Navaho land, and above the mine rises Mount Taylor, that sacred symbol to the Navahos of the fragility of nature.

3   Two weeks ago I was in Australia. We have 70% of the world's richest uranium. It is on aboriginal sacred tribal land, and there is a rainbow snake coming down the side of a mountain, a waterfall. And this mountain is Mount Brockman, and it's full of uranium. And the aboriginal dreamtime myth says, if the rainbow snake is disturbed, it will devour the world. That uranium from Gulf and all the multinationals who want our uranium in Australia is going to power nuclear reactors here, and thirty-five countries have nuclear reactors, and they can all make atomic bombs.

4   What happened in Harrisburg? Did we hear it would have produced devastation of an area the size of Pennsylvania? Twenty percent of the time, the winds blow towards Washington, New York, and Boston. Eighty percent of the time they blow towards Washington, D.C., where the Congress lives, the Pentagon lives, and the N.R.C. [Nuclear Regulatory Commission] lives.

5   What would have happened if they would have melted down? And by the grace of God, it did not melt. It was nothing to do with men that it did not melt. By the grace of God. Three thousand people would have died immediately. Ten to one hundred thousand people right now would be going bald. They would be getting ulcers on their skin, severe vomiting and diarrhea, and, as their blood cells died, they would be dying of massive hemorrhage or infection. Thousands of men would be rendered sterile from the radiation on their testicles. Thousands of women would stop menstruating permanently. Thousands of babies would be born with microcephaly, small heads, because the radiation attacks the developing brain. Thousands more babies would be born as cretins, mentally retarded for life. There would be an epidemic of leukemia five years later, and hundreds of thousands of cases of cancer appearing fifteen to fifty years later. It would have killed approximately half a million Americans.

6   Did any of you hear the government officials on national television tell you these facts? No! Why not? It's like what Eisenhower says: "Confuse the public; let them die in ignorance."

7   What's happened at Harrisburg? They don't know how much radiation they've let out. They let out a lot of primary coolant, and rule number one is, you never let out primary coolant, like if you are a surgeon, you never cut the patient's head off. They have let

out so much radiation, they weren't measuring it. And Califano [Secretary of Health, Education, and Welfare], who is not a doctor, says that ten people will die.

8   We physicians are very afraid that many more children are going to get leukemia and cancer in five, ten, fifteen years. Hershey's Chocolate is twelve miles from that nuclear power plant. They are powdering the milk, because they say the radioactive iodine will decay in a couple of weeks. That's true, but what about the strontium 90 that lasts for 600 years and gets recycled and recycled through the soil, the grass, the milk, the babies, the soil, the grass, the milk, the babies, and human breast milk. It's the babies who are twenty times more sensitive to radiation than adults. It is a children's issue, this.

9   This is a medical problem. Have you seen any doctor testifying on the hill about Harrisburg? Not one. We have to teach President Carter what radiation means. He took Rosalynn Carter into the reactor. He doesn't understand. They shouldn't have any more babies.

10   Nuclear power is the biggest threat ever to face the world, the biggest public health hazard. Now it's a medical issue. We eliminated smallpox. We stopped typhoid. We've stopped malaria. This is preventive medicine. We doctors will take responsibility for educating ourselves and our patients and the politicians.

11   As president of Physicians for Social Responsibility, within two years we will have the whole medical profession of America educated about nuclear power, radiation, and nuclear weapons. We call for phasing out of all nuclear reactors. We call for cessation of exporting any more nuclear technology. Do you know that America is going to be the repository for the whole free world's nuclear waste—so nobody can make bombs out of it? We call for extensive studies on the radiated populations which are not presently being done, and we call for elimination of all nuclear weapons. For nuclear war is the ultimate in medical insanity.

12   I have a vision. Within two years this country will turn this race towards mutually assured destruction towards life. We have no more time than two years to turn this around. We will educate all the profession, with the A.M.A. taking the lead, with the pediatricians, the psychiatrists, the obstetricians, the gynecologists, the surgeons, everyone teaching and getting involved. And you, the people, taking the lead to elect the right politicians.

13   I call for President Carter to pass a law immediately that every new house being built is a solar house. I call for reversal of the Department of Energy research and development budget so that 4% is spent on cleaning up the nuclear waste and 96% is spent on solar power, energy conservation, and the like.

14   All people love their children. Every single person in the world loves their children. Every single person wants to survive, and nobody wants to get cancer, even the men who build the weapons, who sit in Congress, who are on the oil companies, who own the uranium mines, the nuclear reactors, and build the bombs. In fact, none of them wants to die. We will help them and show them how to develop the beautiful sides of their souls and atrophy the evil in their souls.

15   America who has led the world in nuclear development will take the creative initiative to lead the world towards life, maturity, and mutual respect of all nations and turn this federal budget towards life. By paying our federal tax dollars, 46¢ out of every federal tax dollar is used by the military-industrial complex for death. By paying our federal tax dollars, we are all sitting at the Pentagon Kool-aid vat. Our chances of survival, people estimate now to the year 2000, are less than 40%.

16   We are a beautiful species. We are capable of incredible love, creativity, music, art, and so are the Russians. We now hold the whole of life in the palm of our hand. We are at the crossroads of time. We are the curators of every organism on earth because of our brilliance. But we can turn our brilliance towards life, love, and creativity, and we will save the world. And this is the embryo movement. This is this size. In two years time it will be millions of Americans.

After you have made a descriptive analysis, answer these questions:

1.   What are the differences between an oral style adapted to address a large audience outdoors at a rally and a written style adapted to address a thoughtful reader? Does this speech read badly? If so, why?

2.   How are issues of fact and value intermingled in this advocacy of policy?

3.   Describe the kinds of warrants that Caldicott uses. How are these adapted to her audience?

4.   Examine the speech in terms of the continua of rhetorical action:

  a.   In what ways is the purpose consummatory as well as instrumental? In what ways is any rally a consummatory event?

  b.   How is ritualistic argument used? Note particularly the religious symbolism in paragraphs 2, 3, and 16. What does it mean to say, "Forgive us our *trespasses*"? How is logical argument used?

c. In what ways is the structure logical; in what ways is it based on associations grounded in the speaker's experience?

d. In what ways is the evidence a mixture of the empirically verifiable and the psychologically appealing? How is evidence used to arouse fears? What problems might arise from Caldicott's reliance on her own authority as a physician and pediatrician? Is this a novel perspective?

e. How does the style combine the literal and the figurative?

5. How does the speech work to create an audience, to overcome the obstacles of selective attention and exposure, especially in relation to television coverage?

6. What kinds of objections to her claims might be raised by someone who is not an opponent of nuclear power? Does her speech ignore or respond to competing rhetorical action?

EXERCISE

Selecting a President

The class is divided into groups of five or six students and given these instructions:

Read silently the descriptions of the problem and the applicants. Then, through group discussion, select the applicant you think best. Designate one group member as the speaker who will present the group's arguments in support of its choice. Each designated speaker should make a short speech supporting the group's choice.

The Problem

Antiphon College is a private, midwestern, coeducational institution of about 10,000 students. It is a 4-year liberal arts college known for its progressive academic programs and its involvement in and responsiveness to the needs of the surrounding communities, factors important in attracting students and in maintaining alumni support.

Most students come from nearby cities and towns, although some are out-of-state and foreign students. The student body is about 60 percent white, 25 percent black, and 15 percent Chicano. Most students are from middle-class families. Tuition is $3,000 per year.

Antiphon has a financial problem: an annual deficit of nearly $1 million. As a result, the college has been forced to cut certain academic offerings and is in danger of losing its accreditation. The college is not in danger of bankruptcy, however, because it owns a substantial amount of real estate. The value of its holdings has been increasing rapidly so the college has been reluctant to sell them to raise cash. Now, a president must be selected to replace the one who is retiring. The following people are the final pool of applicants. Which would make the best choice?

The Applicants

1.   Richard Bransford, black, male, 35 years old, married, no children. Currently professor of biological sciences. Author of one book and several monographs on recombinant DNA. Active in the National Urban League and in the NAACP.

2.   Andrew Cabot, white, male, 58 years old, single. Currently vice president of a large data-processing firm; formerly a professor of linguistics. Author of numerous articles and books on computer language. An avowed supporter of black civil rights efforts and a frequent contributor to liberal magazines and newspapers.

3.   Sheila DeWitt, white, female, 46 years old, twice-divorced, married, no children. Recently retired from an investment firm she founded and of which she was president. Received a bachelor's degree in business administration through correspondence courses 10 years ago. She has been extremely successful in business and is now a multimillionaire.

4.   Joseph Herrera, white, male, 43 years old, divorced, three children. Currently president of St. Francis University, a private, Catholic, liberal arts college; formerly a professor of philosophy. Author of several widely used ethics textbooks and editor of a leading philosophy journal. A prominent spokesman for Chicano causes, he has been jailed twice for his involvement in demonstrations against discrimination in employment and housing.

5.   Lars Martin, white, male, 50 years old, married with two college-age children. Currently professor of classics at an Ivy League school. Author of numerous articles on Roman civilization, he is now at work on a monograph on the phonological shifts in irregular Latin verbs. Martin is a Danish citizen who has taught in the United States the last 12 years. He has indicated his willingness to become a U.S. citizen if offered the presidency.

6.   Catherine Wright, white, female, 40 years old, single. Currently professor of economics at a Big Ten school, president of a state chapter of the National Organization of Women, and author of books and articles on economics, particularly on women in the marketplace. Speaks and writes on topics related to women's rights.

Class Discussion

List the applicants chosen by the groups and the arguments made in their support on the board. Then discuss the problem and the applicants. Consider these questions:

1. What capacities or abilities would an ideal president have? Examine the problem closely to determine the basic needs of Antiphon College.

2. Which applicants meet all the needs of the college? Were these the applicants chosen by the groups? How were other applicants justified? Discuss how speakers argued or how you might argue that one need takes precedence over the others. Is this possible for each of the basic requirements?

3. Which facts about the candidates are relevant to the needed capacities or abilities of a college president? How were you and others influenced by age, sex, race, nationality, marital status and history, or children? What kinds of inferences were drawn about degrees obtained by correspondence, being jailed for demonstrating, or activities in organizations? Did speakers use these to suggest nondiscursive arguments?

4. Discuss how a brief description could create an ethos for an applicant. What are the problems involved in drawing conclusions from very limited and undetailed facts?

CHAPTER 10
THE RESOURCES
OF ORGANIZATION

Organization is a kind of argument. It is a process of structuring materials so that ideas are clear and forceful for an audience. Ideally, the pattern of development should reflect a consistent point of view on a subject, clarify the relationships among ideas, and make a case effectively.

In his *Rhetoric*, Aristotle wrote: "A speech has two parts. You must state your case, and you must prove it" (1414a. 30–1). This is good advice for making an outline to develop your thesis, but, as Aristotle recognized, you need to adapt your ideas to an audience. First, I talk about the thesis and its development. Then, I discuss introductions, conclusions, and other ways to adapt your presentation for an audience.

The key to organizing ideas rhetorically is your *thesis*. As noted in Chapter 3, a good thesis statement:

1. Is a simple sentence (states one and only one idea)

2. Is a declarative sentence (a statement, assertion, or claim) or an imperative sentence (a command, e.g., Join the National Organization of Women!)

3. Limits your topic (narrows your subject)

4. Suggests your purpose (implies the kinds of response you want)

5. Is a capsule version of everything you will say or write

Please note that you may never state your thesis just as it appears in your outline, but your central idea ought to be clear to your audience when you have finished.

OUTLINING

An outline is a visual representation of the relationships among ideas. As a result, it is a useful tool for testing the consistency of your approach and the strength of your case. To understand how this can be, consider this skeleton of an outline:

I.*
    A.
        1.
        2.
    B.
        1.
            a.
            b.
        2.

This outline says many things. It says that there is one central, all-inclusive idea, Roman numeral I. In a speech or essay, this would be the *thesis*. It says that this central idea is divided into two relatively equal parts, letters A and B. It says that A and B are divided into two parts, but that the idea expressed at B. 1. requires further development, perhaps for more detailed explanation or proof. Overall, this format indicates which ideas are larger and which are smaller, which ideas are parts of other ideas, which ideas will receive special emphasis.

In this outline, A and B are *main points*, A. 1. and A. 2. and B. 1. and B. 2. are *subpoints*, and B. 1. a. and B. 1. b. are *sub-subpoints*. Notice,

---

* Rhetorical acts inevitably violate ordinary outline form because they are unified by a single central idea, the thesis or specific purpose. In all of the illustrative outlines, Roman numeral I. indicates the thesis.

however, that there are three similar relationships in this outline
form:

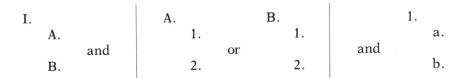

In each case, a larger idea is subdivided into two parts. If the content
of the outline reflects the form, these subdivisions should have three
characteristics. They should be:

1. *Subordinate,* that is, they should be ideas of smaller scope than
the claim they support or explain.

2. *Coordinate,* that is, the subdivisions should be of relatively
equal scope and importance.

3. *Mutually exclusive,* that is, they should cover different aspects
of the larger idea; their content should not overlap.

For example, here is the basic outline of a speech given by an agricul-
ture student about how to choose the cattle for a dairy farm or beef
ranch:

I. The breed of cattle you should buy depends on the product you
want to market.
   A. Guernseys produce a higher percentage of butterfat.
   B. Holsteins produce a greater quantity of milk.
   C. Herefords produce more calves.
   D. Black Anguses produce a higher grade of beef.

Notice that each point is subordinate because each specific breed is
an idea smaller than breeds in general. Each point is coordinate because a breed is examined in terms of the product it is best able to
produce. There is little overlap because each point examines a different breed. These main points are stated in parallel form: "Guernseys
produce . . . Holsteins produce . . . Herefords produce . . . Black
Anguses produce . . ." This helps the audience recognize that they

are main points, and it may help them to remember these major ideas.

Another student talked about rising suicide rates among college students. This was the basic outline of her speech:

I. You can help prevent suicides among your fellow students.
   A. You can recognize the warning signs of potential suicide.
   B. You need no special expertise to follow the basic procedures recommended by crisis centers.
   C. You can keep hotline and counseling center numbers near your phone for reference.

Once again, each point is subordinate in developing one facet of the thesis. The points are relatively coordinate, although point C includes a list of available places for counseling and their telephone numbers. Each point is relatively discrete. Point A develops ordinary warning signs that anyone can recognize. Point B develops simple procedures to follow in an emergency. Point C overlaps point B because one of the first things to do if you suspect that someone has taken potentially lethal drugs, for instance, is to call for medical assistance, but the point is distinct in providing places for different kinds of help— medical aid, psychological long-term counseling services, and crisis intervention hotlines. In this case, the points are parallel only in beginning with "you" and in implying that the "you" referred to is a layperson.

Main points such as these develop, divide, explain, and prove the thesis. Each of the main points in the example about breeds of cattle explains just what the thesis means. Each of the main points in the example about suicide proves the thesis to be true. The subdivisions of a thesis or of any point in an outline usually answers one of these questions: What do you mean? How do you know? How does it work? Why? In other words, there is a necessary relationship between a main point and its subdivisions:

I. Capital punishment should be legalized. (Why?)
   (Because) A. It deters would-be murderers. (How do you know?)
                  1. Comparisons of similar jurisdictions reveal that those with capital punishment have lower murder rates.

In other words, an outline is (1) a way to plan how you will develop your ideas, (2) a way to lay them out so you can examine the relationships among them, and (3) a way to make relationships among ideas clear to your audience.

While some outlines need not be composed of sentences, it is essential that rhetorical outlines be sentence outlines. The reason is simple. The building blocks of rhetoric are arguments, and arguments only exist in sentences. A claim must be an assertion, a declarative sentence; and summaries of evidence and statements of justification (reasons or warrants) require expression in sentences. In short, you cannot make the sort of outline you need or use the outline to test the coherence of your ideas unless you use sentences.

Here is an outline that served as the basis for an excellent speech:

I. Traumatic shock is a dangerous condition for which every injured person should be treated. (thesis; purpose is to alter perception of the condition known as shock and to create understanding in order to affect behavior.)

(Why? Because)

A. Traumatic shock is potentially fatal. (What do you mean?)

   1. Shock is a substantial reduction in the vital functions of the body caused by a decrease in the volume of circulating blood. (defines shock and explains what it is)

   2. If shock is allowed to persist, the person will die. (details results of shock on an injured person)

(Why treat every person?)

B. Traumatic shock can result from almost any injury.

   1. Common household accidents can produce shock.

   2. Psychological factors may speed the onset of shock.

C. There are no reliable indications of the presence of shock.

   1. The symptoms of shock can be misinterpreted or misunderstood.

   2. A person can experience shock without showing any of the usual symptoms.

D. Treatment of shock is simple. (feasibility)

   1. Keep the person in a prone position.

   2. Keep the person warm but not overheated.

   3. Try to reduce contributing psychological factors by reassurance.

This outline leaves out a number of things that happened in the actual presentation. But the outline is strong because it divides the topic and explains its dimensions, and the main points prove that the thesis is true (if A and B and C and D, then I must follow). In effect, the outline says you treat every injured person for shock because shock is very dangerous, it can result from any injury, you can't tell whether or not it is present, and it is relatively easy to treat.

FORMS OF ORGANIZATION

There are three basic ways to develop your thesis: chronologically, topically, and logically. Each of these general patterns can be varied in several ways, and all three patterns may be used to develop parts of a single piece of rhetoric, as illustrated in the analysis of the editorial on teen-age pregnancy in Chapter 2.

Chronological Structure

Chronological structure organizes an idea in terms of its development over time. This may involve division in terms of historical periods or by stages or steps in a sequence. Chronological organization argues that you (as a member of the audience) cannot understand this subject unless you understand how it developed over time, or that you cannot achieve your goal without following a certain sequence. The most obvious form of chronological structure follows historical development. For example:

1. Contemporary feminism has gone through a series of ideological changes.
   A. Until 1968, it was a conservative, reformist movement.
   B. From 1968 until 1977, it divided into conservative and radical factions.
   C. Since the Houston Conference of 1977, the factions have unified into a less conservative but highly political coalition.

Chronological organization is also used to develop the steps or stages in a process. For example:

1. Follow a sequence in preparing for rhetorical action.
    A. Choose your subject.
    B. Research available materials.
    C. Select a thesis.
    D. Structure your ideas.
    E. Practice or rewrite your presentation.

Organizational patterns that develop ideas historically or sequentially are common in rhetoric, but another, less common form of chronological organization is highly effective and impossible to outline. This occurs when ideas are shaped into a dramatic narrative, when a speaker or writer tells a story to develop a thesis. An example of a rhetorical story appears in John Fowles's novel, *The Magus*. The protagonist, Nicholas, is being taught about life by a man who is a *magus* or magician. As part of his instruction, Nicholas is given this story entitled "The Prince and the Magician."*

> *Once upon a time there was a young prince, who believed in all things but three. He did not believe in princesses, he did not believe in islands, he did not believe in God. His father, the king, told him that such things did not exist. As there were no princesses or islands in his father's domaines, and no sign of God, the young prince believed his father.*
>
> *But then, one day, the prince ran away from his palace. He came to the next land. There, to his astonishment, from every coast he saw islands, and on these islands, strange and troubling creatures whom he dared not name. As he was searching for a boat, a man in full evening dress approached him along the shore.*
>
> *"Are those real islands?" asked the young prince.*
>
> *"Of course they are real islands," said the man in evening dress.*
>
> *"And those strange and troubling creatures?"*
>
> *"They are all genuine and authentic princesses."*
>
> *"Then God also must exist!" cried the prince.*

---

* From *The Magus: A Revised Version* by John Fowles. Revised edition and Foreword copyright © 1977 by John Fowles. First edition copyright © 1965 by John Fowles. Reprinted by permission of Little, Brown and Company.

"I am God," replied the man in full evening dress, with a bow.

The young prince returned home as quickly as he could.

"So you are back," said his father, the king.

*"I have seen islands, I have seen princesses, I have seen God,"
said the prince reproachfully.*

The king was unmoved.

"Neither real islands, nor real princesses, nor a real God, exist."

"I saw them!"

"Tell me how God was dressed."

"God was in full evening dress."

"Were the sleeves of his coat rolled back?"

The prince remembered that they had been. The king smiled.

"That is the uniform of a magician. You have been deceived."

*At this, the prince returned to the next land, and went to the same
shore, where once again he came upon the man in full evening
dress.*

*"My father the king has told me who you are," said the young
prince indignantly. "You deceived me last time, but not again. Now
I know that those are not real islands and real princesses, because
you are a magician."*

The man on the shore smiled.

*"It is you who are deceived, my boy. In your father's kingdom
there are many islands and many princesses. But you are under
your father's spell, so you cannot see them."*

*The prince returned pensively home. When he saw his father, he
looked him in the eyes.*

*"Father, is it true that you are not a real king, but only a magi-
cian?"*

The king smiled and rolled back his sleeves.

"Yes, my son, I am only a magician."

"Then the man on the shore was God."

"The man on the shore was another magician."

"I must know the real truth, the truth beyond magic."

"There is no truth beyond magic," said the king.

The prince was full of sadness.

He said, "I will kill myself."

The king by magic caused death to appear. Death stood in the door and beckoned to the prince. The prince shuddered. He remembered the beautiful but unreal islands and the unreal but beautiful princesses.

"Very well," he said. "I can bear it."

"You see, my son," said the king, "You too now begin to be a magician."

The story is an attempt to teach Nicholas about the nature of reality or truth as seen by his teacher. But the story cannot be reduced to an outline form. It is a nondiscursive or nonlogical structure, and it follows a different pattern of development. This pattern is followed by most stories, dramas, and jokes, and it looks something like this:

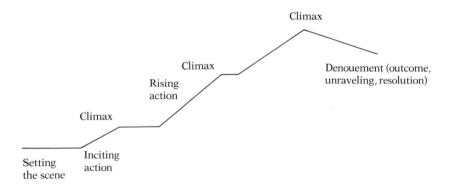

The story by John Fowles follows this pattern rather closely. The first paragraph sets the scene. It tells us that this is a fantasy or fairy story ("Once upon a time . . ."), it introduces us to the points of conflict (whether or not islands, princesses, and God exist), and we meet the main characters. The inciting action is the prince's decision to run away. There is rising action until the king reestablishes his position of authority. A new pattern of rising action begins after this minor resolution when the prince returns to the next land and reencounters the man in full evening dress. There is a pause in the action as the prince returns pensively home, but rising action as he discovers that his father is also a magician. The conflict intensifies to the last climax as the prince encounters death. The final sentences are the denouement, an unraveling or outcome, a kind of resolution.

This story is a useful illustration for several reasons. First, it is clearly intended to teach and persuade. Nicholas receives it under circumstances that leave us in no doubt of that, and the story itself unfolds to make a point, to draw a moral. Second, it teaches and persuades in an entirely nondiscursive way. There are no arguments, and no data are presented. The story is wholly outside logical and empirical reality. If it teaches us and gains our assent, it is because it is a good story that exploits the resources available in drama and narrative.

Good stories have certain qualities. They are filled with concrete details that we can see or imagine, and the details have universality or general application (the story of this particular prince and king is a classic tale of the struggle for maturity). They develop one or more vivid characters with whom we can identify. They are organized around a conflict that increases in intensity so that we are drawn into the story and come to care about how it is resolved. The rhetorical strength of a story comes from its verisimilitude, that is, its formal resemblance to events and persons in our world of experience. While there are few kings and princes (and almost none in our experience), there are fathers and sons. Children run away from their parents to try out their wings and to test themselves in larger worlds. The young are often idealists and absolutists like this young prince; they often see the old as deceptive pragmatists and feel keen disappointment at their feet of clay. There is a kind of "magic," a kind of faith, involved in adjusting to the absurdities of human life (and death). Coming to terms with life as it is is often a very painful experience. These parallels between the story and experiences of the audience (there are others that you might note) help to make this story effective as instruction or persuasion.

A work that is structured as a dramatic narrative exploits the literary and poetic resources of language. On the simplest level, such a speech or essay is an extended *example,* with all of the strengths and weaknesses of this kind of evidence. But dramatic narratives have compensating strengths. They can reach out to the audience to create identification and participation. In a dramatic narrative, we are induced to share the point of view of the narrator, to participate in the experiences described. The rhetor's claim is expressed, not as an abstract proposition, but as a series of concrete experiences or dramatic encounters. If the story is well constructed, it is hard to reject such "claims." They become part of our experience, not simply an idea or an argument.

Narrative-dramatic development is less common than other forms of organization in rhetorical discourse, but when it appears, it illustrates these resources. The most famous example is probably "Toussaint L'Ouverture," a speech delivered many times by the abolitionist orator, Wendell Phillips.* It is the story of the Haitian leader and revolutionary, and his story is intended to demonstrate that blacks deserve full citizenship. The story itself is strong proof because a single contrary instance is enough to disprove a "biological law." If one black is clearly a human being of superior abilities, blacks as a group cannot be biologically inferior. But the story steps outside the usual antislavery–proslavery argumentation to involve us in the life and hopes and tragedy of one person. We share his experiences; we identify with him. Phillips's speech transcends the obstacles of cultural history and engages his listeners and readers in a more direct and participatory way.

There are other contemporary examples. Eldridge Cleaver structured the story of his first encounter with the Black Panther Party as a story–drama that allows us to see the Black Panthers through his eyes, that involves us in dramatic events, that induces us to feel as he did about them.† Paul Ehrlich constructed a fictional narrative to warn us about the dangers of catastrophe posed by assaults on the environment,‡ and the story is a vivid way of allowing us to imagine just what such a disaster would really mean. John Anjain, the magistrate from an atoll in the Marshallese Islands, structured his testimony before a Senate Committee as the story of his people and of his son. As a result, despite great differences in culture and experience, Americans were able to understand, in concrete and human ways, just what atomic testing in the Pacific had meant for Anjain and his people.§ In each of these cases, a dramatic narrative transcends the obstacles created by cultural history or diminishes hostility or reaches across the chasm of cultural differences to create identification between rhetor and audience.

You should choose some form of chronological structure–historical or sequential or narrative-dramatic development–if you wish to emphasize development over time or in steps or stages. It is a good choice if the audience knows little of your subject, because it is a

---

* *American Speeches*, ed. W. M. Parrish and Marie Hochmuth (New York: Longmans, Green and Co., 1954), pp. 311–332.

† "The Courage to Kill: Meeting the Panthers," *Post-Prison Writings and Speeches* (New York: Ramparts, 1969), pp. 23–39.

‡ "Eco-Catastrophe," *Ramparts* (September 1969), pp. 52–56.

§ "Speech before the Senate Committee on Energy and Natural Resources," in *Critical Anthology of Public Speeches*, ed. Kathleen M. Jamieson (Chicago: Science Research Associates, 1978), pp. 12–13.

pattern ideally suited to provide background and to develop relation-ships among events. It is also a kind of structure easily adapted to hold the attention of the audience because it emphasizes progress through time, completion of a process, or movement toward a climax.

Topical Structure

Topical structure develops a subject in terms of its aspects or facets or dimensions. Sometimes the divisions are integral parts of the subject, such as the executive, judicial, and legislative branches of the U.S. government. More frequently, however, the topics are familiar perspectives we take on many subjects—the economic, legal, and so-cial implications of, say, affirmative action programs in the auto-mobile industry or of discontinuing federally funded programs to create jobs for inner city youth or of congressional efforts to end Medi-caid funding for abortion. In other words, a typical topical outline might look like this:

1. Youths are systematically exploited by adults.
    A. They are exploited *economically* by child labor laws and en-forced school attendance.
    B. They are exploited *legally* by the paternalism of the juvenile justice system.
    C. They are exploited *militarily* by the selective service system.*

Topical organization is ideally suited for selecting some parts of a subject for discussion or for emphasis. For example, a contemporary feminist wants to talk about the forms of social control that limit the options open to women. Because there are many forms of social con-trol, she must narrow her focus and select only some forms for discus-sion. Her outline might look like this:

1. Women suffer from overt and covert social controls.
    A. The *law* controls women *overtly*.
        1. *Marriage laws* are the most oppressive controls.

---

* See Edgar Z. Friedenberg, "The Generation Gap," in Karlyn Kohrs Campbell, *Critiques of Contemporary Rhetoric* (Belmont, Calif.: Wadsworth, 1972), pp. 174–187.

    2. So-called *protective labor legislation* limits access to jobs, promotions, and higher wages.

B. *Socialization* controls women *covertly.*

    1. A female child is *reared* to believe that she is limited.

    2. *Education* discourages women from many fields of endeavor.

    3. *Popular culture* reinforces stereotypes and gender-related limitations.*

In this case, topical organization structures main points A and B in relation to the thesis as well as A. 1. and 2. and B. 1. and 2. and 3. Under A, the rhetor selects two kinds of laws for attention. Under B, she discusses three elements of socialization: child-rearing, education, and popular culture.

Topical organization can explore natural divisions of a subject (fiction and nonfiction, commercial and public television, print and electronic media, for example). It can explore selected parts of a subject (soap operas and situation comedies as outstanding examples of kinds of television programming). Or it can apply familiar perspectives to a subject (the legal, economic, psychological, social, medical, etc., aspects of adolescent pregnancy or capital punishment or nuclear power).

Because there is no necessary relationship between the points in a topical structure, this kind of organization can also be put to nondiscursive use. In such a case, the work develops associatively, in a manner analogous to the structure of the lyric poem, and becomes an exploration of the aspects of an attitude or feeling. Such organization is uncommon in rhetorical acts, but it can be highly effective.†

When it is used effectively, topical organization divides a subject into parts that seem appropriate to the audience, parts that reflect a clear appraisal by the rhetor of what is important, what is typical. In addition, these parts should be arranged into some sort of hierarchy so we move from one point to another with a sense of progression. For example, the outline on the exploitation of youth moves from forms of exploitation that merely take away money to forms of exploitation

---

* See Jo Freeman, "The Building of the Gilded Cage," in Campbell, *Critiques,* pp. 152–173.

† Karlyn Kohrs Campbell, "Stanton's 'The Solitude of Self': A Rationale for Feminism," *Quarterly Journal of Speech* 66 (1980):304–312.

that limit freedom or punish to forms of exploitation that take away life.

The outline on the social control of women works differently. The development and proof of point A, that women are overtly discriminated against in law, prepares us for point B, that they are subtly controlled through socialization. If we assent to point A, we are far more likely to assent to point B; the relationship between the two ideas is *a fortiori:* if the first is true (overt discrimination by law), how much more likely it is that the second is true (covert discrimination in socialization).

Topical structure is an ideal pattern for narrowing a broad subject to a manageable size. It is also a method of emphasis by which you can indicate what parts of a subject are most important.

Logical Structure

Logical structure argues that ideas or situations stand in a conceptual relationship to each other. This pattern expresses processes of cause and effect or defines a problem and its solution. As you will guess, logical organization is ordinarily used to develop questions of policy. The relationship between questions of policy and logical structure is illustrated by most television commercials (commercials ask you to change policy by buying a new product or by switching brands or to resist the appeals of competing products). Many ads are little problem-solution dramas. For example, a man in a commercial is shown anxiously discussing the lack of interest his girlfriend is showing. His friend suggests the solution of a toothpaste for sparkling teeth and sweet breath. We then see the man with his sexy girlfriend in a scene that leaves no doubt that his romantic problems are over. In other words, if you have a problem being attractive to someone, solve it by buying Brand X.

Here is a simple example of a problem-solution outline:

I. Hot water can be instantly available in your tap.
   A. In most homes, water cools in the hot water pipes, causing a delay when you turn on the tap.
   B. Circuit hot water plumbing keeps hot water at the tap level at all times.

In this case, the thesis implies a goal (hot water should be instantly available) and indicates that there is a course of action to reach it. Point A states the cause of the problem, and B indicates its solution.

Many speeches combine topical and logical structure, as in this outline:

I. Capital punishment should be legalized.
   A. Murder rates are rising steadily.
   B. Prisons are increasingly overcrowded.
   C. Citizens are losing faith in the criminal justice system.
   D. Capital punishment can lessen all of these problems.

The thesis of this outline is a policy statement. Points A, B, and C develop problems that this advocate thinks can be solved, in part, by capital punishment. Point D explains how capital punishment might diminish these problems; it is a shorter version of the stock issues that there is a practical and beneficial alternative policy.

Cause-effect structure is a variation of this that ordinarily focuses on the first stock issue of a question of policy—the need for a change. Emphasis is placed on effects (the scope of the harm) and their cause (inherency). For example:

I. High rates of minority unemployment are caused, in part, by a lack of skills.
   A. Education in urban ghettoes and in the rural South does not provide basic reading and arithmetic skills.
   B. Few vocational training programs are available.
   C. Minorities are denied access to union apprenticeship programs.
   D. Federal programs do not teach marketable skills.

Once again, this outline combines topical and logical structure. The thesis asserts a cause-effect relationship, but the main points are a topical list of the major causes of the problem of lack of skills.

As these examples illustrate, logical structure is ideal for treating questions of policy. It allows you to meet the requirements for defending a change of policy, and it can be used to explore causal relationship. In all cases, logical structure reflects necessary relationships between ideas or events.

There are, then, three basic forms of organization for development of your thesis. These, in turn, can be subdivided, and each type of structure has certain strengths or advantages.

I. The forms of organization available are the following:
  A. Material can be organized chronologically.
      1. It can be developed by historical periods.
      2. It can be presented as steps in a sequence or stages in a process.
      3. It can be told as the story of a dramatic conflict.
  B. Material can be organized topically.
      1. It can divide a subject into its natural parts.
      2. It can examine a subject in terms of a variety of familiar perspectives.
  C. Material can be organized logically.
      1. It can divide material into cause(s) and effect(s).
      2. It can examine a problem and its solution.
II. Each form of organization has certain advantages.
  A. Chronological structure emphasizes development over time.
      1. It is ideal for providing information and background.
      2. It takes advantage of the appeal of progression through time or of a process that moves toward a climax.
  B. Topical structure selects and emphasizes.
      1. It allows you to narrow a broad subject.
      2. It allows you to indicate what is more important.
  C. Logical structure develops necessary relationships.
      1. It allows you to defend changes in policy.
      2. It is ideally suited to affix responsibility.

Each form of organization is a kind of argument. Each structure provides a particular kind of perspective on a subject. You can combine these different forms in a piece of rhetoric, but in each case, you should choose the kind of structure best suited to the kind of argument you are trying to make.

ADAPTING
STRUCTURE TO THE AUDIENCE

In the early part of this century, the American philosopher John Dewey published a book entitled *How We Think*.* The book developed

---

* (Boston: D.C. Heath, 1910).

the stages in reflective thinking, the processes by which we recognize problems and then go about solving them. These stages included:

1. Perceiving a felt difficulty or recognizing that a problem exists.
2. Analyzing the problem, including attempts at definition.
3. Exploring possible solutions and evaluating them.
4. Selecting the best solution.
5. Discovering how to implement the selected course of action.

Dewey's analysis reflects the stock issues of a question of policy, especially in stages 2, 3, and 4. But the first and last steps are additions, and they are clues to one kind of structural adaptation that needs to be made in presenting material to an audience. Step 1 is introductory; it establishes the facts and values that suggest that we ought to be concerned about something, that we ought to find out what sort of problem this is and whether and how it can be solved. Step 5 goes beyond the stock issues to ask how can we go about implementing the change we have decided would be a good one. It concerns concrete action—for example, how do we go about getting John Anderson on the ballot now that we have decided that the solution to our political woes is a third candidate?

Dewey's book was probably the stimulus for the motivated sequence that Alan H. Monroe developed.* This structural form illustrates the adaptation of logical organization for presentation to an audience. The steps in the motivated sequence are as follows:

1. Attention: call attention to the problem; in Dewey's terms, make the difficulty felt.

2. Need: demonstrate that a need for a change exists (that is, develop the first issue of a question of policy to prove harm, scope, and inherency).

3. Satisfaction: show the audience that the need can be met (that is, that there is a practical and beneficial alternative policy).

4. Visualization: describe vividly and concretely what will happen if the problem is or is not solved (that is, picture good or bad consequences).

---

*Principles and Types of Speech, 2d ed. (Glenview, Ill.: Scott, Foresman, 1939).

5. Action: call for immediate action from the audience; show them how to bring about the solution.

As you examine this sequence, you will see that steps 2 and 3 develop the stock issues of a policy question. In other words, the motivated sequence is a form of logical organization that is appropriate only for advocating policy change. However, steps 1, 4, and 5 are structural elements designed to adapt materials for presentation to the audience. Step 1 precedes the thesis in order to interest the audience in the subject. Step 4 is designed to increase the motivation of the audience by vividly depicting what their world will be like with or without the policy proposed. Step 5 presumes that the audience needs specific instructions on how to bring a solution about—where to go, what to do, who to write or call, and so on. It is designed to bring the proposed policy closer to reality. Steps 4 and 5 also require additions to the outline forms described above. They require special sections that make your ideas vivid and concrete and that give the audience assistance in implementing policy change. The motivated sequence is an excellent pattern to follow in adapting logical organization for presentation to an audience, but all rhetorical action requires similar adaptations. At a minimum, it is necessary to begin with an introduction and to end with a conclusion.

Introductions

In Chapter 3, I listed the basic functions of an introduction: to get attention, to create accurate expectations in the audience for what follows, and to suggest the relationship between the subject and the audience. These functions are good general touchstones for anyone preparing for rhetorical action. But the introduction also serves a vital purpose in overcoming the rhetorical obstacles that you face on any given occasion. For this reason, the introduction is the first attempt to cope with these difficulties. The choices a rhetor makes should be guided by the answers to these questions:

1. What is the relationship between the rhetor and the audience? Do they share many experiences and values, or is the rhetor seen as an alien or outsider?

2. What is the attitude of the audience toward the subject and purpose? Will the audience perceive the subject as overworked and complex or as fresh, vital, and intelligible? Is the reaction to the purpose likely to be hostile and indifferent or sympathetic and interested?

3. What is the rhetor's relationship to the subject? Is she or he an expert or an interested amateur?

As these questions indicate, introductions should be adapted to the attitude of the audience toward your subject and purpose, to the relationship between you and your audience, and to the relationship between you and your subject. It is in light of these considerations that you need to gain attention, create accurate expectations, and develop connections between the subject and the audience.

Kenneth Burke wrote, "Only those voices from without are effective which can speak in the language of a voice within."* His statement emphasizes the importance of identification between a rhetor and audience and recalls the role that the rhetor plays as a context for the message. One of the most important functions of an introduction, therefore, is to create common bonds between speaker and audience, that is, to overcome the perception that the rhetor is different, not like the members of the audience. Very often, personal experience is used to create connections and to establish common grounds. For example, here is part of an introduction I used in the early 1970s before a small-town women's group.

> When I listened to Mrs. P's introduction, I thought to myself that if I were sitting out there where you are, I'd be feeling a bit wary about this Dr. Campbell who's about to speak. After all, she's got a Ph.D., she teaches in a university, and she lives in a city. Why, she's not like us.
>
> Well, I want to let you in on a secret. I grew up on a 138-acre farm in central Minnesota where I spent the first 17 years of my life. My first memories include using a child-sized hand to push down the cabbage in the two-quart jars my mother used to make sauerkraut. I may be a city slicker now, but I started out as a "sod." It's true that my life is different now, but I hope I can combine some of what I learned growing up on a farm with some of what I've learned in school and in my career to talk to you about

---

* Kenneth Burke, *A Rhetoric of Motives*, (1950; reprint ed., Berkeley: University of California Press, 1969), p. 39.

> something that concerns all women—farm women and town
> women and city women, young and old, housewives and
> professionals, mothers and grandmothers, married and single.

This part of the introduction tells you that I thought the first and
major obstacle I faced would be the perception of me as not like the
audience. If I was going to say anything about contemporary
feminism that they were going to hear, I had to create a relationship
between them and me. The introduction acknowledges our differences, it attempts to create some identification, and it suggests that
the experiences of different women are relevant to the subject to be
discussed.

But as I saw it, that wasn't the only problem I faced. Women's
liberation is controversial, a subject and a phrase that is likely to
spark immediate and intense emotional reactions (*cultural history*).
So, my introduction had a second part:

> I want to begin by telling you a story of a woman very like my
> mother who lived down the road from us. She worked on the farm,
> as my mother did, all of her life. Like most farm women, that
> didn't mean just working in the house, cleaning and cooking and
> sewing and canning. It also meant work outside—feeding the
> animals, gathering eggs, working in the fields. This woman had
> never heard of joint tenancy nor had she ever read the marriage
> laws in Minnesota. She had two sons. One was killed in W. W. II on
> one of those Pacific Islands with strange names. The other died in a
> tractor accident. When her husband died at age 61, she was all
> alone, but she hoped to stay on the farm, rent out the land, keep her
> garden, and raise chickens. But the law wouldn't allow that. It said
> that, since there was no will and everything was in her husband's
> name, only one-third was hers. The rest of his estate went to his
> nearest relative, a cousin she'd never met and who wanted his
> share now. The farm had to be sold, and there she was without a
> home and cheated out of most of what she had worked so hard to
> create.

> When people hear the phrase "Women's Liberation," they don't
> think of women like that. They think of Betty Friedan or Gloria
> Steinem. But women's liberation is about laws that cheat wives,
> laws that assume that women's work isn't real work. It's true that
> the women who write and speak are often educated and from the
> city, but that's true of most people who write and speak and are
> covered by the news. But the problems of women aren't urban and
> educated, they are legal and economic, and they affect all women.
> What I want to talk about tonight are these major concerns of the
> contemporary feminists.

This part of the introduction is an attempt to affect the audience's perception of the subject, to lessen their resistance to it, and to suggest that the subject involves issues that concern them. It is attention-getting in telling a story, and it creates expectations about what will follow in the rest of the speech.

What remained to be done was to establish a relationship between the rhetor and the subject, to describe just what expertise the speaker could claim. Thus, the introduction had a third part:

> I am not a lawyer, however, and I am not here to give you legal advice, although some of what I say may suggest that some laws need to be changed. I am here as the teacher of a course called the rhetoric of women's rights in which I and my students study the speeches and documents of 19th and 20th century feminists. Since I am personally a committed feminist, I'll present their views somewhat energetically and share with you some of the evidence these women use to support their positions. But my purpose is to try to give you what I think is an accurate picture of feminism, perhaps to correct some of the strange ideas created by the television news or headlines in the newspaper.

This part of the introduction establishes what my expertise is and is not, it reveals my bias toward feminism, and it states my purpose. It appeals to the audience to learn, to gain a more complete picture of women's liberation before making a final decision about it.

Introductions may be composed of almost any of the resources available to a rhetor—examples, analogies, statistics, quotations from authority, a literary reference, personal experience, explanation, description, and so forth. What an introduction needs to do in a given case depends on the specific obstacles you face. You always need to gain attention, create appropriate expectations, and seek to involve the audience with your subject. But how you accomplish these depends on the audience's attitude toward your subject and purpose, your relationship to the audience, and the nature of your expertise on the subject.

Conclusions

In Chapter 3, I wrote that a good conclusion (1) summarizes the major ideas that lead to the claim that is your thesis, and (2) fixes the specific purpose in the audience's mind. This is good general advice, but some refinements are now in order.

The conclusion ought to be both an ending and a climax. It should be an ending in the sense that it provides a sense of closure, a feeling of completion. Rhetorical action should end, not just stop or peter out. A conclusion can be an ending in the simplest and most obvious way—as a summary that recalls the processes by which rhetor and audience drew a conclusion. Unless the act is unusually short or the structure is very simple, a review of the arguments is highly desirable and probably necessary. If you doubt this advice, listen closely to some television commercials and note the amount of repetition that occurs even in these relatively short bits of rhetoric.

Ideally, the conclusion ought also to be the climax or emotional highpoint, and the material in the conclusion should epitomize (typify, embody) the thesis. Such a conclusion might include a story that captures the essence of what you are saying. It might present a metaphor or analogy that represents the idea. Obviously, a literary allusion or quotation, a citation from an authority, or other kinds of resources might be used as well. Here are some examples:

Many years ago when I was a student in a persuasion class I made a speech about the problem of rape. I argued that rape was a psychological crime, and that as part of the process of prevention, psychological counseling ought to be made available to any person convicted of a so-called sexual offense, however minor. At that time, the newspapers of the city where I lived were filled with stories of a rape that had ended in murder. As I was preparing my speech, the alleged perpetrator was arrested. As it turned out, he had committed a series of minor sexual crimes previously. He had also requested psychological help and been refused. In a news story just a few days before the speech, the man's mother was quoted as saying that if her son had gotten help then, perhaps the woman he had killed would be alive now. That's how I ended the speech. Admittedly, I was very lucky to have such a dramatic example of my thesis filling the headlines. But the story is an example of an epitome conclusion, that is, a conclusion in which a story (or some other device) is used to typify or embody the central idea.

Around 1970, long before the issue of Haitian refugees made headlines, a Haitian student who had emigrated to the United States with great difficulty made a speech about the unfair treatment by the U.S. government of Haitians who sought relief from their repressive government. He argued that, to be true to its principles, the United States should act as a haven for those seeking political freedom. He ended his speech this way:

Almost everyone knows the story of the good Samaritan, but almost no one remembers why Jesus told it. According to the Bible, after Jesus said that we should love our neighbors as ourselves, a young lawyer tried to trip Jesus up by asking the difficult question, but just who is my neighbor? In answer, Jesus told the story of a man beaten and robbed by thieves who was ignored by a lawyer and a priest but who was helped by a man from a place the Jews didn't think much of. As you remember, the Samaritan bandaged the man, put him on his donkey, took him to an inn, and paid for his lodging. When he finished, Jesus turned to the hair-splitting lawyer and asked him the question I'd like to ask you, "Now which of these men do you think was neighbor to him who fell among thieves?"

Outside the context of his speech, that conclusion seems melodramatic. The intensity of his feelings and his personal experience, however, made us willing to listen to such an emotional appeal. The conclusion is vulnerable because it uses a familiar story (allusion) and is highly emotional. However, its strength is the power of the story itself and of the Christian values, held by many Americans, to which it appeals.

ADAPTING YOUR
OUTLINE TO THE AUDIENCE

If you were to follow the form of your outline in presenting your ideas to the audience, your rhetorical action would be presented deductively, starting from a general conclusion and moving to illustrations and applications of it. In fact, all outlines are deductive in starting from a thesis and moving to its divisions. But such a pattern may not be the ideal way to present your ideas in all circumstances. For example, if an audience is hostile to your purpose, or if the subject is controversial, announcing your thesis might stir up resentment and prevent the audience from hearing or considering your ideas. In such a case you might want to present your ideas inductively.

Deductive Structure

The advantages of presenting your ideas in deductive order, as in your outline, are that (1) such a structure avoids ambiguity and possible misinterpretation, and (2) such a procedure is perceived as honest and straightforward. The disadvantages are that hostility may be created or increased by a blunt statement of the thesis and by a failure to acknowledge opposing viewpoints or arguments. The problems of hostility can be handled to some extent through the introduction. The clarity of this pattern is a very strong advantage. As you will note in the section on two-sided arguments (p. 245), it is possible to incorporate a deductive approach into a two-sided presentation of the pro and con arguments on an issue. However, in all cases, your choice of the pattern in which you present your materials should be a conscious one that you make after having considered carefully the obstacles that you face and the strengths and weaknesses of alternative modes of presentation.

Inductive Structure

Logically, induction is a process of going from specifics to a general conclusion. In fact, in traveling from data or evidence to a claim, induction involves the "leap" described in Chapter 9 (p. 194). You will probably follow such a pattern of thinking in the preparation of your speech or essay. But it would be strange indeed if you were to operate inductively *while you were speaking to or writing for an audience.* That would mean that you were drawing your conclusions and deciding on your thesis at the same moment you were presenting them to the audience. As a thoughtful rhetor, you will have reached conclusions before you present your ideas to an audience. However, an inductive structure is an attempt to relive for the audience the process by which you arrived at your conclusions. Obviously, you cannot replicate that process exactly. But you might shorten and streamline the process you went through while giving the listener or reader a sense of how you came to draw the conclusions you are advocating.*

The inductive format has several advantages. It is likely to increase audience involvement, as they will participate more directly in the processes by which conclusions are drawn. This form of presentation also minimizes hostility. The audience has fewer opportunities to disagree, fewer chances to dispute the positions taken by the author. But there are disadvantages. Inductive presentation takes more time or space for development. Also, unless the audience participates very actively—listens acutely or reads intently—they may miss the point, fail to draw the conclusion, and misunderstand your purpose.

---

* An exceptionally fine example of this is Virginia Woolf's *A Room of One's Own* (1929; reprint ed., New York: Harbinger, 1957).

Two-Sided Structure

As described, an outline is a brief or series of arguments developing reasons for taking one position rather than another. But many subjects of rhetorical action are controversial issues. There will be arguments on both sides that need to be considered and examined. When speaking about such an issue, you might wish to explore the opposing arguments as part of the process of explaining why you have decided to advocate another position. In effect, you look at the pool of available arguments in order to show that the weight of the evidence and of argument falls on one side or the other.

Two-sided argumentation is also more appropriate for certain audiences. A two-sided presentation allows you to incorporate refutation into your presentation. That is essential under several conditions: (1) when you know that the audience is familiar with opposing arguments or will be exposed to competing persuaders; (2) when a one-sided presentation may motivate the audience to seek out opposing views; and (3) when your opposition is also a significant part of your audience.

In the first situation, opposing arguments are already in the minds of the audience or they soon will be. As a result, it is essential that you respond to questions they have in their minds or that you prepare them for the arguments they will hear from competing persuaders. When arguments already exist in the minds of audience members, you ignore them at your peril, as they are competing with you whether you know it or not. When the audience will eventually be exposed to opposing arguments, you can inoculate them by suggesting weaknesses in the arguments, which will make them less susceptible to the appeals of competing persuaders. Without such inoculation, the arguments of opponents may become the novel arguments that shift the balance and alter opinion.

As indicated in Chapter 5, there are three conditions in which audiences seek information that challenges their beliefs or values: when audience members are of generally higher levels of education, when the information is very useful, and when the audience members' past history of exposure leads them to believe they have heard a biased or one-sided presentation. Thus, two-sided presentations are desirable with knowledgeable audiences—a highly biased or one-sided presentation can create a desire on the part of the audience for competing information. That is particularly true when the position you take is extreme or unusual. If you claim that laetrile cures cancer but don't acknowledge contradictory views, you may drive your audience to seek out competing medical studies. If you claim that there is no evidence that smoking is dangerous to health or that the amount of cholesterol in foods we eat has no effect on heart condition, you are likely to send your audience off to competing persuaders to look at the opposing evidence. At a minimum, you will need to qualify your claims. At best, you will acknowledge opposing arguments.

Finally, there are situations in which those holding opposing views are part of your target audience. One of the finest examples of two-sided argumentation is an essay on the birth of the "Black Power" slogan written by Dr. Martin Luther King, Jr.* King's opposition included more militant civil rights activists who were using the black power slogan and a more violent approach to civil rights protest. But those same persons were part of his primary audience, because he sought to reconcile these competing groups and to unify the effort for civil rights. However successful his efforts at persuasion might have been, he would have failed if he had not demonstrated to his opponents that he understood their position and respected it. As a result, the essay is both a persuasive statement for a nonviolent approach and a moving statement of why the slogan and a more militant approach have become attractive to civil rights workers. The essay is so balanced that it is an excellent source of information about the motivation of more militant civil rights groups. Despite his fair treatment of the opposition, King makes a powerful case for his own point of view. But a two-sided presentation was ideally suited to the conditions in which he found himself: competing with those whom he needed to persuade. When your opposition is also your audience, you must not only make a two-sided presentation, you must also present opposing arguments fairly and sympathetically.

Summary Outline: The Resources of Organization

  I. An outline that enables you

    A. To see the relationships among ideas

    B. To test the consistency of your development of the thesis

  II. Specific ways of developing your thesis

    A. Chronological organization

---

*"Black Power" is the second chapter of King's book, *Where Do We Go From Here: Chaos or Community?* (New York: Harper and Row, 1967). It is reprinted in Robert L. Scott and Wayne Brockriede, *The Rhetoric of Black Power* (New York: Harper and Row, 1969), pp. 25–64.

  B. Topical organization
  C. Logical organization
III. Methods of adapting materials for presentation to the audience
  A. The motivated sequence, adapted to advocate changes in policy
  B. The introduction, adapted to obstacles arising from:
    1. The relationship between rhetor and audience
    2. The relationships between audience and subject
    3. The relationship between rhetor and subject
  C. The conclusion, adapted
    1. To recall the process of argumentation
    2. To create a sense of closure
    3. To provide an emotional climax
  D. Deductive presentation, adapted
    1. To avoid ambiguity and misinterpretation
    2. To make a case straightforwardly
  E. Inductive presentation, adapted
    1. To minimize hostility
    2. To increase audience participation
  F. Two-sided presentation, adapted
    1. To refute or to inoculate against competing persuasion
    2. To present a fair and balanced view
    3. To show respect and understanding when the opposition is also the target audience

MATERIAL FOR ANALYSIS

The Vietnam War created intense controversy in the United States. Americans came to differ profoundly about the meaning of patriotism. The essay that follows deals with these controversial topics. A major strategy used by the author is structure. It was written by C. D. B. Bryan, who also wrote *Friendly Fire,** an account of how the death of a soldier in Vietnam affected his parents in Iowa. The essay appeared in the *New York Times* on Memorial Day, 1977.

---

* C. D. B. Bryan, *Friendly Fire* (New York: Putnam, 1976). This novel was made into a television movie starring Carol Burnett.

Memorial Day in Stony Creek, Conn.*

1   Last year, in time for the Bicentennial, the men of Rescue Fire Company 5 of Stony Creek, Conn. published a small "miscellany," in part to celebrate their volunteer fire company's 75th anniversary and partly to raise funds for a new fire house. The booklet contained this historical anecdote which haunts me:

2   "The British tried to make a landing at Stony Creek during the Revolutionary War but were driven back by the Stony Creek Guards. One of the British was killed, for men in the yawl boat called back: 'You've killed our Billy.' There is a bullet hole in the framework of a doorway in the Rogers homestead."

3   What I cannot drive from my mind is the anguish in that cry, "You've killed our Billy."

4   Stony Creek is the next little shoreline town down from where I live. Its amateur historians have taken careful count of its citizens who have gone off to our wars: 16 to the Revolutionary War, four to the War of 1812, and so on.

5   I went to Stony Creek's Memorial Day ceremony last year because a new monument was being dedicated to the Stony Creek men who had served during the Korean and Vietnam Wars. The polished pink granite monument came from the local quarry, and it stands now on Stony Creek's "Green"—a pie shaped wedge of grass and scraggily boxwoods so small that a less self-confident community would hesitate to call it anything more than a highway divider.

6   The Green contains a flagpole and three monuments: one with the names of the 36 men who served in World War I, another to the 116 men who served in World War II, and the third one I mentioned above. I don't know how many names are on it. I went back down there the other day to count, but I kept getting angry, losing my place, and gave up. There are too many names on it. Leave it at that.

7   Another reason I attended Stony Creek's Memorial Day service is that only about 750 families live there. My town's population is approaching 16,000, enough to guarantee that at least one politician would feel compelled to speak.

8   Pete Dougherty, the speaker at Stony Creek, is no politician. He runs the local fuel-oil company and was instrumental in having that new monument put up. The Korean- and Vietnam-era vets

---

* C. D. B. Bryan, "Memorial Day in Stony Creek, Conn." © 1977 by The New York Times Company. Reprinted by permission.

asked him to say something at its dedication, so he did. Dougherty was in the Navy in the Mediterranean during World War II, but he never joined any veterans organizations after the war. As far as I know, the only organization Dougherty joined is Rescue Fire Company 5.

9 I also went to the Stony Creek ceremony because a very small town will sometimes project a true image of this nation's mood as a whole. Small-town speakers say what they think, not what they think should be said. I went because I could not then, and still cannot, make it through a Memorial Day without getting mad, without thinking of Vietnam and being lied to, and young men being wasted.

10 In Stony Creek I hoped to gain a little perspective. The ceremony began at 8 in the morning. It was cool and misty, I remember; a light fog must have blown in from the Sound. The Stony Creek Drum Corps (with its fifes, of course) was there in its handsome Revolutionary War uniforms and with its younger members' long hair pulled neatly back and tied with ribbons.

11 The Drum Corps honor guard carried the 13-starred 1777 flag and the 1775 Cambridge flag (that's the red-and-white-striped flag with a Union Jack in the upper left-hand corner) and the current 50-star flag, too—the one Nixon wears as a lapel pin.

12 Pete Dougherty's fellow members of Rescue Fire Company 5 were also on parade; they wore dark-blue pants, stiff "railroad conductor's" caps, white ties, white web belts and bright red shirts so shiny and new I'm sure they itched. They looked very smart, though a bit shy. The whole town turned out for the ceremony around the Green. The new priest said a prayer and then Tim Zmijewski, a former Marine Vietnam vet, read the names of those on the new monument. He was chosen because he'd been badly wounded in Vietnam. And then it was Pete Dougherty's turn to speak.

13 I suspect Dougherty had practiced the first few lines about how the monument came to be because he got through that part smoothly enough, but then suddenly he sounded sore as hell.

14 Dougherty was talking about how "these kids one day got on a bus and went away, went to places we'd never heard of before until suddenly we started hearing about them a lot—the Mekong Delta, Hue, Danang, and a bloodbath was going on where our kids had been sent. They hadn't wanted to go, but they did. They went and don't you forget them!"

15 Dougherty's anger was bringing him close to tears. *"Don't you forget them!"* he told his town, and that was about all he said.

16   The Stony Creek Drum Corps struck up the National Anthem, we all sang it as best we could, and the parade to the cemetery began.

17   The town's one police car led the way, followed by three fellows in uniforms, then a combined veterans organizations' color guard; next came an old man in an old Uncle Sam suit, and the Drum Corps honor guard, followed by the Stony Creek Drum Corps, then the men of Rescue Fire Company 5; then Cub Scouts, and Brownies, and children in Colonial costumes, all carrying flowers and flags. And when they had gone by, the rest of us joined in, the whole town just sort of tagged along up Thimble Islands Road past Paine's general store, and under the New Haven Railroad tracks, left away from Bowhay Hill with the tiny islands glistening now off to port; we went by Capt. Richard N. Howd's gray-shingled Cape Cod with the hawser-rope fences, and under the shade of the big maples by Mr. Koblyanski's, then across Route 146, and on through the Stony Creek Cemetery's gates.

18   A wreath was placed at the flagpole there, the colors were dipped, a volley fired, a prayer said, and then we all followed the drummers and firemen and Scouts and Uncle Sam back onto Route 146, to a right turn on School Street, and then to Thimble Islands Road, and back down to the Green, where the march had begun.

19   It was not really much of a parade at all. It was simply a town bearing witness, honoring and remembering its dead with sadness. What Stony Creek demonstrated was a pride in its acceptance of its responsibilities—responsibilities not unlike those of its Rescue Fire Company 5 whose members every day show their willingness to risk their lives for those conflagrations that are important enough, but who shouldn't be, and are not, expected to risk their lives for those structures which might just as well burn to the ground.

20   Dougherty's rage reflected exactly Stony Creek's own anguish that it had let its young get scorched by Vietnam. What I was so struck by was that Dougherty's shock and grief and anger and sadness came across as crystal clear as that British oarsmen's cry 200 years ago: "You've killed our Billy." Dougherty and a *great many others* will be damned before we let the politicians do that to the young of our towns again.

This essay was written for an occasion, Memorial Day, and it is commemorative, part of the ritualistic process of remembering the past and those who sacrificed their lives for the nation in war. The essay is somewhat unusual because it is both an act of commemoration and an act of protest. After you have made a careful descriptive analysis, consider these questions:

1. What elements of the rhetorical problem are confronted by the author?

2. What strategies are used by the author to avoid arousing the usual sorts of controversy over the Vietnam War? How does the author use details in the narrative to define the abstract concept of patriotism? How does his definition contribute to his purpose?

3. How does Rescue Fire Company 5 function in this essay, and how does it contribute to the purpose of the essay?

4. How does the author's choice of personal narrative to structure the essay change your response? Discuss specific details of the narrative in your answer.

EXERCISE

Two-sided Presentations

Prepare a speech or write an essay organized to present two sides of a controversial topic. Select one of these obstacles as your focus:

1. Inoculating the audience against the arguments of competing persuaders or refuting the major arguments of the opposition.

2. Moderating the views of extremists, for example, urging extreme conservatives to moderate their demands on politicians, urging abortion foes to permit abortions in cases of rape, incest, or where there is a threat to the mother's life, or urging pro-abortion advocates to limit their appeals to the first trimester, and the like.

3. Acknowledging the justice of arguments on both sides while taking a point of view, for example, acknowledging the problems of censorship while arguing that the linkage of sex and violence in pornography is more significant, or acknowledging the evils of pornography while arguing that the evils of censorship are more significant.

Focus attention on the strengths and weaknesses of this form of organization and attempt to locate the particular rhetorical situations in which it is likely to be most effective.

CHAPTER 11

THE RESOURCES
OF LANGUAGE:
STYLE AND STRATEGY

The language of a rhetorical act may be casual (I can't believe I ate the whole thing!) or formal (Fourscore and seven years ago, . . .), vague (Coke adds life!) or precise (Only 2 calories in an 8 oz. glass.), figurative (A day without orange juice is like a day without sunshine.) or literal (Better things for better living through chemistry.). But whatever its style and whatever strategies are used, language is a powerful and significant resource.

However else it may be defined, rhetoric is the art of using symbols. All the resources of rhetorical action have their foundation in language. Given its importance, the student of rhetoric needs to understand the characteristics of language that allow it to play such a special role in rhetorical action.

THE NATURE OF LANGUAGE

In its ordinary sense, *language* refers to verbal symbol systems such as Japanese or English. However, language also includes other symbol systems based on space, movement, sound, pitch, time, color, and so on. In their most developed forms, such symbol systems are dance, music, sculpture, painting, architecture, and the like. Through symbol systems, we order our experiences and assign them meaning. Instead of being bombarded by billions of distinct stimuli, language enables us to make sense of the chaos so that we can perceive and respond to a world of recognizable objects and events.

There are three dimensions of language: naming, abstracting, and negation.

Naming

The first dimension of language is naming—the process by which we notice, recognize, and label certain elements or qualities in ourselves and in our world. Names permit us to identify and isolate significant events. For this reason, the vocabulary of an individual or community is a rough index of what is or has been important to that person or group, a relationship reflected in the "verbal ability" sections of many college entrance examinations.

Naming is a process of ordering the world and of focusing our attention. A name does not label one single thing but a category of relatively similar objects or events. As labels that refer to categories, names permit us to ignore the differences among objects and events and to lump them together into groups to which we can respond similarly. For example, if I identify an object as a "chair," I respond to it as a man-made object with arms or a back, intended for a category of actions labeled "sitting," and I ignore the unique characteristics of this particular chair. However, if this process of labeling and responding is to work well, there must be standards to determine when a particular object, person, or event may be included in a particular category, that is, when it may properly be labeled with a particular name. Such standards are set by definitions.

A *definition* specifies the essential qualities that something must have to be labeled in a particular way in a given linguistic community. Definitions, collected in dictionaries, give the *denotative* meanings of words. But people do not learn meanings from dictionaries. They learn meanings in situations, by having experiences with words and with the persons, events, and objects to which words are applied. In these real, concrete situations, people not only learn denotative meanings, they learn to associate the feelings they experience in these situations with the words. Such meanings are called *connotations* (*com* = together with, *notare* = to mark or note), and they refer to the associations a word calls up.

For example, some years ago while reading a William Faulkner novel, I came across the word *vicegeral.* I looked it up with some irritation (why don't I know that word? why does Faulkner use such unusual words in his novels?) and discovered that it is defined as "acting as an agent." I expected that, once I had learned it, it would reappear, but it did not. Finally, after several years had passed, I went to a performance of the play *Hadrian VII*, and heard actor Hume Cronyn make a speech that referred to the pope as acting in a vicegeral capacity. For me, *vicegeral* not only means to act as an agent, it also means one of the unusual and sometimes irritating words in a Faulkner novel, the kind of role played by a pope, a word used in the play *Hadrian VII*, and a good example to use in this book explaining how connotative meanings develop.

Semanticists (students of meaning) say that meaning is in people, not in things or even in words. The connotative meanings associated with all symbols illustrate this idea. They also show that names are not just factual or descriptive. Words are labels for our experiences so that names are *evaluative* as well as descriptive. Meanings include subjective qualities and associations—connotations.

Names are evaluative at the most basic levels because they are signs of interest and relevance. For example, if you already know the meaning of the term *vicegeral*, your knowledge would indicate past experience with the word. Like me, you may have encountered it in a novel or a play, you may be a student of the papacy, you may even have run across it in the dictionary. But I doubt that the term produces strong reactions, because it is unlikely to be a word that you associate with intense or disturbing experiences.

Contrast *vicegeral* with *masturbation*. The latter term is, for many, associated with disquieting sexual feelings and taboos. In a class on the psychology of sex at K.U. the students asked the professor not to use that word because it was so upsetting. The students decided they preferred *self-pleasuring*. Denotatively, *masturbation* and *self-pleasuring* are identical, but connotatively they are not. Masturbation calls up many highly charged associations, but self-pleasuring, a less familiar term, is unlikely to have been used to label forbidden feelings and behaviors. As a result, hearing and using it are less disturbing.

When we speak of *loaded* language, we are referring to words that produce strong feelings; the person who hears or reads them has vivid, intense associations because of emotion-laden experiences with them. No term understood by a person is simply neutral or factual. It is always bound up with experiences and will always contain evaluations resulting from feelings associated with those experiences. However, in some cases, the response is so strong that it interferes with communication. For many people, it is not possible to talk calmly about abortion or rape or welfare or busing or communism.

Connotations change. For example, at the beginning of the 1960s *Negro* had positive connotations as a term of respect. In the course of that decade, protesting blacks changed its connotations so that it was associated, negatively, with persons who sought approval from whites and who were ashamed of their culture, their past, and their physical characteristics. By contrast *black*, a term that had had very negative connotations, became associated with racial pride.

Naming, the first dimension of language, enables us to order, call attention to, focus, define, and evaluate. Names have *denotative* meanings, found in dictionaries, that define the accepted conditions for their use. Names have *connotative* meanings that reflect our experiences and associations with a term and its use. The connotations of terms can change for us as individuals and for us as members of a culture as our experiences with terms change.

Abstracting

The second dimension of language is abstracting. Abstracting is a process of leaving out details; the most basic kind of abstracting occurs with names. As a title for a category, names leave out all the distracting details. You call what you sit in a desk, ignoring its color, the gum underneath the seat, the initials written in ball-point ink, the difference between it and the desks your professors have in their offices. The most basic element in abstracting is omission—leaving out or ignoring details in order to treat different objects in similar ways.

Abstracting moves us farther and farther from concrete, specific details. In fact, we can go on and on leaving out more and more details. The word *abstract* is defined as "not concrete or specific, without reference to a specific instance, theoretical, not easily understood, abstruse." Such definitions will alert you to problems in communication that arise from abstracting. As we move farther from concrete detail, an idea or concept becomes more and more difficult to grasp. However, abstracting is also a major linguistic resource.

Symbols are abstractions that permit us to talk about an absent world. We write books about the remote past, most of whose details have vanished; we read books and talk about places we have never been; we argue about a future that is outside our experience; we explore concepts we can never see or touch. Here is an example of abstracting as a process of including more and more experience but omitting more and more detail.

Most abstract ↑	5. All of the activities and experiences involved in obtaining knowledge and skills.	"An education"
	4. All of the activities, academic and non-academic, of this institution.	"The university"
	3. All classes offered to students leading to degrees at this institution.	"The curriculum"
	2. All of the classroom experiences on MWF at 11:30 in Smith 101, Spring 1982.	"Rhetoric 102"
Least abstract	1. Concrete experiences with the individuals now in this classroom.	Abstracted by labels such as "students" and "teachers"

Even at the most concrete level in the here and now, abstraction occurs. It occurs as we label our experiences, as for example, when we ignore individual differences and label people as "students" and "teachers." As we move up each level, we include greater amounts of experience as we omit more and more details. Level 2 lumps together many hours of varied activity under a single label. Level 3 lumps together all the courses offered to students and orders them into one giant pattern. And so on.

The advantages of abstracting are evident; they are an ability to combine, for thinking and talking, ever-larger areas of experience while ignoring varied and complex detail. As we move up the ladder of abstraction, it becomes more and more difficult to understand these abstractions—they are farther and farther from our lives. It is also easy to ignore significant differences—to forget that students differ in background, age, social skills, verbal ability, maturity, and so on, and to treat them as stereotypes. Abstraction allows us to manipulate large hunks of the world verbally; it tempts us to forget that these great hunks are made up of highly varied concrete events, objects, and persons. The capacity of language to abstract permits us to talk about the absent, the past, and the future, and it allows us to conceptualize ideas such as love, truth, beauty, and rhetoric that lie far beyond our concrete experience.

Negating

Negating is the third dimension of language. Definitions are based on negating because when we say what something is we are also saying what it is not. The rhetorical power of negation is reflected in the Judeo-Christian cultural heritage. As the Ten Commandments state, "Thou shalt not . . ." But negation is very tricky, because such prohibitions imply their opposites. Carl Sandburg explained such reversals in these delightful lines from *The People, Yes:*

> "Why did the children
> pour molasses on the cat
> when the one thing we told the children
> they must not do
> was pour molasses on the cat?"*

Negation is also involved in abstracting. To abstract is to omit (negate) details and ignore (negate) differences. In fact, the ability to use symbols at all requires an understanding of negation. Whatever a name is, it is not what it stands for. "Dog" is a bit of black ink or a few sound waves, not this creature that barks, bites, wags its tail, and scratches its fleas.

Negation underlies all comparisons and contrasts, including those involved in literal and figurative analogies. As discussed in Chapter 8, literal analogies allow us to evaluate and to predict. But comparisons are also involved in definitions.

A *dialectical definition* defines by contrast. For example, if you wish to define capitalism, you might compare it to socialism and conclude that what is distinctive about it is the private ownership of the means of production. Such a definition uses socialism as a perspective through which to look at capitalism; it ignores similarities and emphasizes differences. We can also compare capitalism and democracy. In this case, the focus shifts to assumptions made about individuals. Capitalism presumes that some will have more economic power (capital) while democracy affirms the right of each individual, regardless of economic or other differences, to an equal voice in how he or she is

---

* Carl Sandburg, *The People, Yes* (New York: Harcourt, Brace and Company, 1936), no. 41, p. 82. Reprinted by permission. The nondiscursive argument implied by the Daisy spot also relies, in part, on a reversal by negation: if LBJ believes in life and love, Goldwater, his opponent, must not.

governed. If we compare capitalism and feudalism, the focus shifts to the reciprocal obligations of liege and lord and the absence of such mutual obligations between capitalist and laborer. Comparisons between capitalism and communism might emphasize the difference between production controlled by the market and production determined by state planning. In each case negation, in the form of contrast, directs our attention and shapes the definition that results. Dialectical definitions are effective ways to define highly abstract terms.

Negation is also the basis for the figurative analogy and for metaphorical language generally. The moon is not "the North Wind's cookie" or "a piece of angry candy" or "a ghostly galleon tossed upon cloudy seas." We can understand and use such metaphors precisely because we recognize that they are *not* literally true. This form of the negative extends the range of our symbols to include comparisons between anything and anything.

These, then, are the three fundamental dimensions of language: the capacities to name, to abstract, and to negate. From them come all the powers of language to influence our perceptions and our attitudes. And from them arise the specific resources of style and strategy.

STYLE

Style is what is distinctive about the language of a rhetorical act, and all rhetorical action, willy-nilly, has a style. The style of an act can vary. It can be more or less formal, more or less precise, more or less literal, and more or less redundant.

Formality

Whenever we speak or write, we make certain assumptions about what kind of language is appropriate to the situation at hand. Basically, this amounts to deciding how formal or informal we will be. Rhetorical style ranges from the formality of a presidential address or a scholarly article on the one hand to the informality of a newspaper article or a conversation with a friend on the other. Generally speaking, as style becomes more informal it becomes more conversational or colloquial.

The factors influencing the degree of formality are those already discussed as the parts of the rhetorical problem: the audience, the subject and purpose, and the rhetor. Whatever is serious and important will be presented in a more formal style. The more authoritative the rhetor is or wishes to appear, the more formal the style. The relationship between rhetor and audience also affects formality. Formal prose creates distance between rhetor and audience while informality minimizes distance.

The differences between formal and informal prose are chiefly matters of grammar, sentence structure, and vocabulary. Formal prose is strictly grammatical and uses complex sentence structure and a lofty or technical vocabulary. Informal prose is less strictly grammatical and uses short, simple sentences and ordinary, familiar words. Informal style may include sentence fragments and some colloquialisms or slang.

How formal or informal should you be? Obviously the answer depends on your subject and purpose, the role you will play, and your relationship to your audience. Most public rhetorical action observes conventional niceties of grammar, is modestly complex in sentence structure, and avoids an excessive use of colloquialisms (words or phrases found more frequently in conversation than in writing). That is, it is relatively formal, although the rhetor must determine just where on the continuum from highly formal to informal a particular rhetorical occasion should be placed.

Precision

Language can be highly precise, specific, and verifiable, or it can be ambiguous and vague. Precise language expresses ideas clearly and distinctly. It is exact and sometimes technical. Ambiguous langue is open to more than one interpretation, and vague language is inexplicit and indefinite. For the most part, good style aims for precision and avoids ambiguity.

Precise language is a symptom that a rhetorical act is emphasizing empirical evidence and logical proof. Only clearly stated arguments can be evaluated logically; only exact statements are capable of verification. Precision in language indicates purpose and reflects the rhetor's assumptions about the audience. More complex, technical subjects require the use of formal, technical vocabulary. In addition, precision reflects the expertise of the speaker or writer.

However, some apparently precise terms can be highly ambiguous. Many advertisements illustrate how technical words can confuse and mislead. "If it isn't Goodyear, it can't be Polyglas," says the ad, and

the unwary consumer may assume that Polyglas refers to an ingre-
dient unique to Goodyear tires. In fact, Polyglas is a trade name,
copyrighted by Goodyear, that conceals the fact that many brands of
tires, including Goodyear's Polyglas, are made of fiberglass belts.
Similar examples can be drawn from the jargon of the Vietnam War.
"Limited air interdiction" meant a bombing strike and "pacification"
meant total destruction.* In these cases, apparently precise terms
turn out to be vague and confusing.

The persuasive advantages of vagueness are illustrated in many
advertisements. Television commercials tell us that Coke adds life,
that Magnavox gives you more, that a brand of shampoo will make
your hair feel new again. These are pseudoclaims, statements that
sound like conclusions, but that assert nothing. What is it to add life?
What does Magnavox give more of? What does new hair feel like? In
these cases, imprecise statements are used as cues to suggest arguments or claims to viewers, and if the ads are successful, viewers
create arguments in their minds.

Some imprecision in language is inevitable. No word means one
thing only. The abstraction of language makes ambiguity inevitable.
We need some vague terms such as *middle-aged* to refer to conditions
that have no definite boundaries. We require the ambiguity of
euphemism (substituting an inoffensive term, e.g., *passed away* or
self-pleasuring, for one considered offensively explicit, e.g. *died* or *masturbation*) to deal with some highly controversial, emotionally
charged subjects. We need figurative language to make concepts vivid
and to enlarge the bases for comparison.

Stylistic precision is good for complex subjects and for exact proof.
Precision implies that the rhetor is expert. The ambiguities of
abstraction, euphemism, and figurative language are important resources for persuasion, but at the same time they open wide vistas for
confusing, misleading, and deceiving audiences.†

Literalness

The style of a rhetorical act can vary in its use of figurative or
metaphorical language. Figurative language grasps and defines the
intangible qualities of experience. Such language can be used to ex-

---

* Paul Dickson, "Demeaning of Meaning," *New York Times*, 15 April 1972, p. L 31.

† See M. Lee Williams, "The Effect of Deliberate Vagueness on Receiver Recall and
Agreement," *Central States Speech Journal* 31 (Spring 1980):30–41, for empirical evidence about the advantages and disadvantages of precision and vagueness.

plain or illustrate a difficult concept. Although it may not be verifiable, it involves another kind of precision—the vividness of immediate sensory experience. In a parody of the clichés mouthed to college graduates, Tom Lehrer wrote a song that told them "Soon you'll be sliding down the razor blade of life." Such an image is painfully vivid.

Figurative language holds our attention. The Emery Freight Company repeatedly tells us how quickly and efficiently it can move virtually anything, but we are more likely to listen to their ad because it describes objects as "pints of pickled peppers" or "tons of toothpicks," and to attend to their claims of speed phrased as picking up "red sails in the Canadian sunset" that are delivered "before the moon comes over Miami." Like the figurative analogy, the metaphor connects what is known and familiar with what is unknown and unfamiliar.

Metaphors reflect attitudes. If life is a dance, it follows a pattern and is influenced by individual artistry. If life is a chess game, it is a competitive struggle of wits. If life is a crap game, it is ruled by chance.

Metaphors evaluate. Sensory images express our values. Bad books are dry. A conservative refers to hemophiliac liberals bleeding for every cause.

There is an ongoing tension between literal and figurative language in rhetorical action. Literal language is precise and exact. It is part of the effort to produce careful proof. Metaphorical language enlivens ideas and arouses our participation. Effective rhetoric requires both.

Redundancy

Style varies in its use of repetition or restatement. Advice to writers usually suggests that they aim for economy of language, avoiding wordiness and circumlocutions. The amount of repetition needed depends on the complexity of the subject and argument and on the knowledge of the audience.

Oral style, whether in live public speeches or in radio and television commercials, differs from written style. Most commercials repeat their claims at least three times. Highly creative ads, like the Emery Freight commercial, restate an idea in several amusing ways. Some repeat the same words over and over. "Plop, plop, fizz, fizz, oh, what a relief it is," says the ad, and then says it again and again. An engaging melody and the faces and actions of actors help relieve the monotony.

Oral style must be more redundant. Because you can reread material and pause to think between paragraphs, a writer need not repeat and restate. But listeners do not have such options. As a result, successful speaking requires internal summaries, transitions connecting ideas, repetition of the major steps in the argument, and the like. Such redundancy increases both comprehension and impact for listeners. Used in print, such devices become irritating under all but the most unusual circumstances.

No other quality consistently distinguishes oral and written style. Both oral and written rhetoric range along the other dimensions. Both can be highly formal or informal. Both reflect the possibilities of precision and ambiguity, although formulations demanding the most precision appear in writing. Both exploit the possibilities of figurative language and require literal expression for careful proof. Because oral style is often related to informality, it is likely to be more personal, with greater use of personal pronouns. But the impersonality and formality of presidential addresses indicate that such qualities are not an inevitable part of oral discourse.

Evaluating Style

Good style is clear, vivid, appropriate, and consistent.

Clarity   To say that style has clarity is to say that it is immediately intelligible to the audience. There is no delay in understanding it; no translation is required. The vocabulary is familiar to the audience, the syntax meets the norms of listeners and readers, and the discourse develops according to a pattern that can be followed easily. Obviously, if you write or speak on a technical subject, all of your language will not be immediately clear to most audiences. The standard simply requires that unfamiliar terms and concepts be defined and illustrated so they can be understood by the audience. No rhetorical act can achieve its goals if it leaves the audience puzzled, confused, at sea.

Vividness   Good style is vivid. It comes alive. It makes us see and hear and imagine. It evokes feelings. It creates virtual experience. Vividness is essential to catch and hold the attention of the audience, a prerequisite to successful rhetorical action. It also speaks to the psychological dimension of proof—we must give assent not just recognize facts. Vivid style depicts, dramatizes, personifies, and describes. It employs the resources of language to focus and emphasize, to make ideas memorable. Vivid style creates associations and enriches the connotations of words and ideas.

Appropriateness   Like all other elements of rhetorical action, style is contingent upon audience, subject and purpose, occasion, and rhetor. Your style should reflect the formality of the occasion and the seriousness of your purpose. It should be suitable for the complexity of the subject, and it should be adapted to the expertise and attitudes of the audience and to them as members of a linguistic community. Your style must be appropriate to you—to your expertise on the subject, to your relationship to the audience, to the persona you present in this situation.

These statements reflect general admonitions to apply your analysis of the rhetorical problem to stylistic choices. The Material for Analysis sections at the end of most chapters provide models for rhetorical analysis; and the choices made by these specific speakers and writers should be used to refine these comments.

Consistency   Good style is consistent. All elements fit together so your discourse is a unified whole. Your language should reflect your tone, your persona, your purpose, and your relationship to the audience. Style may vary, but avoid contradictions among the elements of your rhetoric or major shifts in your perspective.

The importance of consistency should focus special attention on introductory statements. Opening lines establish tone and create expectations. As a result, stylistic choices made at the outset become important commitments for the statements that follow.

Strategies are one route by which speakers and writers achieve some of their stylistic goals.

STRATEGIES

A strategy is a plan of action, a maneuver designed to overcome the obstacles in a particular rhetorical situation. Strategies are part of rhetorical invention. They are discovered or found in your materials as you prepare for rhetorical action, and they are part of the creativity of your role as a rhetor. Strategies are used to cope with controversial and complex issues, with hostile and skeptical audiences, and with difficulties in establishing your credibility and expertise as a source.

Many of the resources already discussed can and should be used strategically. Evidence should be selected and presented strategically to speak to the audience, to refute competing persuaders, to present your subject and perspective clearly. Each organizational pattern is a strategic way of unfolding a position. The arguments you select should be chosen strategically for the response you seek and the audience you want to reach. Introductions and conclusions are particularly important as strategic responses to the rhetorical problem. In the speeches and essays you analyze, consider how speakers and writers have used opening and closing statements to respond to the obstacles in a particular situation.

Despite the strategic character of most rhetorical choices, specific strategies are usually devices that exploit the capacities of language. Although their purposes overlap, strategies are designed to assist in proof, to make ideas vivid, and to create connotations. All strategies require participation by the audience and illustrate the fact that rhetorical action is jointly constructed by rhetor and audience.

Strategies of Proof

Strategies of proof resemble or mimic logical arguments. Through the identification and participation of the audience, they appear to justify a claim or conclusion.

Rhetorical Question   A *rhetorical question* is a question to which no answer is expected or to which only one answer can be given. It is an idea put in the form of a question for greater effect. It is a question whose answer is known by the audience. Presidential campaigns often include rhetorical questions. In 1952, Dwight D. Eisenhower said, "The Democrats say you never had it so good. Do you want it any better?" That's a particularly effective rhetorical question because few people would answer no. But it was a highly strategic choice for Ike in this campaign. It allowed the audience to supply the defects of the Democrats so that the heroic candidate did not have to stoop to making nasty charges. In 1980, Ronald Reagan asked, "Can anyone look at the record of this Administration and say, 'Well done'? Can anyone compare the state of our economy when the Carter Administration took office with where we are today and say, 'Keep up the good work'? Can anyone look at our reduced standing in the world today and say, 'Let's have four more years of this'?"* Once again, the questions need no answer. Note that they also present Reagan as merely expressing what all of us know (the questions work as enthymemes) rather than as making charges against our president, and that the questions direct our attention to economic and foreign policy issues.

A Fortiori   *A fortiori* is an organizational strategy. It connects two claims so that if we accept the first, it becomes more likely we will accept the second. For example, if it can be shown that a politician betrayed a close friend who trusted him, it becomes more plausible that he would betray his constituents. An example of this kind of structure was given in Chapter 10 to illustrate topical structure. If it can be shown that women are discriminated against overtly in law, it becomes more plausible that they are discriminated against covertly in socialization. Again, the strategy aims at proof. Where arguments are in an *a fortiori* relationship, the claim in the second is made more likely by proof of the first.

Enumeration   *Enumeration* is a bill of particulars, a list of examples. If done well, we are swamped with a mass of details, and each particular or example gains force from all those that have preceded it. For example, feminist Jo Freeman used enumeration as part of her proof to show the effects of socialization on women:

> To understand how most women are socialized we must first understand how they see themselves . . . [one study] showed that women strongly felt themselves to be such things as uncertain, anxious, nervous, hasty, careless, fearful, dull, childish, helpless, sorry, timid, clumsy, stupid, silly, and domestic. On a more positive side women felt they were: understanding, tender, sympathetic, pure, generous, affectionate, loving, moral, kind, grateful, and patient.†

This long list of adjectives functions strategically to overwhelm us with evidence of the negative attitudes women have toward them-

---

* "Acceptance Speech," *New York Times,* 18 July 1980, p. A 8.

† "The Building of the Gilded Cage," in Karlyn Kohrs Campbell, *Critiques of Contemporary Rhetoric* (Belmont, Calif.: Wadsworth, 1972), p. 165. The study cited was that by Edward M. Bennett and Larry R. Cohen, "Men and Women: Personality Patterns and Contrasts," *Genetic Psychology Monographs* 59 (1959):101–155.

selves. However, note that the list works only if you see these self-descriptions negatively. If these are qualities you believe desirable in a "true woman," the strategy will fail.

Refutation   *Refutation* involves answering and rejecting the arguments of the opposition. In an organizational pattern that examines arguments pro and con, it can work strategically to answer questions in the minds of the audience and to inoculate them against competing persuaders. One form of refutation, however, deserves special mention. *Debunking* refutes opposing positions by making fun of exaggerated claims. Debunking is a process of deflating pretense, of shrinking opposing arguments to their "proper" size. It is often done through names that serve as labels. For example, a public speaking text discusses the problems of using slang and jargon, and the authors write:

> The observations about the use of slang apply also to the use of the special terminology and jargon of, let us say, sports commentators, the entertainment world as represented in the publication *Variety*, and such cults as the libbers and the discotheque enthusiasts.*

Feminists are being debunked as "libbers" and as extremists and fanatics (a cult). That it is feminists who are being debunked is most evident if we rewrite the paragraph to make the style consistent: "the special terminology and jargon of, let us say, sports jockeys, show biz gossip, and such cults as the libbers and disco freaks." Now each group is treated with equal informality, and all are debunked by unflattering labels.

Once again, note that the strategy depends on the beholder. The strategy is most evident to feminists who resent such chummy labels and is least evident to those who share the authors' views. Note that the list of examples also functions as *enumeration*.

Definition   Those with experience in debate will know that *definitions* are strategic. Definitions are critical elements in determining just what must be proved in order to establish a claim. The dialectical definitions discussed earlier are also examples of strategic definitions. Definitions explain highly abstract terms, and they are often used in an attempt to change the perceptions of the audience. For example,

---

* Donald C. Bryant and Karl R. Wallace, *Fundamentals of Public Speaking*, 5th ed. (Englewood Cliffs, N.J.: Prentice-Hall, 1976), pp. 320–321.

the civil disobedience practiced by civil rights protesters met with strong disapproval. Dr. Martin Luther King, Jr., used the strategy of definition to deal with this problem:

> Agape is more than romantic love, agape is more than friendship. Agape is understanding, creative redemptive good will to all men. It is an overflowing love which seeks nothing in return.
> Theologians would say that it is the love of God operating in the human heart. So that when one rises to love on this level, he loves men not because he likes them, not because their ways appeal to him, but he loves every man because God loves him. And he rises to the point of loving the person who does an evil deed while hating the deed that the person does. I think this is what Jesus meant when he said, "love your enemies."*

King's statement combines a number of strategies. It defines by *enumerating* the various meanings of agape and by referring to a statement made by Jesus in the Bible (an *allusion*). This definition will be most effective for Christians in the audience. Note, however, that if accepted, this definition will create more positive attitudes toward civil disobedience in those being addressed.

Other strategies aid the rhetor in making arguments and substantiating claims, but these are the most important. These examples should illustrate the nature of these strategies and the fact that strategies appear in combination and depend on the participation of the audience.

Strategies to Animate and Vivify

Nearly all strategies catch and hold attention and, in that sense, make ideas more vivid. But some strategies have this as their chief function. They are intended to make people and events come alive before our eyes, to create virtual experience by allowing us to see and hear and feel what the rhetor is talking about.

Description   *Description* provides the detail that makes a scene or person come alive before our eyes. It creates the sensation that you

---

* "Love, Law, and Civil Disobedience," in *Contemporary American Speeches*, 4th ed., ed. Wil A. Linkugel, R. R. Allen, and Richard L. Johannesen (Dubuque, Iowa: Kendall/Hunt, 1978), p. 79.

are there watching events as they occur. For example, the Walker
Report used this eyewitness account to describe the kinds of confron-
tations that occurred between police and demonstrators in Chicago in
1968:

A federal legal official relates an experience of Tuesday evening.
I then walked one block north where I met a group of 12–15
policemen. I showed them my identification and they permitted
me to walk with them. The police walked one block west. Numerous people were watching us from their windows and balconies.
The police yelled profanities at them, taunting them to come down
where the police would beat them up. The police stopped a number
of people on the street demanding identification. They verbally
abused each pedestrian and pushed one or two without hurting
them. We walked back to Clark Street and began to walk north
where the police stopped a number of people who appeared to be
protesters, and ordered them out of the area in a very abusive way.
One protester who was walking in the opposite direction was
kneed in the groin by a policeman who was walking towards him.
The boy fell to the ground and swore at the policeman who picked
him up and threw him to the ground. We continued to walk toward
the command post. A derelict who appeared to be very intoxicated,
walked up to the policeman and mumbled something that was
incoherent. The policeman pulled from his belt a tin container and
sprayed its contents into the eyes of the derelict, who stumbled
around and fell on his face.*

This instance illustrates the convergence of evidence and strategy.
The cited material is *testimony* (an eye-witness account) that provides
a series of *examples* of police behavior. Because the eye witness is
described as "a federal legal official," his observations move toward
authority evidence: he may be competent to judge what is improper
behavior and his status gives his reports greater credibility. But it is
the descriptive details that give this evidence its force. The police
"yell," "taunt," "abuse," and "push." As described, the attack on the
"boy" is wholly unprovoked and because it is an attack on a boy, it is
doubly offensive (note that the fact that the policeman can pick him
up and throw him to the ground lends credence to this label). The

---

* Daniel Walker, "A Summary of the Walker Report," in *Counterpoint: Dialogue for the
70s,* ed. Conn McAuliffe (Philadelphia: J.B. Lippincott, 1970), p. 153.

description gives us the sense of walking down the street with this group and watching what occurs. We come to see the events as the observer does and to judge them, unfavorably, with him. Such descriptions are particularly effective ways to induce readers to participate in creating the proofs by which they are persuaded.

Depiction   *Depiction* literally means to represent in picture or sculpture or to picture completely. It is a particularly vivid form of description, and it usually involves *dramatization,* presenting material as a drama of characters in conflict. If successful, it should create virtual experience. The most famous example of depiction in rhetorical literature occurs in a speech by Senator Daniel Webster of Massachusetts given in reply to Senator Robert Y. Hayne of South Carolina in 1830. The crux of the debate was the issue of slavery and the power of the federal government to regulate it. Hayne advocated state nullification, and Webster argued that this doctrine must inevitably lead to war. But Webster chose to make his case through depicting what must happen if a state should nullify a federal law. He uses the tariff law and nullification by South Carolina as his example:

> We will take the existing case of the tariff law. South Carolina is said to have made up her opinion upon it. . . . She will, we must suppose, pass a law of her legislature, declaring the several acts of Congress, usually called the tariff laws, null and void, so far as they respect South Carolina, or the citizens thereof. So far, all is a paper transaction, and easy enough.

(At this point, Webster has set the scene for his depiction.)

> But the collector at Charleston is collecting the duties imposed by these tariff laws. He, therefore, must be stopped. The collector will seize the goods if the tariff duties are not paid. The State authorities will undertake their rescue, the marshal, with his posse, will come to the collector's aid, and here the contest begins.

(The depiction includes a drama, and Webster prepares us for conflict.)

> The militia of the State will be called out to sustain the nullifying act. They will march, Sir, under a very gallant leader; for I believe the honorable member [Hayne] himself commands the militia of

that part of the State. He will raise the *nullifying act* on his standard, and spread it out as his banner! It will have a preamble, setting forth, that the tariff laws are palpable, deliberate, and dangerous violations of the Constitution! He will proceed, with his banner flying, to the custom-house in Charleston,

> All the while,
> Sonorous metal blowing martial sounds.

Arrived at the custom-house, he will tell the collector that he must collect no more duties under any of the tariff laws. . . . But, Sir, the collector would not, probably, desist, at his bidding. He would show him the law of Congress, the treasury instruction, and his own oath of office. He would say, he should perform his duty, come what might.

Here would ensue a pause; for they say that a certain stillness precedes the tempest. The trumpeter would hold his breath awhile, and before all this military array should fall on the custom-house, collector, clerks, and all, it is very probable some of those composing it would request of their gallant commander-in-chief to be informed a little upon the point of law; for they have, doubtless, a just respect for his opinions as a lawyer, as well as for his bravery as a soldier. . . . They would inquire, whether it was not somewhat dangerous to resist a law of the United States. What would be the nature of their offence, they would wish to learn, if they, by military force and array, resisted the execution in Carolina of a law of the United States, and it should turn out, after all, that the law *was constitutional?* He would answer, of course, Treason. No lawyer could give any other answer. . . . How, then, they would ask, do you propose to defend us? We are not afraid of bullets, but treason has a way of taking people off that we do not much relish. How do you propose to defend us? "Look at my floating banner," he would reply; "see there the *nullifying law!*" Is it your opinion, gallant commander, they would then say, that, if we should be indicted for treason, that same floating banner of yours would make a good plea in bar? "South Carolina is a sovereign State," he would reply. That is true; but would the judge admit our plea? "These tariff laws," he would repeat, "are unconstitutional, palpably, deliberately, dangerously." That may all be so; but if the tribunal should not happen to be of that opinion, shall we swing for it? . . .

Mr. President, the honorable gentleman would be in dilemma, like that of another great general. He would have a knot before him which he could not untie. He must cut it with his sword. He must say to his followers, "Defend yourselves with your bayonets"; and this is war,—civil war.*

This excerpt from Webster's speech is justly famous as an outstanding example of the depiction of a *hypothetical* encounter, and like many strategies, it combines animation and demonstration. As proof, it *spells out the consequences* of Hayne's position, but the proof depends on the plausibility of the scene for the listener. It is highly effective *refutation* that shows that, contrary to Hayne, nullification means civil war. The humor of the depiction serves to *debunk* Hayne's position, to reduce it to absurdity. Webster also uses an *allusion* to the story of Alexander the Great cutting the Gordian knot as a figurative analogy to illustrate that Hayne's position must end in violence. Webster's depiction is structured as a drama. He sets the scene, presents characters, sets forth the conflict, presents the dialogue between Hayne and his militia, and even provides the theatrical spectacle of banners and trumpets. The conflict within the doctrine, dramatized in the dialogue, escalates to a climax, which is followed by a denouement that draws his conclusion: "This is war,—civil war."

The detail Webster provides is worth noting. The marshall and his posse, supporting the federal customs collector, confront Hayne and the state militia. The acts of the collector are detailed. The dialogue between Hayne and the militia men spells out the internal contradiction in Hayne's position.

Webster might easily have chosen to detail these consequences in a logical argument, but depicting this scene animated his claim, a process that was essential if civil war was to be averted. Webster attempted to create virtual experience, to allow his listeners to imagine a scene in all its detail, so that they would perceive, in human terms, the results of Hayne's position.

Personification and Visualization   Closely allied to description and depiction are the strategies of personification and visualization. *Personification* represents an object or an abstract idea as if it were a human being or had human capacities. Advertisers personify products as cartoon characters, such as Mr. Clean or the Michelin tire man. The cleaning power of a detergent and the strength of a tire cannot be seen or experienced. The strategy of personification at-

---

*Daniel Webster, "Reply to Hayne," in *Famous Speeches in American History*, ed. Glenn R. Capp (Indianapolis: Bobbs-Merrill, 1963), pp. 57–58.

tempts to overcome this problem. *Visualization* puts an idea into visual form. A familiar example is the long-running series of commercials that shows a person drinking a glass of iced tea and then falling backwards into a swimming pool. The ad visualizes how you feel when you drink a glass of cold, refreshing iced tea.

Enactment   *Enactment* is both proof and a way to present evidence vividly. Enactment occurs when the speaker or writer is proof of the claim that she or he is making. For example, Rep. Barbara Jordan gave the keynote address at the Democratic National Convention in 1976. In her speech she said, "And I feel that, notwithstanding the past, my presence here is one additional piece of evidence that the American dream need not forever be deferred."* The very fact that she, a black woman, had achieved the stature to be asked to give the address was proof that blacks and women can reach the highest levels of achievement in America here and now. Similarly, recall the student speech on the 55 mph speed limit. The student, covered with scratches and bruises, was himself proof that travel over 55 mph was hazardous. Enactment is powerful evidence because members of the audience see and hear the evidence for themselves, directly. The proof is particularly vivid—it is alive in front of them!

Other Animating Strategies   *Alliteration, assonance, rhyme,* and *rhythm* are some of the ways of arranging words so that ideas and phrases become more vivid and memorable. *Alliteration* is the repetition of initial consonants, a strategy Spiro Agnew used effectively. He called antiwar critics, for example, "*n*attering *n*abobs of *n*egativism." Commercials also use this technique to make ideas vivid, as in the previously cited, "*p*ints of *p*ickled *p*eppers" and "*t*ons of *t*oothpicks from *T*ucson."

Assonance is the repetition of a vowel sound, and it produces a kind of rhyme. In his inaugural address, for example, John F. Kennedy spoke of "the st*ea*dy spr*ea*d of the d*ea*dly atom." The repetition made the phrase memorable and the creeping vowel seemed to mirror the creeping danger. Actual rhymes occur less frequently in both oral and written rhetoric. The most interesting contemporary examples occur in the speeches of Malcolm X, who said, "We have to stop *singing* and start *swinging*." The historian Daniel Boorstin used rhymes to create associations. In an attack on student and black protesters, he con-

---

* The *New York Times*, 15 July 1976, p. 26.

trasted *egalitarians* with *egolitarians* (these protesters) and called them apa*thetes* who resembled the aes*thetes* of the past.* Such rhymes not only make ideas vivid, they work to change the attitudes of the reader.

Parallelism is a strategy that creates rhythm in prose. It can also enhance the precision of language and create an impression that the rhetor thinks in a very orderly fashion. Perhaps the most famous example is the repeated "I have a dream . . ." in Dr. Martin Luther King, Jr.'s famous speech of that name. Like King's speech, it may take the form of a series of sentences or paragraphs, all of which begin with the same phrase. For example, in his inaugural address, John F. Kennedy addressed his statements, "To those old allies, . . . To those new states, . . . To those peoples in the huts, . . . To our sister republics . . ." He began each of his statements addressed to adversaries with the phrase, "Let both sides . . ." Such parallelism creates patterns that are easy for listeners to follow, and such patterns help fix ideas in our minds.

Parallelism can also create contrast and emphasis. *Antithesis* is a kind of parallelism that contrasts one idea with another. Two examples in contemporary speeches have proved particularly memorable. In 1960 John F. Kennedy said, "Ask not what your country can do for you: Ask what you can do for your country." In 1964 Barry Goldwater accepted the Republican nomination for the presidency and said, "I would remind you that extremism in the defense of liberty is no vice! And let me remind you also that moderation in the pursuit of justice is no virtue!" Antitheses juxtapose two ideas, and the contrast not only defines the speaker's position more clearly, it animates it with emphasis.

Climax constructions are also a form of parallelism. In a climax construction, repetition builds to a high point of excitement or tension, a climax. For example, consider the climax created in paragraph 9 of Edward Kennedy's speech to the midterm Democratic convention in 1978 (see page 144). Kennedy argues that Democrats "are the heirs of a great tradition in American public life." He supports that statement and then uses it to call for passage of national health insurance based on this climax construction: "Our party took up the cause of jobs for the unemployed in the great depression. Our party took up the cause of civil rights for black and brown Americans and the cause

---

* "The New Barbarians," in *The Rhetoric of No*, ed. Ray Fabrizio et al. (New York: Holt, Rinehart and Winston, 1970), pp. 94–102.

of equal rights for women in America and the people of the District of Columbia. And in that same tradition of leadership it is time for the Democratic Party to take up the cause of health." Notice how the strategy seems to make this outcome inevitable. In this case, if we accept the great tradition of the past, we must be committed to this policy. A similar climactic process is found in the conclusion of the last speech of Dr. Martin Luther King, Jr., which is reprinted at the end of this chapter.

Finally, recall that parallelism also appears in patterns of organization. Ideally, main points in an essay or speech will be stated in parallel form so that major ideas will stand out for the reader or listener.

Once again, these are only some of the strategies that can be used to make ideas vivid. Sources cited at the end of the chapter will lead you to more extended discussions of such devices.

Strategies to Change Connotations

The strategies described in this section are directed at our attitudes. They are attempts to change associations so that we will become more positive or negative toward an idea or position. Successful rhetorical action changes verbal behavior. Our speech reflects our perceptions, understandings, and attitudes, and if these change, our speech will change. But the reverse is also true: if we change the way we talk, changes in perception and attitude will follow.

The preceding statement is highly controversial although the protest movements of blacks and chicanos illustrate the power of a name change to mobilize a social movement.* The argument is at the heart of disputes over whether or not the pronoun "he" or the word "man" can function generically to include both men and women. Feminists present examples to show that they cannot, as in "Man, being a mammal, breast-feeds his young." They also argue that shifts in words, such as the use of *chair* or *chairperson,* and in pronouns, "s/he" or "he *and* she," raise consciousness about the sexism of our society.†

---

* See Karlyn Kohrs Campbell, "The Rhetoric of Radical Black Nationalism," *Central States Speech Journal* 22 (Fall 1971): 151–160, and Richard J. Jensen and John C. Hammerback, "Radical Nationalism among Chicanos: The Rhetoric of José Angel Gutiérrez," *Western Journal of Speech Communication* 44 (Summer 1980): 191–202.

† See, for example, Wendy Martyna, "Beyond the 'He/Man' Approach: The Case for Nonsexist Language," *Signs* 5 (Spring 1980): 482–493.

In all these cases, all the parties involved behave as if the words we use are very, very important.

Labeling   *Labeling* is the commonest strategy used to alter attitudes, and it is often related to *debunking.* A label is a name, an epithet, chosen to characterize the nature of a person or thing. For example, one conservative, referring to Ronald Reagan's choice of George Bush as a running mate, said that Reagan sounded like Winston Churchill but behaved like Neville Chamberlain. Because of the Munich agreement, Chamberlain has become a symbol of compromise and betrayal. By associating Reagan's actions with those of Chamberlain, we are asked to view them unfavorably. In this case, the label is also an historical *allusion.*

Labels work by creating associations. The language Spiro Agnew used in his attacks on the news media illustrate this process. Instead of using short, ordinary words, Agnew always chose complex, unfamiliar, Latinate terms. He referred to media criticism as querulous (nitpicking), he said that newsmen disparage (not belittle), he spoke of veracity (not truth), of expunging (not erasing), and so on. The use of such 50¢ words dignified and intellectualized what were rather nasty attacks. They made him seem more authoritative, more competent to criticize journalistic excesses. In this case, labels not only alter associations negatively, but affect our perception of the speaker's tone, persona, and style (ethos).

Slogans   *Slogans* are expanded labels. They are highly effective because they condense into a single phrase or sentence a whole world of beliefs and feelings. This power to sum up is illustrated in phrases such as "the American dream," "a new deal," "the iron curtain," and "rugged individualism." They are powerful unifiers because, while all of us have our own ideas of just what they mean, the level of abstraction is such that all disputes over meaning are avoided.*

An effective slogan draws together a whole world of ideas in a short, cleverly expressed phrase or sentence. Advertisers seek such catchphrases: "Progress is our most important product." "Join the Pepsi generation!" "Everything you always wanted in a beer. And less." Every presidential campaign manager tries to find such a slogan, because, in a short, memorable phrase, it can sum up many associations and evoke strong reactions.

---

* Murray Edelman, *The Symbolic Uses of Politics* (Chicago: Markham, 1971), pp. 6–11, discusses the powerful role of condensation symbols in political rhetoric.

Metaphors   Many labels and slogans are also *metaphors*. Figurative language not only makes ideas vivid, it changes our attitudes toward them and it clarifies meaning. A particularly famous example comes from the speech Booker T. Washington made at the Atlanta Exposition in 1895. Washington, a black, tried to allay the hostility of whites while urging them to support the economic and educational development of blacks. The metaphor he used illustrates how metaphors can clarify, vivify, and change connotations. He said, "In all things that are purely social we can be as separate as the fingers, yet one as the hand in all things essential to mutual progress."*

Allusion   Closely related to metaphors are *allusions* to items from our shared cultural knowledge, such as references to history, the Bible, Greek mythology, Shakespeare's plays or other works of great literature, or items from the popular culture such as television programs or comic books. James N. Rowe used allusions to define the conditions of a prisoner of war:

> It is not the Hogan's Heroes concept that many people have, because in South Vietnam and in North Vietnam, we found that an American prisoner of war is not a military prisoner, he is a political prisoner. . . . The American prisoners find themselves being manipulated and being made more pliable by Communists using principles that we have read about in Koestler's *Darkness at Noon*, perhaps in *1984*.†

In this case, Rowe is struggling with the cultural history of a subject that has been distorted by a television program depicting prison camp life in humorous terms. Rather than merely describing conditions, Rowe uses allusions to two novels as a kind of shorthand to suggest the grim conditions prisoners faced.

Biblical materials are also a common source of allusion. Such materials are frequently used to demonstrate that God is on our side or we are doing God's will. For example, in defending American involvement in Vietnam, Richard Nixon said, "Let historians not record that when America was the most powerful nation in the world we

---

* Booker T. Washington, "Atlanta Exposition Address," *Famous Speeches in American History*, ed. Glenn Capp (New York: Bobbs-Merrill, 1963), 115.

† James N. Rowe, "An American Prisoner of War in South Vietnam," in *Contemporary American Speeches*, ed. Linkugel, Allen, and Johannesen, p. 57.

passed on the other side of the road and allowed the last hopes for peace and freedom of millions of people on this earth to be suffocated by the forces of totalitarianism."* The allusion is to the story of the good Samaritan, and Nixon's allusion is intended to convince us that in Vietnam we are behaving as good neighbors.

Allusions can be used to perform acts that would not be acceptable to an audience if they were done directly and explicitly. Most audiences, for example, do not take kindly to being threatened. Yet, in what is surely one of the most controversial of all Fourth of July addresses, the black abolitionist orator Frederick Douglass used the story of Samson in Judges 16:23–30 to threaten the audience:

> The Fourth of July is yours, not mine. You may rejoice, I must mourn. To drag a man in fetters into the grand illuminated temple of liberty, and call upon him to join you in joyous anthems, were inhuman mockery and sacrilegious irony. Do you mean, citizens, to mock me by asking me to speak today? If so, there is a parallel to your conduct. And let me warn you that it is dangerous to copy the example of a nation whose crimes, towering up to heaven, were thrown down by the breath of the Almighty, burying that nation in irrevocable ruin!†

If you know the story of Samson (captured by the Philistines, blinded, taken to Gaza, brought to the temple for sport on the feast day of their god Dagon, praying for strength, pulling down the temple, and killing more Philistines in death than he had in life), there are powerful parallels between it and the situation of Frederick Douglass on July 4, 1852. But if you do not know the story, you may not recognize the allusion, much less feel its impact. Allusions work only if the audience recognizes them and can fill in the necessary details. Biblical allusions are powerful, if they are familiar, because our culture is Judeo-Christian and many persons accept the Bible as the word of God. For contemporary readers, that is only half the problem. To appreciate the parallels one must know biographical facts about Douglass (an escaped former slave speaking in a state, New York, in which slavery

---

* Speech delivered November 3, 1969, printed in *Congressional Record*, Vol. 115, Part 24, pp. 32784–32786.

† An excerpt from this speech that includes the allusion can be found in *Critical Anthology of Public Speeches*, ed. Kathleen M. Jamieson (Chicago: Science Research Associates, 1978), p. 20.

was still legal) and the place and period in which he spoke. These problems illustrate the limitations of allusions, which depend on knowledge in the minds of the audience.

Identification   Finally, the strategy of *identification* uses language to create positive associations between the rhetor and the audience; it suggests shared experience or common viewpoints. For example, Robert Kennedy, in the introduction to his Law Day Address at the University of Georgia, both created identification and made fun of the strategy itself:

> For the first time since becoming Attorney General, over three months ago, I am making something approaching a formal speech, and I am proud that it is in Georgia. Two months ago I had the very great honor to present to the President, Donald Eugene McGregor of Brunswick, Georgia. Donald McGregor came to Washington to receive the Young American Medal for Bravery. . . . And, as the President said, Donald McGregor is a fine young American—one of a long line of Georgians who have, by their courage, set an outstanding example for their fellow Americans.
>
> They have told me that when you speak in Georgia you should try to tie yourself to Georgia and the South, and even better, claim some Georgia kinfolk. There are a lot of Kennedys in Georgia. But as far as I can tell, I have no relatives here and no direct ties to Georgia, except one. This state gave my brother the biggest percentage majority of any state in the union and in this last election that was even better than kinfolk.*

The first paragraph creates identification in a traditional and serious way. The speaker praises someone who is also admired by his audience, and he praises qualities admired by them. He does honor to his audience by identifying this brave young man as one of a long line of Georgians with similar qualities. The second paragraph creates identification indirectly by honestly acknowledging differences: the speaker has no family ties with Georgians or Southerners. However, the statement that Georgia gave strong support to his brother in the last election suggests that the speaker and the audience have strong ties of party, ideology, and policy.

---

*Glenn R. Capp, ed., *The Great Society: A Sourcebook of Speeches* (Belmont, Calif.: Dickenson, 1967), p. 75.

Speakers and writers traditionally identify ties of kinship, shared beliefs, and common experience as ways to create bonds between themselves and the audience. When the urbane and highly educated Adlai Stevenson spoke at a plowing contest in Kasson, Minnesota, he said "I am myself a farmer, I own farm land in Illinois, and I come from a family that has lived in the heart of the Corn Belt for over a hundred years." When Winston Churchill, a British subject, spoke before a joint session of the American Congress, he referred to his "American forebears" and reminded the audience that his mother had been an American: "By the way, I cannot help reflecting that if my father had been American and my mother British, instead of the other way around, I might have got here on my own." Later in his speech he described his political philosophy as a commitment to "the Gettysburg ideal of government of the people, by the people, and for the people." This last reference not only establishes shared values, but it locates them in the words of an American president, Abraham Lincoln, and in an American document, his Gettysburg Address. In addition, the phrase that he quotes, "of the people, by the people, and for the people," is an *allusion* and a phrase that functions as a kind of *slogan* that sums up the most basic ideas of democracy.

These, then, are strategies that serve primarily to alter attitudes toward people, objects, events, or ideas. The most basic is the *label*, which designates in an evaluative way so that the name colors our perception or response. The label works by *association*, connecting the qualities associated with a category with the person or thing or idea labeled. Closely related to the label is the *slogan*, which sums up a whole series of feelings and experiences in a cleverly put and memorable statement. *Allusions* to items in popular culture, literature, the Bible, or history also serve to change the emotional valence. Allusions may work to compare or contrast or they may serve to designate. Allusions may be used subtly to make an argument, as in the threat made by Frederick Douglass. *Metaphorical* language serves both to make ideas vivid and memorable and to alter an audience's emotional response to an idea. Finally, language that creates *identification* between rhetor and audience works to alter the audience's attitude toward the rhetor and the rhetor's purpose.

These are some of the strategies available for rhetorical action. Strategies are techniques that use language to prove, vivify, and alter attitudes. Each of these functions is a central element in rhetoric. Strategies provide important resources by which to overcome the obstacles of the rhetorical problem.

SUMMARY

The fundamental capacities of language, to name, abstract, and negate, enable us to perform these and other symbolic actions. Style is an encompassing term that describes the possibilities that exist in word choice and grammar. Style can vary in formality, precision, literalness, and redundancy. Good style is clear, vivid, appropriate, and consistent. The resources of style are increased by strategies that contribute to proof, animate, and change connotations.

Summary Outline

I. Language (here, verbal symbol systems) has three dimensions.
  A. Naming is the process of noticing, identifying, and labeling elements in ourselves and our world.
    1. Names have denotative meanings (definitions).
    2. Names have connotative meanings that reflect our experiences and feelings.
  B. Abstracting allows us to omit details.
    1. Naming involves abstraction.
    2. We can omit more and more details, referring to ever-larger wholes.
  C. Negating reflects the relationship between words and things.
    1. Whatever a word is, it is not what it signifies.
    2. Naming requires us to ignore differences.
    3. Abstracting requires us to omit details.
    4. Figurative language rests on negation.
II. Stylistic choices are rhetorical choices.
  A. As style becomes more informal, it becomes more conversational.
  B. Precision reflects an emphasis on empirical evidence and logical proof, but ambiguity can be persuasive.
  C. Figurative language grasps and depicts intangible qualities of experience.
  D. The level of redundancy should reflect the subject's complexity and the audience's knowledge.
III. Good style is clear, vivid, and appropriate.
  A. Good style is immediately intelligible.
  B. Good style creates virtual experience.
  C. Good style fits the subject, occasion, purpose, and rhetor.

IV. Strategies are linguistic resources for overcoming rhetorical obstacles.

    A. Some strategies resemble logical arguments.

    B. Some strategies create virtual experience.

    C. Some strategies change connotations and alter attitudes.

SOURCES

Blankenship, Jane. *A Sense of Style: An Introduction to Style for the Public Speaker.* Belmont, Calif.: Dickenson, 1968. A more extended treatment of style for the public speaker.

Langer, Susanne K. *Philosophy in a New Key,* 3d ed. Cambridge, Mass.: Harvard University Press, 1942. Basic reading for those who wish to understand the dimensions and capacities of language.

Newman, Robert S. *Language for Writing.* Belmont, Calif.: Dickenson, 1967. An excellent introduction to style for writing.

Osborn, Michael. *Orientations to Rhetorical Style.* Chicago: Science Research Associates, 1976. An excellent short work on the resources of style and strategy in rhetorical action.

Strunk, William, Jr., with revisions by E. B. White. *The Elements of Style,* 3d ed. New York: Macmillan, 1979. Elementary rules of composition, usage, and style are provided by this clear and readable work.

MATERIAL FOR ANALYSIS

The speeches of the Reverend Dr. Martin Luther King, Jr., are well known as masterpieces of rhetorical adaptation and as models of rhetorical style. When he made his last speech in Memphis, Tennessee, on the night that he was murdered, he faced many obstacles. A strike by sanitation workers had begun on February 12, 1968, and little progress had been made.* A protest march led by King earlier,

---

* For a detailed analysis of how the rhetoric of the municipal establishment contributed to a lack of progress, see John Bakke, "A Study of Establishment Rhetoric during the Sanitation Strike in Memphis, 1968." (Manuscript housed in the Missouri Valley Collection, Memphis State University Library.).

on March 28, 1968, was poorly planned and organized, and ended in violent encounters between marchers and police. The momentum of the civil rights movement as a whole had lessened, and King was struggling to be an effective leader. The need to encourage his audience of striking sanitation workers, to raise their morale, was great, but the past history of the strike was hardly cause for optimism. In the face of such obstacles, here is what King said in his peroration (conclusion):

Conclusion of the last speech of Dr. Martin Luther King, Jr., Memphis, Tennessee, April 4, 1968.*

1 And I want to thank God once more for allowing me to be here with you. You know several years ago I was in New York City autographing the first book that I had written. And while sitting there autographing books, a demented black woman came up. The only question I heard from her was, "Are you Martin Luther King?" And I was looking down writing, and I said yes. The next minute I felt something beating on my chest. Before I knew it, I had been stabbed by this demented woman. I was rushed to Harlem hospital. It was a dark Saturday afternoon. That blade had gone through and the x-rays revealed that the tip of the blade was on the edge of my aorta, the main artery. And once that's punctured, you drown in your own blood; that's the end of you. It came out in the *New York Times* the next morning that if I had merely sneezed, I would have died.

2 Well, about 4 days later, they allowed me, after the operation, after my chest had been opened and the blade had been taken out, to move around in a wheel chair in the hospital. They allowed me to read some of the mail that came in, and from all over the states and the world, kind letters came in. I read a few but there's one of them I will never forget. I had received one from the president and the vice president. I've forgotten what those telegrams said. I'd received a visit and a letter from the governor of New York, but I've forgotten what that letter said. But there was another letter than came from a little girl, a young girl who was a student at the White Plains high school, and I looked at that letter, and I'll never forget it. It said simply, "Dear Dr. King, I am a ninth grade student at the White Plains high school." She said, "While it should not matter, I would like to mention that I'm a white girl. I

---

* This is a transcription by the author of the conclusion as delivered. From "I've Been to the Mountaintop," by Martin Luther King, Jr. Copyright © 1968 by The Estate of Martin Luther King, Jr. Reprinted by permission of Joan Daves.

read in the paper of your misfortunes and of your sufferings. And I read that if you had sneezed, you would have died. I'm simply writing you to say that I am so happy that you didn't sneeze."

3 Because if I had sneezed, I wouldn't have been around here in 1960 when students all over the South started sitting in at lunch counters. And I knew that as they were sitting in, they were really standing up for the best in the American dream and taking the whole nation back to those great wells of democracy which were dug deep by the founding fathers in the Declaration of Independence and the Constitution.

4 If I had sneezed, I wouldn't have been around here in 1961 when we decided to take a ride for freedom and ended segregation in interstate travel.

5 If I had sneezed, I wouldn't have been around here in 1962 when Negroes in Albany, Georgia, decided to straighten their backs up. And whenever men and women straighten their backs up, they're going somewhere, because the man can't ride your back unless it is bent.

6 If I had sneezed, I wouldn't have been here in 1963 when black people of Birmingham, Alabama, aroused the conscience of this nation and brought into being the civil rights field.

7 If I had sneezed, I wouldn't have had a chance later that year in August to try to tell America about a dream that I had had.

8 If I had sneezed, I wouldn't have been down in Selma, Alabama, to see the great movement there.

9 If I had sneezed, I wouldn't have been in Memphis, to see a community rally around those brothers and sisters who are suffering. I'm so happy that I didn't sneeze. And they were telling me, now, it doesn't matter now, it really doesn't matter what happens now.

10 I left Atlanta this morning, and as we got started on the plane, there were six of us. The pilot said over the public address system, we're sorry for the delay. But we have Dr. Martin Luther King on the plane, and to be sure that all of the bags were checked, and to be sure that nothing would be wrong on the plane, we had to check out everything carefully. And we've had the plane protected and guarded all night. And then I got into Memphis. And some began to say the threats or talk about the threats that were out, what would happen to me from some of our sick white brothers. Well, I don't know what will happen now.

11 We've got some difficult days ahead but it really doesn't matter with me now, because I have been to the mountain top. And I don't mind. Like anybody, I would like to live a long life; longevity has its place. But I am not concerned about that now. I

just want to do God's will. And He's allowed me to go up to the mountain, and I've looked over and I've seen the promised land. I may not get there with you, but I want you to know tonight that we as a people will get to the promised land. So I am happy tonight. I am not worried about anything. I'm not fearing any man.

12   Mine eyes have seen the glory of the coming of the Lord.

In this instance, the conclusion is a major part of the entire speech. Describe it carefully; then consider these questions:

1.   What language strategies can you identify? How does each contribute to the effectiveness of the speech in creating identification and in inducing audience participation?

2.   How does the ethos of the speaker affect audience response to the conclusion? What persona does he adopt? What role is the audience expected to play? What risks are involved in these choices?

3.   Much of the conclusion involves enthymemes that depend on knowledge of events in the civil rights movement. What must you know to participate in this rhetorical act? What must you believe?

4.   How does King go about creating his audience, convincing those listening that they can be effective agents of change? What view of the success of the movement is assumed in the conclusion?

5.   King says that he has "been to the mountain top," an allusion to the death of Moses. Read Numbers 27:12–14 or Deuteronomy 32:48–52. How does more detailed knowledge about Moses and his death affect your reaction to the speech?

6.   The final sentence is an allusion to the Battle Hymn of the Republic. Who wrote it, and under what circumstances? With what events is the song associated? Is it an appropriate ending?

7.   Subsequent events have changed the meaning and significance of this speech. How is your reaction to the conclusion affected by your knowledge that this speech was delivered on the night of King's assassination? Compare that fact with its role in the Memphis sanitation strike. Which is more important, and why?

CHAPTER 12

NONVERBAL ELEMENTS
IN RHETORIC

Anyone who has played charades knows that words are more effective than gestures for expressing complex and abstract ideas. The ideas in this or any other book could not be presented nonverbally unless the gestures were part of a symbol system like the sign language of the deaf. However, all speech is accompanied by nonverbal elements such as a drawl, a frown, a stare, a handshake, or a bow.

This chapter is not an extended analysis of all nonverbal communication, but sources that will allow you to pursue these ideas are provided at the end of the chapter. The focus of this chapter is the role of nonverbal elements in oral rhetoric. I address these questions: (1) How do nonverbal elements affect the meaning of and response to oral rhetoric? (2) What can be communicated nonverbally? (3) What are the strengths and limitations of nonverbal rhetorical acts?

Nonverbal communication includes the human actions that *accompany* speech, nonverbal acts *perceived* as communicative, and nonverbal acts *intended* to be rhetorical. The problem of rhetorical intention, discussed in Chapter 1, recurs here. Some nonverbal elements are random, idiosyncratic, and unintentional. Others are part of established symbolic patterns shared by a pair of friends, a family, an organization, or a culture.* Random, unintentional, idiosyncratic

---

* See C. David Mortenson, *Communication: The Study of Human Interaction* (New York: McGraw-Hill, 1972), pp. 211–217, for a discussion of the problems of analyzing and interpreting nonverbal behavior.

behaviors may be taken as communicative, as when a squinting attempt to see something on the blackboard is interpreted as a frown of disapproval. As critics and analysts, the potential influence of such behaviors has to be considered. However, rhetorical action can only encompass intentional behaviors that can reasonably be expected to communicate conventional meanings to others.

NONVERBAL ADJUNCTS TO SPEECH

No oral communication takes place in a vacuum. In any act of oral communication, there are senders and receivers (rhetors and audiences are both), and they must be in some physical relationship to each other (from face-to-face to back-to-back), at some distance, in some posture (standing, kneeling, slouching). These relationships are studied in the area of nonverbal communication called *proxemics*. Every oral message is accompanied by body movements ranging from obvious gestures to tiny facial movements and general muscle tension. These behaviors are studied in *kinesics*. Every oral message includes vocal modifiers (volume, rate, pitch, quality) and noises of the vocal tract that carry meaning but aren't thought of as language (e.g., mm-hmm, tsk-tsk, coughs, laughing). These are studied in *paralinguistics*. People who participate in rhetorical acts have bodies of different sizes and degrees of attractiveness, and with more or less hair; they are clothed in different ways, and adorned by a variety of objects (earrings, watches, pipes, handbags). Their interactions occur in environments (in halls, on streets) and on certain kinds of occasions (a birthday party, a political convention, a class meeting). All of these are nonverbal elements that inevitably accompany spoken language.

Nonverbal behavior is learned just as language is learned. As a result, it varies from culture to culture. Americans nod in agreement while Arabs shake their heads in assent. Important cultural differences in the use of distance, time, voice, and gestures can create misunderstanding and generate resentment.* One reason for studying nonverbal behavior is to improve our ability to communicate with people from other cultures.

Problems can also be created nonverbally between people of different subcultures or ethnic backgrounds. For example, some studies show that patterns of eye contact between blacks and between whites

---

* See, for example, Robert L. Saitz and Edward J. Cervenka, *Columbian and North American Gestures: A Contrastive Inventory* (Bogota: Centro Colombo Americano, 1962).

in the United States differ. For some blacks, looking another person directly in the eye is considered rude, a putdown or a confrontation, and avoiding eye contact is a way of communicating recognition of authority.* Since norms among most U.S. whites differ, requiring direct eye contact to indicate attention and interest, problems arise for these blacks in interactions with whites, particularly when whites are in positions of authority.

Researchers do not agree about the origins of nonverbal acts. Some presume them to be caused biologically. Others argue that "the observed 'sex differences,' 'race differences,' and 'class differences' in nonverbal behavior may be traced to differences in power; and that these are learned differences which serve to strengthen the system of power and privilege that exists."† No one denies that observed behaviors differ; but there are at least two explanations of them.

Whatever their origin, nonverbal behaviors communicate power and reflect patterns of dominance and status in a culture. For example, a pair of experiments carried out by a team of Princeton investigators illustrates how nonverbal cues can reinforce racist stereotypes.‡ In the first experiment, white male subjects believed they were interviewing applicants for a team position in a group decision-making experiment. Black and white male "applicants," actually confederates, were trained to act in a standard way, and their performances were rehearsed until all applicants appeared equally qualified. But the white interviewers behaved differently toward the black applicants. They placed their chairs at a significantly greater distance from them, they made more errors of grammar, usage, and pronunciation, they showed less immediacy (a measure combining eye contact, forward lean, and shoulder angle), and they ended the interviews significantly sooner.

The second experiment tested the effects of such nonverbal differences on applicants. In this case, the interviewers were trained confederates and the applicants were naive subjects, white males who believed they were being interviewed as part of a training program

---

* Albert Scheflen, *Body Language and the Social Order* (Englewood Cliffs, N.J.: Prentice-Hall, 1972), pp. 95–96; Kenneth R. Johnson, "Black Kinesics—Some Non-Verbal Communication Patterns in Black Culture," *Florida FL Reporter*, Spring/Fall 1971, p. 18.

† Nancy M. Henley, *Body Politics: Power, Sex, and Nonverbal Communication* (Englewood Cliffs, N.J.: Prentice-Hall, 1977), p. 2.

‡ Carl O. Wood, Mark P. Zanna, and Joel Cooper, "The Nonverbal Mediation of Self-Fulfilling Prophecies in Interracial Interaction," *Journal of Experimental Social Psychology* 10 (1974):109–120.

and who were given a monetary incentive to compete for the job. Interviewers were trained to exhibit either immediate or nonimmediate behaviors to applicants, that is, to vary proximity, speech errors, and interview length. The applicants responded in kind, reciprocating the degree of immediacy of the interviewer. Judges who observed the applicants without knowing about the experiment rated those receiving nonimmediate behaviors as performing less well generally and as having less composure during the interview. The subjects also rated less immediate interviewers as less competent and friendly. These experiments illustrate several principles of nonverbal communication. Nonverbal cues are read very quickly and accurately.* They are reciprocated to alter the transaction that occurs, and they are taken as reliable signs of ethos. In this case, they also functioned as a self-fulfilling prophecy (behavior that guarantees a predetermined result).

The person who tries to overcome such problems faces large obstacles. As Henley notes, for example, you cannot teach women to violate norms of femininity in assertiveness classes and then expect that all will be well. A woman who does not conform to the submissive female stereotype may be ignored, her action may be misinterpreted as a sexual invitation, and she may be punished physically (nonverbally) or labeled as a deviant, a bitch, or a lesbian. Or her expression of dominance may be accepted.† It is possible to change nonverbal behavior, but the results may not be what are desired. Once again, the receiver will play a significant role in determining the kind of action that takes place.

Nonverbal elements always accompany oral communication. Like language, these behaviors are learned. Differences between cultures and subcultures make misunderstanding easy, and nonverbal behaviors influence the relationships between sexes, classes, and ethnic groups.

NONVERBAL MEANING

Just what can we communicate nonverbally, and how significant are such messages in the total pattern of meaning? Most researchers

---

* See, for example, Robert Rosenthal et al., "Body Talk and Tone of Voice: The Language Without Words," *Psychology Today* 8 (September 1974): 64–68. Even when exposures were reduced to only one-twenty-fourth of a second, observers correctly identified the emotions being portrayed on film by an actress two-thirds of the time.

† See Henley, *Body Politics*, pp. 196–205, for a discussion of body politics and women's liberation.

agree that the nonverbal channels carry more *social* meaning than the verbal channels. This means that we communicate attitudes and feelings nonverbally. More specifically, we communicate likes and dislikes, dominance and status, and responsiveness.*

Evaluations

We communicate our evaluations, our attitudes, our likes and dislikes (good-bad, pleasant-unpleasant, beautiful-ugly) primarily through signs of immediacy. We move closer, lean forward, take a face-to-face position, touch, look at, maintain eye contact with, and speak to persons we like; we move away from, lean back, turn away from, avoid, and look away from persons we do not like. Members of an audience will use such nonverbal gestures as data from which to infer the speaker's feelings at a given moment and to make judgments about character. They will also draw conclusions from stylistic signs of immediacy, a point at which nonverbal and verbal communication converge.

Your language can reflect immediacy and involvement or nonimmediacy and distance. The rhetor who talks about "those people" is distancing herself or himself from the people being discussed; "these people" lessens the distance, and "we" is evidence of close identification. Errors of grammar and pronunciation suggest distance and reflect a subject that distresses the speaker or is not of great interest. Stylistic choices that connect speaker and statement are evidence of commitment, as in "I think" vs. "it is thought" or "researchers think." The active voice (I finished it) is more immediate than the passive (It is finished). Such stylistic markers are cues that the audience will use to infer your feelings and attitudes. They are indicators of tone.

Power

We communicate power, dominance, and status nonverbally. The dynamics of such communication are described by Henley: "The humiliation of being a subordinate is often felt most sharply and painfully when one is ignored or interrupted while speaking, towered

---

* This analysis is indebted to Albert Mehrabian's *Silent Messages*, 2d ed. (Belmont, Calif.: Wadsworth, 1981).

over or forced to move by another's bodily presence, or cowed un-
knowingly into dropping the eyes, the head, the shoulders."* As children, as students, as employees, we have all had such experiences.
Our social power is expressed through nonverbal behaviors expressing strength, size, and weight.

Those showing submission speak softly, occupy less space (stand
and sit in tense positions with arms close to the body), keep their
distance, lower their eyes, hesitate to intrude upon another's space,
bow their heads, cringe, and cuddle. Persons expressing dominance
and status speak more loudly, occupy more space (stand with arms
akimbo, sit in relaxed and sprawling positions, and gesture widely),
take the initiative in increasing intimacy, look into the eyes, violate
territory with aplomb, raise their chins, stand erect (often on plat-
forms), and put their hands on or their arms around others.

Audiences use nonverbal evidence to make inferences about the
speaker's confidence, commitment, and expertise. Your knowledge of
the subject will be tested against nonverbal cues that you provide.

Dynamism

We communicate activity and responsiveness nonverbally. We do so
through evidences of life and vitality and through the rate of our
activity. We react, adapt, shift position. By contrast, passivity, lack of
movement, and rigidity reflect a lack of vitality. Dynamism is expressed in the sheer amount of interaction that occurs and in changing facial expressions, vocal variety, and gestures.

These three factors—evaluation, power, and dynamism—interact
and overlap. Evidences of liking may also indicate status, and nonverbal dynamism reflects dominance. Those of higher status feel more
comfortable increasing immediacy, and nonverbal signs of immediacy are also cues of dynamism and responsiveness. These three factors
are closely related to the elements of ethos discussed in Chapter 6.
Immediacy seems to be the counterpart of trustworthiness, power is
related to competence and expertise, and responsiveness, activity and
dynamism seem to be identical both as factors of ethos and as dimensions of nonverbal communication. In other words, overcoming

---

*Henley, *Body Politics*, p. 3.

the obstacles you face as a rhetor, at least in oral communication, is directly related to nonverbal behavior.

Responses to Nonverbal Cues

Nonverbal behavior expresses emotions. The importance of such communication is magnified in this culture in at least two ways. First, we have a tradition of restraint about expressing feelings, but we believe that such feelings will out, if not overtly in speech then covertly in actions. Thus, we look for signs of feelings in nonverbal cues and take them as good evidence of attitude and character. Second, we learn nonverbal behaviors unsystematically and indirectly. Until recently, they were rarely studied, except by actors. As a result, we believe nonverbal cues are produced spontaneously so that it would be difficult to lie nonverbally. Hence, we trust these cues, and when inconsistencies appear, we are likely to believe the nonverbal rather than the verbal message.

The nonverbal adjuncts to verbal messages can be contradictory or inconsistent. The simplest examples are sarcastic and ironic statements. The secretary who does the work of her boss for one-third of his pay says, "Yes, my boss is a fantastic administrator," and she leaves no doubt about her contradictory attitude. Sarcasm and irony illustrate the fact that we use nonverbal cues to interpret the meanings of messages, to decide between alternative possibilities.* As speakers, we use nonverbal cues to indicate what we mean, and nonverbal elements greatly extend the meanings of words. For example, Elaine May and Mike Nichols recorded a dialogue using only the words "George" and "Martha" that some radio stations considered too erotic to broadcast.

Nonverbal messages produce intense responses in receivers. This is not surprising since the bulk of what is communicated involves attitudes and feelings. The fury generated by long-haired, bearded

---

* Henley cites an interesting example: "When Richard Nixon sent transcripts, rather than tapes, of presidential conversations to the House Judiciary Committee investigating the question of his possible impeachment (April, 1974), members quite rightly complained that transcripts could not convey the full or correct meaning of an utterance, having no voice inflection, stress, or other such nuances, and demanded the tapes. This exchange is a landmark in recognizing the legitimacy of paralinguistic communication, those characteristics of speech that affect its interpretation but are not part of the usually recognized language" (*Body Politics*, n., p. 7).

young men in the 1960s is just one example of this kind of reaction. But such responses are mirrored in our dislike of tense and nervous people, in our anger at persons who violate our territory, "barging in without knocking," and in our rebellion at unwanted backslapping and fondling. You can be sure that your audience will not only pick up nonverbal cues, it will react to them, trust them, and use them as a major source of information about your feelings, attitudes, and ethos.

DELIVERING A SPEECH

Concerns about delivery are closely related to stage fright or communication apprehension. Fears about speaking are normal and appropriate. We fear what is unfamiliar and unknown, and most people who come to a rhetoric class have not had extensive experience speaking publicly to others. We fear the consequences of committing ourselves. Initiating rhetorical action requires that you do just that. By speaking you say, "I have made a decision, I know, I believe, and I am ready to urge you to likewise." Most of us are somewhat reluctant to set ourselves up as authorities, to take the responsibility of giving advice. As a result, speaking creates apprehension.

We fear isolation from and rejection by others. In most speaking situations, the audience clusters together in comfortable anonymity while the speaker stands alone. Nonverbally, it feels as if it's you against them. Because rhetorical action asks for and requires the participation of others, every speaker risks rejection. In face-to-face situations, the evidence is immediate and unavoidable. Audience members send hundreds of nonverbal messages registering their responses. As a study reports, it is very uncomfortable to speak to listeners who show total visual disregard while you are speaking.* Under such conditions and faced by such possibilities, some fear is appropriate. All good speakers, even those with much experience, feel some apprehension. On every occasion, a speaker takes responsibility for a commitment, is partially isolated from the audience, and risks rejection. Apprehension is a recognition of what is involved in acting as a rhetor.

However, such fears diminish greatly with practice, and most classroom speakers become quite comfortable after two or three ex-

---

* Ralph V. Exline, "Visual Interaction: The Glances of Power and Preference," in *Nebraska Symposium on Motivation, 1971*, ed. James K. Cole (Lincoln: University of Nebraska Press, 1971).

periences. In addition, if you have prepared carefully and practiced aloud so that you are in command of your material, your fears will be manageable after a few sentences. Human beings are symbol-using creatures, and despite our fears, we take pleasure in communicating with others, in expressing our ideas and feelings. You will enjoy the experience even more if you consider the following bits of advice.

Preparing the Scene

Insofar as it is possible, take control of the scene. Arrive early and case the joint. If possible, move chairs so that you lessen your isolation from the audience. This will make you more comfortable and create an environment in which participation by the audience is easier. If the audience is scattered over a large area, ask them to move forward so that they are closer together. Unless the occasion is extremely formal, ask that lights be arranged so that you can see the audience. Stage lighting separates you from the audience and turns you into a performer.

In general, avoid the use of a lectern and stand in front of tables and desks. A lectern shuts off much of your nonverbal communication and reduces your immediacy. Both lessen ease of audience participation. Use a lectern or table if you will feel more comfortable behind one, but do everything you can to minimize the barrier between you and the audience. Try standing *next to* the lectern. In this way you will be able to rest one hand on the lectern, and yet you won't be as severely "fenced off" from the audience.

Check to ensure that all materials you need are present and working. Test the microphone and look for a blackboard or a place to put visual aids. If any machines are to be used, be sure that they are there and working. Nothing destroys your efforts more quickly than a tape recorder that won't work or a beautiful visual aid that keeps collapsing.

If there are problems that can't be solved, acknowledge them to the audience in good humor. Try to make them your confederates in struggling to cope with a cold room, a noisy radiator, a defective mike, or whatever. Your role as rhetor requires you to take charge of the scene and to be responsive to what goes on in it.

Presenting Materials

Audiovisual aids such as charts, maps, pictures, and taped or filmed materials create special problems. Use them only when they contribute something essential to your presentation, and prepare them carefully. Visual aids are essential when presenting large amounts of statistical material or when ideas and relationships are difficult to explain verbally—for example, locations on maps. Follow these guidelines for using visual aids:

1. Be sure that they are large enough to be seen easily by all members of the audience (check sight lines).

2. Prepare them for easy display. Maps should be on a stiff backing so they can be stood up. Flip charts should be used with your own stand. Printing should be done in thick dark lettering.

3. Keep them simple so the audience can look at them and understand them, but be sure to explain them verbally in your speech.

4. Look at the audience, not at the visual aid. Keep your face toward the audience and talk to them. Remember, you are speaking to the audience, not to the chart or blackboard. Note: An overhead projector is preferable to a blackboard because it permits you to point out things on the visual display without turning your back to the audience.

5. Use them only when they contribute directly to your speech. Any visual aid is a competing, potentially distracting message. Unless an aid contributes to your entire speech, remove the distraction when you have finished using it. Do not pass items around while you are speaking.

Similar principles should be followed in the use of tape and film. Be sure that taped material is loud enough to be heard easily. Have the tape set up and ready to play. Use only that amount of taped or filmed material essential to make your point. Be prepared for mechanical problems!!

Notes are perfectly acceptable in all speaking situations, but some kinds of notes are preferable. Since your aim is immediacy, freedom of movement, and ease of use, print or type your notes so they are easily read on 3"-×-5" or 4"-×-6" cards. These can be held easily so you can stand anywhere, and one hand remains free for gestures. Because they are stiff, note cards can never betray your nervousness by rattling. Use your notes as you practice aloud (as you practice you will learn where items are on the cards). When you speak, refer to them regularly so that you do not lose your place and have to struggle to find a quotation.

Presenting Yourself

Dress   Dress with due consideration for the occasion, the role you will play, your purpose, and the expectations of the audience. Clothing is a major source of messages for the audience, and it can detract and distract. Follow these simple rules:

1. Dress for comfort and ease of movement. Avoid tight, stiff clothing, high heels that wobble, or climbing shoes that creak.

2. Dress to avoid distraction. Avoid bright, busy, loud patterns that attract attention away from your message. Eliminate any item that can rattle, such as coins, keys, or bracelets.

3. Dress in an outfit that is harmonious. Minimize the time the audience will spend remarking on your clothes.

Posture and Gesture   Before you begin to speak, walk slowly to the front of the room. Do not begin to speak until you have taken a position standing firmly on both feet. You will create anticipation for what follows, and you will take charge of the scene. Avoid standing on one foot, rocking back and forth, and slouching. All of these distract from your message and suggest discomfort and lack of involvement. Feel free to move about, but move with purpose and for emphasis.

Hold your notes at chest level in one hand for easy reading and gesturing. Do not clasp your hands in front of you or behind you, fold your arms, or play with your notes. Avoid pointless or repetitious gestures. Aim for movement that will in no way distract from what you are saying.

Your eyes are a major source of contact with the audience. To establish your involvement and to hold attention, you must look at the audience directly. Be sure to include everyone. For the audience, your gaze is a primary indicator of immediacy. And, of course, you can't respond to messages from the audience unless you are looking at them.

Voice   The ideal speaking voice is easy to hear and pleasing to listen to. Good delivery involves vocal variety and patterns of pause and emphasis that increase our understanding of what is said. The 1980 presidential candidates provide some useful illustrations. Ted Kennedy shouts and strains, and after only a few minutes, it is hard to listen. Jimmy Carter is hard to understand because he pauses so inappropriately. It is easier to understand his speeches in print than as delivered. Ronald Reagan does an excellent job. His voice is pleasing and flexible, emphatic but not strident. His training as an actor serves him well.

The most common vocal problem among novice speakers is speaking too fast for clear articulation or comprehension. Writing "slow down" on each note card is a useful reminder, and practicing at slower rates helps to change habits. However, audiences may respond to rapid speech as dynamic, and most native speakers will be able to decode all but the most hurried speech.

These suggestions for delivery are grounded in the principles of nonverbal communication. As a rhetor, your goal is participation by the audience. Initiating joint action requires dynamism on your part. Your eyes, face, arms, and body should communicate your interest and involvement. Participation is made easier by indicators of immediacy such as lessening the distance between you and the audience and maintaining eye contact. As the initiator, you must establish your authority and competence. Gestures, posture, and physical relaxation all bespeak your competence. If rhetorical action is your goal, you must seek it both verbally and nonverbally. And remember that, while these hints may be helpful, preparing your speech carefully and practicing it aloud are probably the best ways to improve oral presentation.

NONVERBAL RHETORIC

Some rhetorical action is wholly nonverbal. For example, consider this button:*

---

* Used by permission.

When I showed it to a class of freshmen students, they interpreted it variously. All recognized the sign Ⓢ, now common on traffic markers, that something is prohibited. But just what was prohibited was unclear. One person said, "No more hangups." Another said, "Don't keep me hanging." Only one person was certain. She recognized the button as one distributed by the National Abortion Rights Action League and translated it as "No more backroom or kitchen abortions."

The button illustrates some of the problems involved in nonverbal rhetoric. Because such acts are highly abstract, they are very ambiguous. The ordinary audience member is free to interpret them in many different ways, some of which may be quite different from what was intended. For that reason, nonverbal rhetoric works best with "true believers," those who already agree. An ideal audience for the button is a member of N.A.R.A.L. who recalls the higher rates of maternal death and sterility that resulted from illegal abortions performed under unsanitary conditions and with improper instruments. In other words, nonverbal rhetoric works best as ritual, as a reaffirmation of belief. The important role of gestures and actions in rituals reflects this fact.

Nonverbal rhetoric is simple, an expression of feeling. It provides no explanations or justifications. There are no qualifiers to modify the claim. It is usually intense, even simplistic. As a result, reactions to such rhetorical acts are also intense. Black protestors rejoiced at the gestures made by Smith and Carlos at the 1968 Olympic Games; one Olympic official was simply infuriated,* and many Americans were very angry. Under such circumstances, there is no opportunity to explain just what is intended, to provide evidence and reasons to justify the claim reflected in the gesture, to discuss what kinds of changes are needed. There is just a dramatic assertion.

Nonverbal rhetoric has compensatory strengths. Most examples are like slogans, vivid symbols that summarize a whole realm of intense associations and thus call up emotional responses in those who see them. They are rallying cries that unify and raise the morale of like-minded groups. Like their weaknesses, their strengths come from their high level of abstraction and their emotional power.

Several years ago, one of my students made a speech against abor-

---

* John Kieran, Arthur Daley, and Pat Jordan, *The Story of the Olympic Games, 776 B.C. to 1976* (Philadelphia: J.P. Lippincott, 1977), p. 431. The official was British, the Marquis of Exeter, Lord David Burghley.

tion and used as a visual aid pictures from a pamphlet called "Life or Death" distributed by the Kansas Right to Life Organization. The pictures are large, colored photographs of aborted fetuses. They are dramatic evidence of the human features that appear during the early weeks of life and of the physical effects of various abortion procedures. But the response of the class was overwhelmingly negative. They said things like, "After I saw those pictures, I just didn't want to think about it." "I was insulted." "Those just aren't appropriate for any speech." Only one person was positive: a student who, like the speaker, took a strong anti-abortion stand.

The pictures are nonverbal rhetoric. They illustrate once again that nonverbal channels communicate emotional materials and that, for those who do not share your views, the channels can easily become overloaded. In that case, the response will be intensely negative. For this reason, nonverbal rhetoric has to be used with great care whether in isolation or in conjunction with a speech. Be aware of its ambiguity and the intensity of its message and of the potential responses, and remember that it is most effective for those who already share the views that it espouses.

SUMMARY

No oral communication takes place in a vacuum. It is always accompanied by nonverbal elements that affect its meaning. Nonverbal behaviors are learned; they differ between cultures; and they are a major source of misunderstanding. The origins of nonverbal behaviors may be biological or social, but they reflect patterns of dominance within a culture.

Nonverbal channels communicate attitudes and feelings, specifically evaluations, power, and dynamism. We tend to trust nonverbal cues as reliable indicators of both momentary feelings and general character. Hence, they strongly affect audience perceptions of the ethos of the speaker.

Fears about delivering a speech are closely related to nonverbal communication. The role of the rhetor is one that puts pressure on a speaker, threatening social relationships and demanding responsibility and commitment. Apprehensions about communication are appropriate responses to such demands. Experience, practice, and preparation are excellent ways to cope. You can also reduce fear and increase effectiveness by the way you prepare the scene and present your material and yourself.

The strengths and limitations of nonverbal rhetoric reflect the general qualities of all forms of nonverbal communication. Such acts are abstract and ambiguous, open to varied interpretations. They communicate highly emotional messages that produce intense responses. They are most effective for a target audience that shares the beliefs and values expressed in the rhetoric. Nonverbal rhetorical acts can symbolize large amounts of experience, but they cannot explain, justify, or qualify. Great care should be taken in using them as visual aids in speeches. Unless the audience shares your point of view, a boomerang effect of intense disapproval may occur.

Summary Outline: A Checklist for Oral Delivery
I. First, prepare the scene.
  A. Judge how formal the occasion ought to be, and then:
    1. Arrange the seating.
    2. Arrange the lighting.
    3. Decide on using a table or lectern.
    4. Set up and check out all audiovisual aids.
II. Second, present yourself.
  A. Dress for comfort and, to avoid distraction, wear an outfit to fit your role.
  B. Situate yourself comfortably before you begin to speak.
  C. Move with purpose and for emphasis; avoid distraction.
  D. Look directly at all of your audience.
  E. Speak with variety and dynamism.
  F. Speak slowly enough to be understood.
III. Third, present your materials.
  A. Use visual aids with care.
    1. Display them so that they can be seen easily by all the audience.
    2. Explain all displays in your speech.
    3. Look at the audience, not at the visual aid.
    4. Don't turn a visual aid into competing rhetoric.
  B. Use notes effectively.
    1. Type or print your notes on cards.
    2. Hold them in one hand at chest level for easy sight and movement.

SOURCES

Argyle, Michael. *Social Interaction.* New York: Atherton, 1969. A survey of theory and research on nonverbal communication.

Benson, Thomas W., and Frandsen, Kenneth D. *An Orientation to Nonverbal Communication.* Chicago: Science Research Associates, 1976. An excellent basic orientation to principles of nonverbal communication.

Birdwhistell, Ray L. *Introduction to Kinesics.* Louisville: University of Kentucky Press, 1952. A pathbreaking work by a pioneer in this area.

————. *Kinesics and Context: Essays on Body Motion Communication.* Philadelphia: University of Pennsylvania Press, 1970. More work by an outstanding theorist.

Goffman, Erving. *Relations in Public.* New York: Basic Books, 1971. As the title indicates, this book focuses on public interactions.

Hall, Edward T. *The Silent Language.* Garden City, N.Y.: Doubleday, 1959. An early work that is still a good basic introduction.

Henley, Nancy M. *Body Politics: Power, Sex, and Nonverbal Communication.* Englewood Cliffs, N.J.: Prentice-Hall, 1977. An excellent survey of research on nonverbal expressions of power.

Langer, Susanne K. *Feeling and Form: A Theory of Art.* New York: Charles Scribner's Sons, 1953. A beautifully written work that focuses on the nondiscursive elements in art forms, including music and architecture.

Mehrabian, Albert. *Silent Messages,* 2d ed. Belmont, Calif.: Wadsworth, 1981. An excellent survey of theory and research in this area.

Sontag, Susan. *On Photography.* New York: Farrar, Straus and Giroux, 1977. A provocative book on the cultural meanings of photographs.

MATERIAL FOR ANALYSIS

As you can imagine, nonverbal rhetorical acts create particularly difficult ethical and constitutional issues. The following essay raises such issues for discussion. As identified in a note, the author was a second-year law student at Hofstra Law School at the time this essay appeared.

Come On, I'm Not a Radical
Terry C. Markin*

1   I was in a protest the other day. It was not an unusual demonstration. Ten of us handed out literature, carried signs and walked together. There was no violence, no yelling, no restriction on people's access to private or public property.

2   Hundreds of similar small protests are held every day around the world. So what makes this particular protest noteworthy?

3   It is significant because the people who watched the protest posed a greater threat to Americans' constitutional rights than the protesters themselves.

4   The incident occurred at Hofstra Law School. As students there, we had studied in depth our constitutional right to dissent. Ten of us decided to put these constitutional principles into action at a controversial event held at the school.

5   We did not disagree with the right to speak of those with opposing viewpoints, and neither prevented anyone from entering the auditorium nor disrupted the presentation.

6   Our goal was simply to present our view on the need for more ethical responsibility in the legal profession.

7   We entered the auditorium with our signs and sat down. I placed my sign so that it obstructed no one's vision, but someone yelled at me to put it down anyway.

8   Why, I thought, did that person oppose my expressing my view? Did he not understand that I was exercising my First Amendment right to freedom of expression?

9   The speaker in the presentation was introduced to the audience. He glanced down at us and began. "I am going to give this speech today," he declared, "even though these demonstrators are trying to prevent me from exercising my First Amendment right to do so." As the presentation proceeded, the demonstrators remained quiet; the audience's disapproval of our protest was becoming evident.

10   Why, I thought, were we being viewed as obstructors of justice? I had many friends in the audience who agreed with our views but objected to our openness in expressing them.

---

* Terry C. Markin, "Come On, I'm Not a Radical." © 1979 by the New York Times Company. Reprinted by permission.

11   Demonstrating in America is simply not a popular activity. The general public labels protesters as either right- or left-wing. One cannot be politically moderate in America and demonstrate for what he believes in, since once one becomes active in a cause he is viewed as a radical.

12   If I had taken down my sign, I would have fit in with a large segment of the audience. By holding up the sign, however, I was viewed as a radical. To the audience, I was a civil obstructionist attempting to deny someone else his constitutional right to speak. In reality, I believe strongly in freedom of expression for others as well as myself.

13   Why is someone viewed as radical in America if he protests even though what he seeks may actually be in conformity with many people's opinions? Many Americans fear a radical revolution and view demonstrations as the springboard for rebellion. Although the public tolerates demonstrations as a First Amendment right, it discourages people from participating by labeling demonstrators radicals.

14   In the end, this sociological viewpoint will do more to encourage radical revolution in America than to prevent it.

15   Thousands of Americans are afraid to demonstrate for ideals they believe in because they will be labeled radical by the community in which they live or work.

16   And those few who have the courage to demonstrate commonly find themselves leaning toward the radical right- or left-wing organizations that often are the only groups supporting their activities.

17   Peaceful demonstrations benefit American society enormously. They provide the Government with a way to discern the public's beliefs. Americans are able to hear new ideas that they may find beneficial. Those citizens who are dissatisfied with society are able to let off steam peacefully rather than wait for it to build up and explode violently in a riot.

18   The Framers of the Constitution provided the first step to free participatory government by legally permitting peaceful demonstrations. It is now time to complete the task by accepting it sociologically.

Read the essay carefully; then consider these questions:

1.   Is the author right about American attitudes toward demonstrations? What evidence about reactions to sit-ins, marches, and other demonstrations exists to support his view? Select one example, such as the right of the American Nazi Party to march in Skokie, Illinois, in order to confront specific pro and con arguments.

2. What Supreme Court decisions define the right to speak nonverbally?

3. Based on what you know about nonverbal rhetoric, explain why the author was asked to put his sign down and why the speaker treated the signs as an effort to prevent him from speaking.

4. What is it about nonverbal rhetoric that might lead an audience to classify its creators as radicals? What special rhetorical obstacles are faced by rhetors using signs, sit-ins, or marches? What might be done to lessen negative reactions?

5. In what ways is your reaction to the essay affected by what you know about the author?

6. What additional information would you like to have about the event described by the author?

INDEX